Internet Marketing Methods Revealed

The Complete Guide to Becoming an Internet Marketing Expert

By Miguel Todaro

Internet Marketing Methods Revealed
The Complete Guide to Becoming an Internet Marketing Expert

Copyright © 2007 by Atlantic Publishing Group, Inc.
1405 SW 6th Ave. • Ocala, Florida 34471 • 800-814-1132 • 352-622-1875–Fax
Web site: www.atlantic-pub.com • E-mail: sales@atlantic-pub.com
SAN Number: 268-1250

ISBN-13: 978-1-60138-265-8   ISBN-10: 1-60138-265-0

Library of Congress Cataloging-in-Publication Data

Todaro, Miguel, 1967-
  Internet marketing methods revealed : the complete guide to becoming an Internet marketing expert / Miguel Todaro.
      p. cm.
  Includes bibliographical references and index.
  ISBN-13: 978-1-60138-265-8 (alk. paper)
  ISBN-10: 1-60138-265-0 (alk. paper)
  1. Internet marketing. I. Title.

  HF5415.1265.T63 2008
  658.8'72--dc22
                          2008025599

INTERIOR LAYOUT DESIGN: Vickie Taylor • vtaylor@atlantic-pub.com

Printed in the United States

Printed on Recycled Paper

Dedication

To Isadora, Leopoldo and Silvana

Acknowledgements

To a considerable degree, this book is the product of collaboration with many persons and professionals who share experiences and extensive investigations.

Thanks to Wallace Murray for all his help and professional support, our conversations have been a real inspiration to me.

I am also indebted to David Nikke from Forrester Research, Elizabeth Month from Hoovers, and Victor Samuel from UBC Research Institute.

Many thanks to the people of **StatCounter.com** for their collaboration in providing extraordinary data that was very useful for the completion of this book.

Alisa Marfield, Jonathan Labbir, and Seven Deen have collaborated enormously in the development of many chapters of the book.

My wife and partner, Silvana Vieytes, was a source of insight and encouragement throughout. This book would not have been written without her fantastic help and support. She also had to alternate this with the tough task of taking care of the amazing Leopoldo, four years old, and the little princess Isadora, two years old.

Thanks to Atlantic Publishers for believing in this project and making it real.

Four others deserve special thanks: Norman Gardner from Google Canada, Michael Obrem, Richard Josephs from Yahoo!, and Analia Vieytes, always helping me with her kind support.

Thanks also to Betty, Susana, and Sebastian.

My sincere thanks to all of you.

We recently lost our beloved pet "Bear," who was not only our best and dearest friend but also the "Vice President of Sunshine" here at Atlantic Publishing. He did not receive a salary but worked tirelessly 24 hours a day to please his parents. Bear was a rescue dog that turned around and showered myself, my wife Sherri, his grandparents Jean, Bob and Nancy and every person and animal he met (maybe not rabbits) with friendship and love. He made a lot of people smile every day.

We wanted you to know that a portion of the profits of this book will be donated to The Humane Society of the United States. *–Douglas & Sherri Brown*

The human-animal bond is as old as human history. We cherish our animal companions for their unconditional affection and acceptance. We feel a thrill when we glimpse wild creatures in their natural habitat or in our own backyard.

Unfortunately, the human-animal bond has at times been weakened. Humans have exploited some animal species to the point of extinction.

The Humane Society of the United States makes a difference in the lives of animals here at home and worldwide. The HSUS is dedicated to creating a world where our relationship with animals is guided by compassion. We seek a truly humane society in which animals are respected for their intrinsic value, and where the human-animal bond is strong.

Want to help animals? We have plenty of suggestions. Adopt a pet from a local shelter, join The Humane Society and be a part of our work to help companion animals and wildlife. You will be funding our educational, legislative, investigative and outreach projects in the U.S. and across the globe.

Or perhaps you'd like to make a memorial donation in honor of a pet, friend or relative? You can through our Kindred Spirits program. And if you'd like to contribute in a more structured way, our Planned Giving Office has suggestions about estate planning, annuities, and even gifts of stock that avoid capital gains taxes.

Maybe you have land that you would like to preserve as a lasting habitat for wildlife. Our Wildlife Land Trust can help you. Perhaps the land you want to share is a backyard— that's enough. Our Urban Wildlife Sanctuary Program will show you how to create a habitat for your wild neighbors.

So you see, it's easy to help animals. And The HSUS is here to help.

THE HUMANE SOCIETY
OF THE UNITED STATES.

2100 L Street NW • Washington, DC 20037 • 202-452-1100

www.hsus.org

Table of Contents

Preface

In 1995, I was advising many corporations about investing in Internet projects, mostly related to marketing and e-commerce, and whether the Internet was worthwhile. There were questions about the durability and potential of the Internet as a new platform for business development.

The Internet has since demonstrated its potential, and corporations invest with the intention of making more money and defining new strategies to survive in the competitive online business market.

This book is more than a "learn how to make money online" guide; it is about understanding the new requirements and rules for marketers and developers in the new digital economy, driven by the Internet and its promising and increasingly known business future.

I remember a big book my parents gave me for my eighth birthday. It was full of short stories with colorful, neat illustrations. I remember well a story of two kids living in a fantastic city in the year 2000. I spent many hours looking at the detailed images — high crystal buildings with futuristic architecture and a blue sky full of sophisticated flying machines with people driving them. I truly believed at that time that the distant year 2000 was going to be, somehow, like that illustration.

I admit my disappointment when the year 2000 arrived and there were no flying machines; transportation in general was pretty much the same. Maybe it was more slick, but it was the same concept. It is easy to overestimate the unknown.

On the other hand, I never could have guessed that now, almost a decade after the year 2000, I would be writing these thoughts with a small device that I have in my pocket. This device, light and handy, is able to play and store movies and music; make a phone call in seconds to anywhere in the world; send and receive electronic letters in milliseconds; identify my geographic location and give me directions to almost any place on the planet; provide weather, traffic, or financial data; connect to a computer and transfer photos, articles, and documents; receive instructions from my voice, identify my fingerprint; and communicate with many other devices through infrared beams. So, on the flip side, it is also easy to underestimate the unknown.

Today's technological reality was beyond the wildest imagination of people growing up 30 years ago. But the most fascinating thing about this is that the device I described cost as much as a dinner in a nice restaurant. The most impressive technological advance so far is accessibility to a new high tech reality that is generating a new economic reality for us all.

Many business analysts are still surprised about the way the Internet is transforming communication, information, and economics.

The reaction of society to this was fast enough to create new trends and habits that virtually redefined the present world. But, for some, this is not sufficient. Many corporations, governments, scientists, and developers tried to accelerate the process of assimilation. In 1991, Al Gore, while senator of Tennessee, wrote: "Gutenberg's invention which so empowered Jefferson and his colleagues in their fight for democracy, seems to pale before the rise of electronic communications and innovations, from the telegraph, to the television, to the microprocessor and the emergence of a new computerized world — an information age."

Gore also propelled the electronic highway and facilitated the platform for electronic development as the Vice President years later. He understood the importance of the upcoming revolution and the need for upgrading professionals in all fields.

Sometimes the market is afraid of uncertain changes. I remember some of the original responses from business analysts and experts around 1994, when the Internet was beginning to "eclipse the sky with its mysterious potential," as referred by Steve Barry. At that time, the big "ghost" was e-mail — there was concern about the system collapsing because of this new menace. It seemed that people were going to stop sending letters and replace them with these new electronic messages. The system did not collapse; society adapted to the comfort of e-mail technology and postal companies incorporated the Internet as a new value to their business offerings. The post office now offers the ability to track online a letter anywhere in the world and identify its exact location — a technology unimaginable 15 years ago.

On the other hand, nobody was able to anticipate the revolution that the Internet created in the music and movie industry. However, the market did not collapse here either. Once again, it adapted and redefined its strategy around the new rules of the game. In order to do that, professionals of all industries needed to upgrade their skills and expand their understanding and creativity. This is an ongoing process, and it is the main objective of this book — to provide substantial data and guidance to upgrade and inform marketers, business people, and developers in order to access new ways of assimilating the Internet from a business perspective.

Today, it is essential to estimate what the future holds, without false assumptions. We are living in the digital revolution, and Internet marketing plays a major role in the business development of the new economic landscape. It is time to get involved.

Miguel Todaro
mtodaro@canada.com

Introduction to Internet Marketing

What You Will Learn About in the Following Chapter

- The Internet evolution and the history of the most important Web sites in the world

- The history of SEO and the basic definition of Internet marketing and its derivatives

- The fundamentals and principles of Internet marketing

- The impact of Internet marketing on media and traditional advertisement

Opening the Door

In 1997, I was in the office of the Vice President of Latin American division of FIAT Auto, Roberto San Pedro, one of the most innovative business people I have ever met. After a relaxed conversation, I told him I wanted to sell cars online.

He looked at me puzzled, trying to decide whether I was kidding. This reaction was quite expected, and it could have been worse; the Internet was still an uncertain soil for business. At that time, companies and organizations had a fair presence on the net, but the idea of doing business online was beyond comprehension.

Two months after that conversation, I was in charge of that project, with the ambitious objective of selling 150 cars on the Internet by the end of that year. Today, this objective would be not a big deal (the automotive industry made more than $85 million in car sales online worldwide in 2005), but considering that e-commerce was invented in 1995 and the technical tools for financial transactions and security online were very poor at that time, the objective was quite a challenge.

I led a team of five developers and we engaged in the execution of the project in a small office in the basement of the information technology (IT) building. After three months, the Web site was online and fully operating. The company supported the launch with newspaper advertisements to promote the idea and attract customers. At that time, the only search engines were Yahoo! and Altavista (with very limited traffic), and the concept of Internet marketing was a dream.

Four months later, we reached our goal with no difficulty. This Web site did not allow the user to go through the whole process of e-commerce as it is known today; we did not have a reliable technological platform at that time, but at least the Web site provided real time information about the stock of cars of each of the dealerships (420 in total) and gave the option to select the color of the car as well as diverse accessories. Finally, the user was invited to go to the closest dealership to finalize the purchase.

The experiment was a marketing exercise in e-commerce; moreover, it was the first strong step into a long process that would finally evolve as a real e-commerce corporate move that has not stopped since, and generates more than 13 percent of the sales worldwide for FIAT Auto today.

When we accomplished our goal, I had the feeling that we were in an extraordinary moment, observing the sunrise of a new, and uncertain, business era. Several years later, I still have that feeling, stronger and with more clear indications. My personal analysis and knowledge about those first indications motivated me in writing this book, which I consider a helpful implementation tool for anyone with desires of learning how to get involved in Internet marketing and making it profitable. Any user with basic knowledge about marketing and how the Internet works will be able to understand it and find it extremely practical; this is my personal promise to you.

Getting Started

Before explaining in detail what Internet marketing is, and what the most effective way to implement it is, I would like to make clear some points that will help you to better understand the relevancy of the topics of this book.

The Internet network was invented in the late '70s, designed originally as a government communication tool; nobody at that time expected it to become the colossal business and commerce instrument it is today. When the interlink and hyperlink system known as the World Wide Web (WWW) was implemented on the Internet in 1989, the network became accessible to everybody. Companies and organizations began to publish their Web portals as a type of virtual brochure with corporate and, to some extent, promotional information.

Slowly, midsize companies and businesses made their appearance on the network, promoting their services and products in a very direct approach. Most of these companies published their Web sites just to "be there," with no real business expectations. At that point, everybody started talking about the Internet, and everybody wanted to be involved somehow; however, nobody had any clear understanding of the operational characteristics and dynamic of this network.

In order to better explain the evolution of the Internet and its associated sub-products (like Internet marketing), I would like to guide you through the following argument:

Figure 0.5

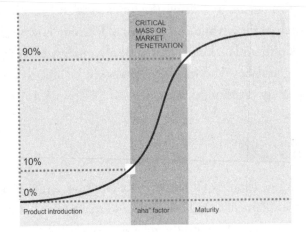

In business, the typical S curve model shows the analytical representation for establishing the market penetration of any product, as shown in Figure 0.5. We know that any product reaches market penetration once it hits 10 percent of the market, also known as hitting the critical mass. If we understand that Internet marketing is a "product," and view all its associated activities as derivatives of that main "product," we could agree that the evolution's laws of any product in the last century are also applicable to it.

Figure 1.0 represents a set of diagrams with the evolution of very significant products according to the S curve analysis and the moment they hit critical mass. There is an extensive period of time that elapses until the product reaches market penetration; this is the emplacement period, in which the market slowly assimilates new technology offers. Once the product penetrates 10 percent of the market, the product sets a new time range until reaching 90 percent of the market; this is also known as the "aha" factor. After this period, the product reaches maturity, and the continuation of the curve depends on several subsequent factors.

As the user can see on the diagrams, the range of time to hit the critical mass of 90 percent of the market has been decreasing in high-tech products. The market capacity for assimilating new products has evolved at a very significant rate, for different market behavior reasons. If we analyze the evolution of electricity, for instance, we may observe that it took 37 years after it was introduced to the public to hit critical mass, and then it took another 47 years to reach 90 percent of the market. Other examples include the telephone and the automobile, which show a similar evolution. On the other hand, products like the Internet, the microwave, and the television represent a different scenario, in which the time for reaching the critical mass is equal to or longer than the time for reaching 90 percent of the market.

Figure 1.0

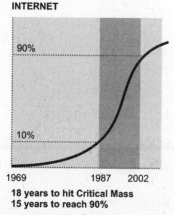

TELEPHONE

27 years to hit Critical Mass
70 years to reach 90%

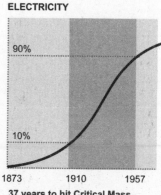

AUTOMOBILE

36 years to hit Critical Mass
50 years to reach 90%

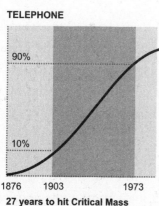

INTERNET

18 years to hit Critical Mass
15 years to reach 90%

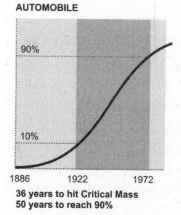

ELECTRICITY

37 years to hit Critical Mass
47 years to reach 90%

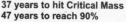

Figure 1.0

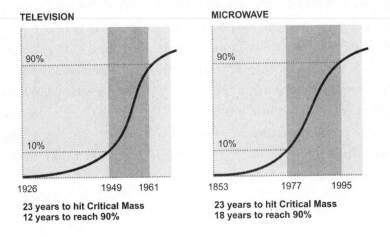

TELEVISION

90%

10%

1926   1949   1961

23 years to hit Critical Mass
12 years to reach 90%

MICROWAVE

90%

10%

1853   1977   1995

23 years to hit Critical Mass
18 years to reach 90%

Internet marketing has not yet reached critical mass, and that is one of the most important reasons for reading this book. At the present time, approximately 100 million people engage in e-commerce activities per year. In the next 10 or 15 years, that number will reach more than 800 million users per year, crushing into 10 percent of the market and then, as predicted, climbing to 90 percent in a frantic way. That is what authors like Don Tapscott define as the upcoming digital economy. Figure 2.0 represents the S curve analysis specifically calculated for Internet marketing, in order to facilitate the comprehension of its market immersion in the next 20 years.

Figure 2.0

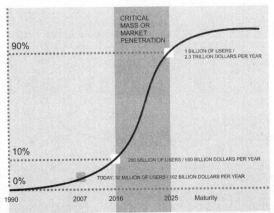

CRITICAL
MASS OR
MARKET
PENETRATION

90%

1 BILLION OF USERS /
2.3 TRILLION DOLLARS PER YEAR

10%

200 MILLION OF USERS / 650 BILLION DOLLARS PER YEAR

0%

TODAY: 32 MILLION OF USERS / 102 BILLION DOLLARS PER YEAR

1990   2007   2016   2025   Maturity

ESTIMATIONS FROM UBC RESEARCH

Figure 2.5 represents the current picture of Internet marketing in numbers and values that provide a strong reference to anyone with a minimal understanding of business. When Internet marketing has an impact on the market's critical mass, it will become one of the most astounding emerging multibillionaire industries ever.

Figure 2.5

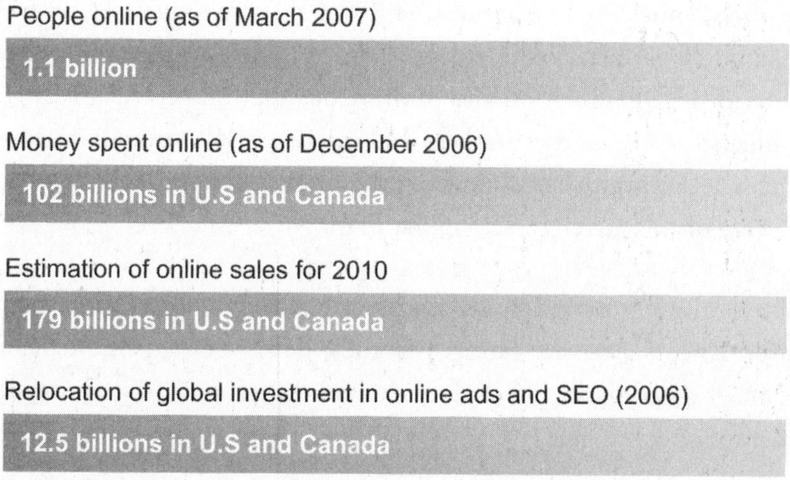

People online (as of March 2007)

1.1 billion

Money spent online (as of December 2006)

102 billions in U.S and Canada

Estimation of online sales for 2010

179 billions in U.S and Canada

Relocation of global investment in online ads and SEO (2006)

12.5 billions in U.S and Canada

Traditional Marketing Versus Digital Marketing

In the late '90s, traditional marketing began to experiment and introduce new services. Internet marketing is the natural evolution of one of those services — digital marketing.

Many professionals and developers started to realize the value of interactive marketing, capitalizing on the propagation of home computers with CD-ROM and the consolidation of the Internet.

As a result, several companies began offering online tools, such as interactive kiosks, multimedia catalogues, interactive games, promotional slideshows, and virtual magazines and brochures. Companies like Ambrosia Software,

Medialab International, Blast Radius, Insigna Systems, Electric Rain, and Xyvision Enterprise, among many others, initiated a new line of marketing that slowly incorporated the Internet as the most relevant channel for promotion and interaction.

These types of companies were the pioneers of Internet marketing, introducing new interactive concepts like banner ads, online catalogues, directories, and virtual magazines. This was also the time when developing companies like Macromedia, Adobe, Xerox, Quark, and Ventura started to deploy advanced animation and multimedia applications for the Internet, in order to conquer the market. For instance, Macromedia introduced Director, an innovative multimedia programming application that became the father of the current and popular Flash MX.

At the beginning of 2000, big corporations began to seriously consider incorporating digital marketing into their promotional plan, allocating a portion of their marketing budget to this new type of advertisement and promotion.

As a result, companies identified several new unique value propositions:

1. **Customer interaction:** Interactivity as a part of the new business interaction, in which the user manages his desire to select, click, open, close, drag, and see the different options presented by the application.

2. **Multimedia:** The integration of multiple channels of communication, combining sound, images, motion, and more.

3. **Tracking of user behavior and reaction:** The ability to identify action paths, patterns, common behaviors, and audience interest with the application.

4. **Electronic commerce:** Engagement of some form of electronic

commerce in order to provide the user with the capacity to initiate a financial transaction or purchase of any type.

5. **Unmatchable Return on Investment (ROI):** With the implementation of online advertisements, low cost, and tracking functionality, unique advantages were created for ROI. For example, sensitive information about how many users saw the ad, for how long, and whether somebody clicked on the link could be tracked and assessed financially.

What is Internet Marketing?

Advertising and its associate activities have been one of the most important actions in the marketing industry in the last 50 years. In the early 1990s, the Internet made a warm entrance into the advertising world, appearing to be the little sister of traditional and significant advertisement channels (newspapers, billboards, and television). Nobody believed at that time that online advertising would produce such a direct impact into the market and affect the business performance of the traditional, multibillion dollar advertising channels.

At that time, online advertising was inexpensive and Web traffic was not significant. Yahoo! was one of the first players trying to establish banners and skyscrapers controlled by a simple programming cycle. Advertising companies did not see any value in the advertisement options on the Internet, and many times during that period, Yahoo! offered banner ads to big corporations for free.

Figure 3.0

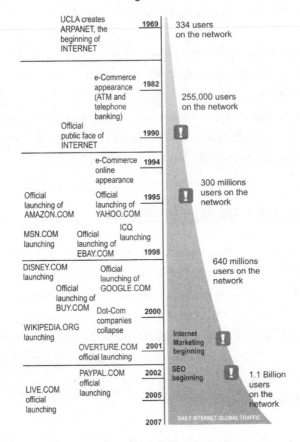

As the technology evolved, the amount of options increased, and more formal techniques started to appear; this was the initiation of Internet marketing. Figure 3.0 represents an interesting snapshot of the time evolution of Internet and all its collaterals; I believe it is important to take a few minutes to understand the major components of the diagram, since we will be referring to this timeline several times in this chapter.

Due to the impressive volume of Internet users, and the characteristics of the different online advertisement options, the impact on the traditional advertisement channels was significant. It is important to understand that online advertising is not only the typical banners ads displayed in the top section of any popular Web site, those just represent a small segment of a diverse set of options. Internet marketing is the evolution of online advertising and e-commerce. The Internet offers a market of 1 billion users daily.

Figure 3.1

Figure 3.1 represents the main components, or sub-activities, of Internet marketing; we will refer to most of them in the upcoming chapters.

One of the most relevant components of Internet marketing is search engine optimization (SEO). This component currently represents more than 70 percent of Internet activity. SEO represents the big initial step toward the Internet marketing revolution; let me explain this in detail. In 1999, Google traffic was about 40 million people per day. The very next year it reached over 100 million. Internet World Stats reported that Google and Yahoo! together, at the end of 2002, managed traffic of up to 190 million people per day.

The Internet exploded. People were actively looking for something on the net, using the search engines: writers, historical events, furniture, books, articles, music, data, hardware, and the list goes on.

Antonio Mercado, director of marketing for Oracle-Latin America and an expert in advance e-commerce, told me in 2001, "the new understanding in business is the traffic, no matter the type of Web site or service you have, if you have the traffic and you are able to keep it, you will make money." This was, and is, an interesting concept. At that time, not too many people understood this "traffic value concept." Many marketing academic experts actually questioned both the Google and Yahoo! business models, without trying to figure out their long term strategy. I remember some colleagues saying that Google was going to collapse before 2005.

The true investment for online companies in the late 1990s and the new century was "traffic." This new understanding required a high comprehension of the trend that had been coming since the late '80s, and had been identified by just a few professionals and business people.

There is not an official start date for Internet marketing, but we can agree on two major episodes that define when it did start:

- The launching of overture services

- The SEO implementation

Overture

On October 8, 2001, Bill Gross decided to re-launch **GoTo.com** as Overture Services. The company managed, through different alliances with search engines like MSN and Yahoo!, a new business model on top of the traditional user's search online, capitalizing on the significant traffic at that time. Overture implemented the pay per click (PPC) system, offering "sponsored results" added to the existing relevancy lists. Usually for every search, the search engine will display the relevancy list and in the right side, a highlighted column with the sponsored result.

As a result, Yahoo! became Overture's best customer, with a profit of $60 million at the end of 2003. In 2004, Yahoo! announced the purchasing of Overture Services for $1.7 billion, re-branding the service as Yahoo! Search Marketing. In 2003 Google joined the PPC war with the launching of AdWords, its own product for PPC campaigns.

Essentially, the PPC service secures the appearance of the sponsor in the sponsored list or links section. The details of this activity will be explained in Chapter 7.

The SEO

Every time a user submits a search, the application (search engine) obtains a result page with a list. That list is called the relevancy list. All search engines use different systems (e.g., robots, spiders, or submission) to cover the global network looking for and classifying Web sites. The relevancy list is the output of complex mathematical algorithms that the search engines apply in order to rank the links, based on data storage criteria.

There is no human intervention in the process of listing results of the relevancy list; the entire process is automated according to the algorithms mentioned before. Since 1996, several Web developers, programmers, and mathematicians have experimented with SEO, an activity that combined Web programming and statistical calculations with the objective of defining the rules that make Web sites friendly for the search engines and easy to rank. In the next chapter, you will find full coverage of SEO and some of its secrets.

SEO became very popular in 2003, when Google introduced a new formula that basically set the standards of SEO. That formula was a combination of keyword analysis, link popularity, contextual content, and parametrical regulations.

Today, big and midsize corporations in North America reallocate more than $30 billion of advertising budgets from traditional promotional activities to Internet marketing options. To understand why, take a look of the following list:

- **Captive market** — The people who are using search engines are definitively looking for something.

- **Attracted buyers** — This market has a high chance to purchase and is receptive to engaging in a transaction.

- **Interested market** — The user's curiosity about the product or service has been established. This is also considered the "engaged market."

- **Traceable market** — The audience and its activity on each Web site can be detailed and identified in order to be analyzed from a marketing perspective.

- **Interactivity factor** — Cross selling and promotional outcomes as a result of users' interactivity with your interface.

It has been predicted that by 2010, the volume of investment allocated by companies in North America will be over $100 billion, which is at the same strength as the TV industry.

The Principles of SEO

The main principle is simple (Figure 3.5), and is called the basic market connection law. There are millions of people surfing the Internet every day, a segment of which represents the manufacturer market. Internet marketing is the activity that builds the bridge between that potential number of customers and the manufacturer.

Figure 3.5

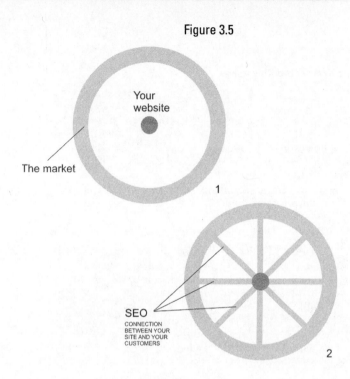

The activities of SEO and PPC services became stronger once e-commerce consolidated and managed around 20 billion in online sales. At that point, a new kind of company started offering Internet marketing services. These companies have become very popular and are defining a new sub-industry. At the back of this book, there is a classification and an overview of these services.

In late 1998, Elliot Anderssen from Alcatel at the University of Toronto said, "The real value of this type of marketing (Internet marketing) is the captive public factor. Remember, there is no communication channel in this industry that could manage millions of people looking for something." Anderssen had a valuable point, although it took a while to understand what he "looking for something" really meant.

Figure 4.0

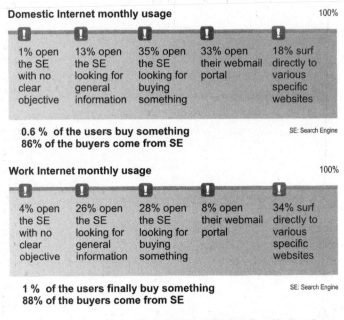

Domestic Internet monthly usage · 100%

| 1% open the SE with no clear objective | 13% open the SE looking for general information | 35% open the SE looking for buying something | 33% open their webmail portal | 18% surf directly to various specific websites |

0.6 % of the users buy something
86% of the buyers come from SE   SE: Search Engine

Work Internet monthly usage · 100%

| 4% open the SE with no clear objective | 26% open the SE looking for general information | 28% open the SE looking for buying something | 8% open their webmail portal | 34% surf directly to various specific websites |

1 % of the users finally buy something
88% of the buyers come from SE   SE: Search Engine

Average statistical analysis performed by the author on
340 users (27-40 years old): 80 female and 260 male

People who open an Internet browser or search engine are going to engage in a hunt that will bring a result as a part of a motivational activity; they do not visit the search engine necessarily to have fun, to relax, or to find some entertainment. Figure 4.0 details some clear statistical data about the average usage of search engines in North America. The information displayed is fundamental in understanding the added value of Internet marketing.

Never before has any type of marketing activity secured a qualified market like the Internet does. Just to be sure, let us go over the following information displayed in the last diagram:

An average of 87 percent of buyers come from a search initiated in a search engine.

If we expand this to a global scale, we can see that from the 320,000 daily average online buyers, around 275,000 will come from a search engine. Imagine the extraordinary potential of a new business channel that could virtually manage an average of 100 million focused buyers per year.

Before moving forward, here is a comparison about the market volume of different promotional and traditional channels:

- Super Bowl TV ads — 80 million viewers

- North America average live TV shows, peak hour — 34 million viewers

- Full-page, traditional magazine ads — 2 million readers

- Local radio program at the peak hour of the morning — 50,000 listeners

- Full-page in a national newspaper — 23 to 49 million readers

Do not forget that this audience is broad and does not represent a targeted market, which means that probably less than 2 percent could be your market, and eventually, a small percentage of that might became buyers.

Now, let us consider the average ROI in all those media channels (average percentages for each dollar invested):

- Super Bowl TV ads — 0.025 / 0.035

- North America average TV live shows peak hour — 0.2 / 0.44

- Full-page, traditional magazine ads — 0.43

- Local radio program at the peak hour of the morning — 0.21

- Full-page in a national newspaper — 0.54 / 0.93

In comparison, the average daily audience of the major representatives of Internet marketing are:

- Yahoo! — 263 million

- Google — 240 million

- eBay — 17 million

- Amazon — 16 million

- MSN — 300 million

Now, let us take a look at the average ROI of these companies (average percentages for each dollar invested):

- Yahoo — 0.97 / 1.22 (based on an average PPC campaign model)

- Google — 1.56 / 2.37 (based on an average PPC campaign model)

- EBay — 0.47 / 0.82 (based on promotional ads)

- Amazon — 1.89 / 2.43 (based on promotional ads)

- MSN — 1.46 / 2.22 (based on promotional ads)

It is not difficult to recognize the difference between traditional and Internet media channels in regard to numbers of people, and most importantly, the ROI. There is also an extra value to consider.

Search engine traffic is called the "focused market," since people sit in front of the computer with a defined objective (the "looking for something" factor). On the other hand, traditional promotional channels make contact with the "unfocused market," people who access them to obtain entertainment or learn information. This market is not necessarily interested in "looking for something." They could potentially become buyers, but they might not.

How many people reading the newspaper or watching TV are interested in the advertising? Leolen Lipovetsky, from **Eye4u.com**, during his speech at Westwood College in Anaheim, California, emphasized this point about today's advertising landscape. "The market's interest has been the most important component in any promotional process. Online buyers have initiated the process and they are far advanced on it at the time they arrive to the right e-commerce site."

Search engines manage about 100 million online buyers per year, with the main objective of Internet marketing being to capitalize on this impressive segment of recognized online buyers. In ten years, the amount of online buyers will be around one billion per year. Imagine the power of a market that size.

Web Site Evolution and the Introduction of Internet Marketing

The evolution of Internet marketing has been influenced by economical and technological factors, represented in detail in Figure 5.0. In 1993, graphic designers and programmers began to experiment and develop Web sites with very basic tools, half programming and half design. The traditional concept of visual communication and the new concept of visual interaction merged to develop Web sites. At that point, the market was fragile and not very promising — the Internet had an uncertain future.

The Internet started to show strong indications of success in 1999, when world-wide net's traffic exceeded 350 million daily worldwide; at that point, companies and developers started to consider how they could make money with Internet.

Figure 5.0

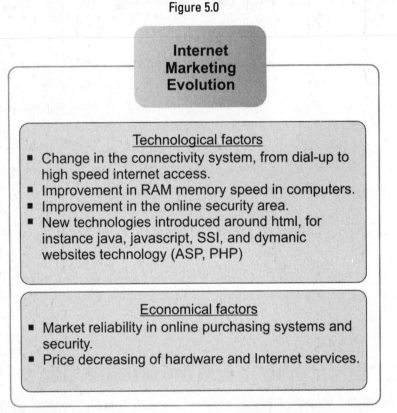

Internet Marketing Evolution

Technological factors
- Change in the connectivity system, from dial-up to high speed internet access.
- Improvement in RAM memory speed in computers.
- Improvement in the online security area.
- New technologies introduced around html, for instance java, javascript, SSI, and dymanic websites technology (ASP, PHP)

Economical factors
- Market reliability in online purchasing systems and security.
- Price decreasing of hardware and Internet services.

The basic Web site approach mutated from being a nice looking Web site with information about the product or company, to being a business tool with economical objectives. The first to do this was **Amazon.com** in 1995. This was a clear signal to entrepreneurs and investors that the dot-com bubble in the '90s was not without merit. The company finally showed real profitability in early 2003.

Definitive Added Value

One thing that clearly defines the success of Internet marketing is its unmatchable value proposition. For a better understanding of this, Figure 5.5 represents a number of elements that conceptually describe this added value.

Figure 5.5

Internet Marketing added value

- **Multimedia:** Motion, animation, sound, etc
- **Tracking:** Visitor behavior recording
- **Selectivity:** Audience segmentation
- **Broad action:** Big range of functionality, from the promotion to the purchase (shopping cart)
- **Dynamic content:** Management of real time and dynamic visual and text content
- **Redistribution:** visitors organization by specific criteria (vertical portals)
- **Real time data:** Connection with databases
- **Proactive:** Email campaigns, newsletters, promotions, automation, etc.
- **24/7 and worldwide:** All the time and anywhere
- **Selective content:** By region (i.e. geographic) or other type of criteria
- **Intelligence:** Real time statistics, visitors activity and sensitive information collection

2

Introduction to SEO

What You Will Learn About in the Following Chapter

- SEO and practical implementation guide
- Conversion rate and its usability
- The fundamentals of ethical SEO
- Professional implementation of Web site optimization

What Is Search Engine Optimization?

As outlined in the last chapter, SEO is the technique that improves the volume or quality of traffic to a Web site from search engines, implementing algorithmic calculations in order to rank in the list of search results. Typically, there is a basic logic behind ranking lists of search engines: as earlier, a Web site is presented in the search results as higher it ranks, which means that site's age is relevant for its own ranking.

SEO can also target different kinds of search, including image search, local search, and industry-specific vertical search engines. Figure 6.0 represents significant statistical information that helps to better understand the fundamentals that forced the evolution of SEO from the business standpoint.

Figure 6.0

75%	SOURCE: TNS

of all online shoppers said that *company size was not a factor* in having their online shopping needs satisfied. Only 15% said they preferred to shop with large retailers

More than 80%	SOURCE: Tech/GVU Users Survey

Of all Internet users find new web sites through search engines. That means that about 650 million people use search engines to find web sites.

More than 89%	SOURCE: Tech/GVU Users Survey

Of search engine users are the most qualified and motivated visitors on the net. The buying rate is 1 of 7 buyers, coming from SE, engage a financial transaction online.

As a marketing strategy for increasing a site's relevancy, SEO considers how search algorithms work and what people search for. SEO efforts may involve:

- Site coding

- Presentation

- Design and structure

- Fixing issues that could prevent search engine indexing programs from fully screening the Web site

- Content indexed by search engines without changing the feeling of the Web site

The previous list represents the basic set of considerations for making a Web site "SEO friendly" or "SEO optimized." In Chapter 4, we will cover in detail the basic and advanced techniques for Web optimization, from the concept stand point to the practical implementation training.

Conversion Rate

The basis of SEO strategy is to establish (and improve) the conversion rate of the Web sites, independently of the nature of the business. Every Web site has traffic, the relationship between that traffic and the amount of people that "buy" every day from the Web site identifies the conversion rate. The conversion rate is extremely important and useful for the design of the overall marketing strategy, as this book will explain in the following chapters.

 In this case, the word "buy" refers to any financial transaction or special engagement that the Web site defined in its business model, regardless of the product or service.

Figure 7.0 represents a diagram with SEO's conversion rate. The important factor of the rate is the following:

> *At least 2 percent of the visitors have to become customers in the overall calculation.*

If this ratio is not present, the Web site is not profitable.

Figure 7.0

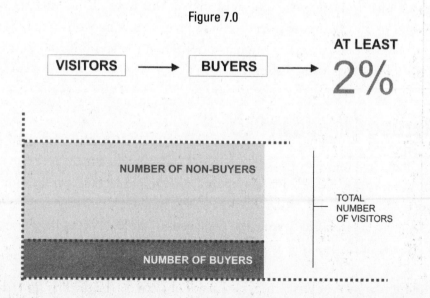

Why You Need to Optimize Your Web site

Considering that there are billions of Web pages on the Internet, it is obvious that not all of them can be listed in the top position of search engines. Search engines only list Web sites that they find applicable to a special topic. If search engines cannot find out what a particular Web site is about, they cannot give that Web site ranking for that keyword. The process of optimizing Web pages consists of making the Web site searchable, so the search engines worldwide are able to qualify and rank it according to the referential keywords.

It is important to reflect on the following data:

> *Only a few Web surfers look further than the first or second result page of a search engine.*

According to Georgia Institute of Technology, 75 percent of searchers never look further than page one. Most search engines display 10 results on the first page, and very few searchers click the links to look at the second page. As usability expert Jakob Nielsen points out, "Users almost never look beyond the second page of search results." Danny Sullivan, ClickZ Search Engine Marketing Columnist, puts it this way, "Being listed 11 or beyond means that more than 2 million people daily may miss your Web site." For that reason, search engine optimization is relevant if you want to be successful with your Web site.

Getting Started in SEO

In 1994, Stephen Holdren, a recognized e-commerce expert and one of the creators of CNET **Download.com**, convinced the board of The Hong Kong and Shanghai Banking Corporation to implement the first project of e-Banking. The project was finally deployed in late 1997, creating a break in the use of the Internet as a simple consulting media.

Holdren's argument was rich in two major objectives – be the first financial institution offering an online banking product and generate a total new channel of profitability in Electronic Banking services.

He succeeded in both. He also made an involuntary contribution to the evolution of the Internet – providing online services beyond any expectations. People had begun to realize that the Internet was much more than a simple new media (similar in many aspects to TV). Today, Internet users around the world make financial transactions with banks for over 13 billion dollars per year.

Holdren contributed to propelling several e-businesses, such as hotel reservations, books cataloguing, and plane ticket reservations online. In the meantime, e-commerce began to show its potential; search engine companies started to identify a new market. Yahoo!, Altavista, Google, America Online, Dogpile, and others were the pioneers of the development of an automated process of identification and classification of Web sites worldwide. The way to achieve this was the creation and deployment of two very important initiatives:

- The Spider or Robot

- The Algorithm

Both are relevant in the effective operation of search engines today. The spiders or robots (also known as Web Crawlers) are smart, responsive programs that analyze the Internet in a particular way, in order to obtain information from the Web sites. The only objective of the spider is to capture sensitive information and report it to the search engines. Each search engine company has its own spider system, similar in operation, but adapted to their own characteristics.

The spider is one type of bot or software agent that starts with a list of URLs to visit called "seeds" (we will discuss seeds in Chapter 5). As the spider visits these URLs, it identifies a set of components that are relevant for the search engines:

- Title and description

- Hyperlinks

- Keywords

- Images

- Content relevancy

The spider also classifies the Web site by comparing it with the set of policies.

The policies (also known as Crawlers Policies) were conceptually introduced by Raymond Shaffer from Stanford University and finally implemented in early 2002 by all search engines. The policies are a set of standardized validation rules, oriented to facilitate the spider's performance and avoid fraud.

Sooner or later, the Web spiders will arrive at each Web site, inspecting and analyzing its structure, integrity, and content. For that reason, any professional Web developer must optimize his site to make it "acceptable" to the Web spider visit.

Figure 7.5

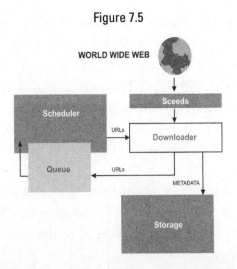

Figure 7.5 represents the basic architecture of the Web spider's functionality; its mission is to capture and filter Web site information, but that is not the only classification method involved in the process. After the spider classifies the Web site, the information is submitted to the search engines to apply the algorithm.

The algorithms are conventional formulas that complement the job of the spiders to identify the relevancy of the URL researched by the software agent. The formula is able to calculate the level of importance of the Web site, analyzing different variables:

- Time or age of the Web site

- Content consistency

- Link coherency

- Level of relevancy (coming from the spider)

- HTML content level

- Frequency of modification

The representation in Figure 8.0 is part of the standard algorithm published by Google. It is important to mention that the algorithm implemented by the search engine companies is always reviewed and adjusted; changing some calculations that eventually might impact the development of the "SEO friendly" adjustments on Web sites. Do not worry, the main components of the calculation listed above are standard, but some new little components might be added or adjusted. Major search engines (Google, Yahoo!, MSN, Alexa, etc.) lead the trend of the universal algorithm formula; the rest of the search engines usually follow the patterns established by those big corporations.

Figure 8.0

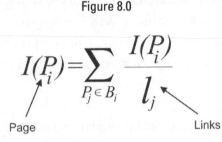

Page   Links

Here's how the PageRank is determined. Suppose that page Pj has lj links. If one of those links is to page Pi, then Pj will pass on 1/lj of its importance to Pi. The importance ranking of Pi is then the sum of all the contributions made by pages linking to it. That is, if we denote the set of pages linking to Pi by Bi.

Tip — As part of the SEO optimization work, the developer/marketer must check periodically the algorithm adjustments from Google and Yahoo! (at least). More information on this topic can be found at **http://www.free-seo-news.com.**

The algorithm itself means nothing; it is just a mathematical formula. The real value is to be aware of the elements that the formula analyzes, in realistic terms, with the purpose of defining an action from the development perspective. Useful information about this topic can be found at the Search Engine Marketing Professional Organization (SEMPO) at **www.sempo.org**.

How Do Search Engines Rank Web Pages?

As we learned, search engines use algorithms to determine the rank of a Web page. The complete mathematical formulas are never revealed by search engine companies; just a part of them is disclosed. I might help you to decrypt those algorithms in a practical way, using the Google algorithm as an example.

Google explains the ranking algorithm on their corporate site as follows:

"Traditional search engines rely heavily on how often a word appears on a Web page. Google uses PageRank™ to examine the entire link structure of the Web and determine which pages are most important.

It then conducts hypertext-matching analysis to determine which pages are relevant to the specific search being conducted. By combining overall importance and query-specific relevance, Google is able to put the most relevant and reliable results first."

PageRank and Hypertext-Matching

PageRank and hypertext-matching analysis is a popular way to extrapolate the information from the spider in order to rank Web pages. To obtain good results from the PageRank, the marketer need good links from related pages that point to the site. It is a simple principle: if page A links to page B, then it is a recommendation from page A to page B.

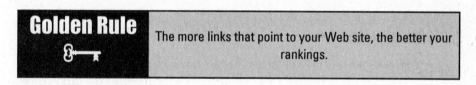

Golden Rule The more links that point to your Web site, the better your rankings.

The quality of the links is also important. A link that contains the keyword for which you want to have high rankings in the link text is better than five links with the text "click here." A link from a Web site that has a related topic is also much better than links from unrelated sites or link lists (see Figure 8.5).

Figure 8.5

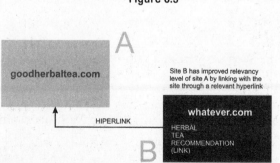

There are many characteristics and measures of link relevancy, which we will cover in detail in Chapter 6. For now, appreciate that hyperlinks are extremely important in the ranking, and require a special strategy. There are applications specially designed to determine the level of hyperlink-matching of Web sites.

The hypertext-matching analysis performed by Google also considers page content, not only meta-tags, but full content of a page and characteristics in fonts, contextual appearance, subdivisions, and the precise location of each word. The calculation also considers the content of adjacent Web pages to ensure the results returned are the most relevant to a user's query.

As Google, for instance, analyzes the full content of your pages, you also have to optimize the full content of your Web pages. It is not enough to edit the meta-tag. It is necessary to optimize all factors that can influence the ranking.

Before Starting

Many Webmasters and developers do not know which page factors can be important for SEO optimization. The objective of this book is to provide all the information required to perform an effective SEO optimization strategy.

There are several different Web page elements that search engines use to identify hypertext-matching level. Following, you will find a list of those relevant elements, and the ideal recommendation with the intention of optimizing any Web site:

- At least one Web page from a different domain has to link to your Web site.

- Links from .edu or .gov domains to your Web site can be beneficial for your search engine ranking.

- You should try to get a link from **DMOZ.org** (Open Directory Project). The best way to do it is to submit the information through their Web site.

- Links that are in bold face or use a big font may be more important than other links.

- At least one link of the site must use the terms of the most important meta-tag keywords.

- Hyperlink text must represent as much as possible the target topic. For instance, if the target is the "about us" page, the link might say "learn more about us in this link."

- Never repeat the same hyperlink text in the same page.

- The maximum number of total characters of the inbound links is between 850 and 930.

- Hyperlink color must be different than the body text.

- Hyperlinks must not contain special characters "&," "#," " percent," "?," "$," or "=."

The list above is just oriented to provide optimization for the hypertext-matching category. Web site optimization is much more complex, and will be covered in Chapter 4.

One Page Is Not Enough for Relevancy

As part of hypertext-matching analysis, Google, for instance, also analyzes the Web content of other Web pages on the same site to ensure that the Web page is relevant.

The intention of this is to avoid anchor Web sites, a technique developed in 2005 by many Web developers to secure high rankings.

Anchor Web sites were simple and independent (own URL) one page Web sites with supportive information and links to the real Web site, with the intention of providing link relevancy. Some companies developed hundred of single-page Web sites as part of their link relevancy strategy. This is not necessarily fraud, but search engines considered it unreal linkage. For that reason, during 2006, a new standard changed the evaluation method for hypertext-matching to the following:

The more pages of your Web site are optimized for keywords about a special topic, the more likely it is that the site will get high rankings for a special keyword that is related to that topic.

Your Web Site Must Have Both Optimized Content and Incoming Links

In Chapter 4, you will learn how to perfectly optimize any Web page for the exact ranking algorithm of Google, Yahoo!, or any other search engine. Additionally, you will also learn how to obtain high quality links to your Web site that significantly enhance search engine rankings.

Search Engines

Fortune Magazine published an interesting article called "Search Engines secret world." One section of the investigation highlighted the reality of the search engines business and all the collateral business that emerged from the SEO fever … many companies promise customers to submit their Web sites to 30,000 or more search engines in the world. This is false, considering there are only 4,200 dedicated and real search engines listed online."

The so-called "search engines" they are using are free directories or special interest Web pages. Submitting your Web page to thousands of those sites does not have any positive impact on your SEO strategy, and probably the only result you will get is millions of spam e-mails in your inbox.

I have performed many experiments with those submissions, and I did not identify a single visitor coming from those "search engines." There are quite a few search engines that can bring visitors to Web sites. The smart marketer or developer must look for quality instead of quantity, since SEO optimization's objective is to bring customers to a site, not just traffic.

At the present time, there are only six major players: Google, Yahoo!, AOL, Alexa, MSN Search, and **Ask.com**. They are leading the market (and traffic) of search engine business, and search engine companies are businesses. The fact that access to their site is free or that you do not necessarily buy something from them does not mean they are not profitable or they do not care about making money.

The majority of the search engines around the world are powered by those major search engine. For example, the search engine on **AOL.com** displays Google results. Another example is **Bloomberg.com**, a robust portal for stock traders and financial agents, which also uses Google as a search engine.

Ethical SEO

Some developers use unethical techniques and tricks to artificially improve the search engine rankings of a Web site. If you know how to do it, or have been taught, do not do it. Unethical SEO techniques reduce the quality of search results; in addition, search engine companies have become stricter about relevancy analysis and policies as a result.

Increasingly unethical SEO techniques forced search engines to reconstruct their algorithms to prevent spammers from flooding the results page with irrelevant or low quality content. Once that takes place, everyone (legal or illegal developers) is obligated to adapt to the new requirements.

If you use a Web site promotion tool that uses these unethical techniques, you will put your Web business at severe risk. The level of penalization of search engines today is severe and does not have considerations. Let me give you an example. In early 2006, the automotive company BMW Germany was penalized by Google for illegal usage of keywords and doorways in its corporate Web site. The company also mentioned competitor brands and other generic and popular words not related to the automotive industry in its meta-tags. As a result, BMW Germany was completely removed from the result list of Google for about 230 days. The details of the episode can be found at **http://blogoscoped.com/archive/2006-02-04-n60.html.**

Ethical search engine optimization methods produce lasting results and do not upset search engines. Unethical techniques are usually considered spam. The following list represents all the spam actions that search engines penalize:

- **Doorway pages** – Several "single page Web sites" in the same IP address and redirecting to the main Web site

- **Cloaking and false redirects** – The Web server returns different pages for search engine spiders and human Web surfers

- **Keyword stuffing** – Meta-tags with competitor brand name or irrelevant words in order to be exposed in popular searches

- **Hidden text or hidden links** – Text has a color that is very similar to the background color, text in very small font sizes, text has been hidden with CSS tags, or similar techniques

- **Pages loaded with irrelevant words** – Irrelevancy between Web site content and the page displayed

- **Duplicated content on multiple pages** – Identical or very similar pages, in order to qualify for coherency and Web size

- **Misspelling of well-known Web sites** – Usage of typos of recognized brands

- **Unrelated and centralized link farms** – Several hidden hyperlinks to popular sites

You might get short term results with these techniques, but it is likely that your site will be penalized and eventually disqualified from search engines if you use them.

The Threats of Spam

Before beginning with an SEO optimization, you must be sure your Web pages are free of any spam element. If you use a spam technique on your Web site, all other search engine optimization efforts are useless. If a search engine has identified your Web site as a spam source, you are in trouble. Even if you remove the spam components of the site, it might take a while for the search engine companies to re-qualify your Web site. Search engines do not like to be cheated.

When you are sure that your Web pages are spam free, you can start with your search engine optimization activities. Better concentrate on ethical methods that are beneficial to you, such as Web surfers and search engines.

SEO Companies and Services

In the last couple of years, several SEO services companies have appeared on the market, offering the impossible. They guarantee that clients will get a special search engine position, often the first place. No company can guarantee a special position in the search engine listings. If a company makes such promises, it is being dishonest. The catch is often that the company selects the search terms. You will discover in this book that there are no big secrets behind SEO, and that it is an ongoing process that could not be managed effectively by an external service company.

Many of those companies generate a satellite or floating SEO strategy, which consists of the implementation of additional Web sites located in dedicated servers around the world, supporting link relevancy and popularity. Of course, those Web sites disappear if you discontinue the service. Some other companies also implement a click farm technique (absolutely illegal) with the purpose of showing their customers an increase in traffic from many parts of the world.

Submitting Web sites to the search engines is free, and has to be done systematically. It is recommended to acquire supportive software for scheduling the process rather than paying third party companies to do it, with no control of the details of the process. In Chapter 5, I will refer to these particular applications for scheduling the submission.

Once again, SEO is the technique that improves the volume/quality of traffic to a Web site from search engines, implementing algorithmic calculations, in order to rank in the list of search results. This process is a delicate, ongoing action that never stops and needs to grow as the business grows, the Web site grows, and the knowledge of the developers and marketers involved grows.

3

Keywords, the Cornerstone of a Successful SEO

Finding the Best Keywords

In the last chapter, we reviewed in detail the way search engines work and the importance of "keywords" for search engines during the process of Web site identification and classification. The present chapter is dedicated to "keywords" in order to ensure you get a deep understanding of this important topic.

As I mentioned before, people look for specifics. People sit down in front of their computer and type referential words or phrases that represent their need or interest hoping they will obtain the expected result. Search engines need keywords to qualify Web sites. For this reason, the "keyword definition" became one of the most important activities in the Internet marketing process, and, as you will learn in this chapter, is an ongoing action, meaning the Internet marketer is always working, creating, and adjusting the set of keywords. Defining keywords is a constant process of creativity and strategy, directly linked to the success of your Web site.

Two vital considerations must be taken into account with keywords:

- They must be related to the theme of the Web site.

- In Internet marketing, we use the term "keywords" for single word keywords and also for keyword phrases, such as "running shoes shop boston."

The basic rule of successful keyword generation is to choose focused and targeted keyword phrases that are common enough that the Web searcher will use them, but selective enough that they do not return millions of matches. Very specific keywords generate extremely qualified traffic.

The first steps in selecting the right keywords are:

- Making them very specific

- Using keyword phrases that consist of two to four words

- Avoiding very competitive keywords

- Being specific

- Defining relevant keywords

For a booming online marketing campaign, it is important to target the right keywords. Most people use a two- to four-word phrase in a search, so phrases are very effective.

Single words cannot be promoted effectively. For instance, it is not likely that someone looking for "free software download" is going to type just "software" into the search box.

The most popular keyword phrases are what make the Web site battle against millions of other pages; it is unrealistic to think that a new Web site could rank number one on a popular phrase like "music."

Tip	Start with multiple word keywords and later extend your keyword list.

Search engines analyze all pages of your Web site and put them into context. Starting with multiple keywords increases the possibility of getting higher rankings. For example, if the objective is to sell paintings, the best optimization is to create multiple keywords that make reference to the specific aspects of the product, such as "alternative painters," "modern figurative art paintings," or "artists oil painting chicago."

Keyword Types

Internet users usually start looking with general keywords. After becoming more knowledgeable about a particular product or service, they use more specific keywords. There are three types of keywords:

- Browsing type keyword
- Buying type keywords
- Association type keywords

Browsing type keywords

These are the keywords used during the first research phase. For example, a general user could be interested in a Replica watch. The keyword a person may use in a search engine could be:

Replica watch

In this case, the user is looking for general information about that product. These types of keywords usually produce a very high volume of results; probability of positioning a Web site within the top 10 is very small.

Association type keywords

Users usually narrow down their selection because they know, with a higher level of detail, what type of product they want. In this case, the user is considered a qualified user. For example, he may type:

Golden Omega replica watch

The keywords of this research are way more specific, and usually are composed of four or five words. Other variations of this type of search are as follows:

- Omega + Replica + gold

- "Omega Replica" + gold

- Replica watch Omega + gold

People who use association keywords are potential buyers; for that reason, they are probably the best keywords to target for any SEO campaign. They often have much lower search volumes than general keywords, but are more effective in terms of results.

Note	Keywords can be in upper or lower case, since search engines do not distinguish between them.

Buying Type Keywords

More aggressive users, who have already decided to buy, use these types of keywords. They look online for the best offer or price. For that reason, these users apply very specific keywords:

- Replica watch + Omega + model 1256266 + gold

- Omega Replica + golden + James bond model

- Omega Replica watch + golden + 007 model

Multiple Keywords

Single words cannot be found effectively. For example, it is not likely that someone looking for "replica omega watch + golden" will type just "watch" into the search box. Multiple keywords provide the highest chance to rank in the search of users applying association and buying type keywords.

Below are real life examples of keywords from Tom Jacobson, a very successful Internet marketer who, in 2004, developed the keyword strategy for the Herbalife Web site. This company, a manufacturer of herbal health products, also wanted to promote its real business objective — a pyramidal structure for people looking for additional income sources. As a result, Jacobson engaged in two different strategies:

1. Natural and health products stream

2. Second income source stream

For the first stream, he designed keywords that represent the product's effectiveness. The keyword list was:

- Lose weight

- Diet products
- Overweight solutions

- Diet center
- Obesity control

- Healthy natural products
- Health center

- Herbal products
- Natural vitamins

- Medicinal herbs

For the second stream, he chose the following keywords:

- Get rich
- Second income jobs

- Business opportunities
- Financial freedom

- Profit increasing
- Personal business

- How to make more money

Another example is from Alexey Milkov, a pioneer of SEO, who created the keyword strategy for the Canon Digital Camera division. He guessed the unique entries from people looking for information about the product, anticipating potential customers wanting to learn more before making any buying decision.

- Digital cameras
- Digital photography

- How to buy a digital camera
- Electronic photos

- Camera reviews
- List of camera manufacturers

- New digital cameras

By analyzing different company keywords, you will find (and learn) how professionals design their keyword strategy, considering basically two important points:

- Words that represent the product, service, or type of business

- Words with a high level of singularity and uniqueness

Analyzing Competitor's Keywords

This is a very common technique that helps to complete and to make adjustments in your set of keywords. Obviously, this technique could also be used by your competitor to analyze your keywords.

Web site pages of any type (e.g., HTML, ASP, and PHP) contain the SEO keywords implanted in the first section of the code, under a special tag named:

<meta name="keywords">

The appropriate syntax is the following:

<meta name="keywords" content="golden watches, men watches, silver watches, metal watches" />

In order to access the keywords of your competitor's Web sites, the first step is to identify a list of URLs using your favorite search engine (it is recommended to analyze at least five URLs). Depending on your level of knowledge in HTML, you can use any HTML editor in order to obtain the keywords directly from the code or apply any free keyword analyzer online. The following list of links represents many of the meta-tag keyword free analyzers available online.

- **http://www.widexl.com/remote/search-engines/ metatag-analyzer.html**

- **http://www.submitexpress.com/analyzer/**

- **http://www.seochat.com/seo-tools/meta-analyzer/**

Figure 10.0 represents the result of the keyword analyzer online applications, providing additional information about Web site description and basic analysis, such as the amount of characters and keywords, and word regularity. After you run this test on every competitor's URL, you will be able to create a simple text document with a list of all the unrepeated keywords. Then, you are ready to incorporate them to your own Web site.

Figure 10

Meta tags report for: http://www.globz.com/

meta tag length value

Title:	49	GlobZ: free single and multiplayer games in Flash
Description:	49	GlobZ: free single and multiplayer games in Flash
Keywords:	159	Flash games, free, multiplayer games, 3d flash, Macromedia Flash, games, dancer, microbe, entertainment, fun, cartoons, toys, virtual creatures, widgets, tools
Robots:	3	all

Meta tags analysis.

Title: Title meta tag contains no errors.
This tag contains 49 characters.

Title relevancy to page content is excellent.
The Title relevancy to page content is 100%.

Description: Description meta tag contains no errors.
This tag contains 49 characters.

The first step is to define which ones you want to add, considering a very important rule:

The maximum amount of words in the meta-tag keywords per HTML page is 25. This number must never be exceeded.

If you identify more than 25 words, and chances are you will, you need to prioritize the ones that reflect what your Web site is offering. Leave the rest for stage two, which I will explain further in Chapter 4. This means that the keyword selection has to be a conscious choice between the keywords you defined for your Web site and the new ones to add from your analysis, without writing more than 25 words.

Keyword Tools

There are several tools available that can assist you with Internet marketing, such as easy-to-use applications; they really simplify tasks and assist in defining keywords. These tools are:

- Wordtracker or reverse lookup

- Keyword suggestion tool

Few companies and organizations develop these types of applications. Following is a list of links for the user. Some of them are freeware and some of them are licensed software. Make your own evaluation; all of them are tested and very reliable.

Wordtrackers:

- http://www.wordtracker.com

- http://www.123promotion.co.uk/ppc/index.php

Keyword suggestion tools:

- https://adwords.google.com/select/Keyword ToolExternal

- http://inventory.overture.com/d/searchinventory/suggestion/

- http://conversion.7search.com/scripts/advertisertools/keywordsuggestion.aspx

- http://freekeywords.wordtracker.com/

- http://www.google.com/trends

Wordtracking

This activity, also called reverse lookup, is a useful commercial service that provides the amount of people per month who search for a particular keyword (and its derivatives).

Wordtracking applications allow the user to enter a keyword and retrieve all the variations, and its corresponding traffic, that were searched in the last 30 days. It is a wonderful tool for defining trends and adjusting your own keywords.

There are all types of trends and collective search behaviors; these applications can easily provide valuable information in order to re-define and create more.

Figure 11.0 shows an example of the typical result obtained from this type of application; in this case, the user entered the keyword "bird food," obtaining a list of results that represent the most searched keywords entered by users, related by approximation with "bird food."

After reading the list of results, the user can have a better idea about which keywords to use with "bird food" in order to be more successful. In summary, wordtracking provides a comprehensive report of the trends of potential markets of any product or service.

Figure 11.0

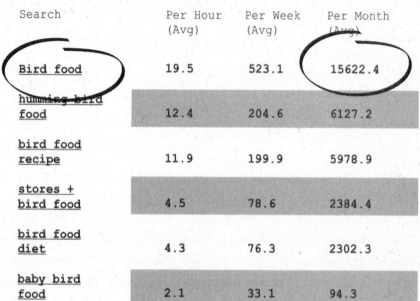

Search	Per Hour (Avg)	Per Week (Avg)	Per Month (Avg)
Bird food	19.5	523.1	15622.4
humming bird food	12.4	204.6	6127.2
bird food recipe	11.9	199.9	5978.9
stores + bird food	4.5	78.6	2384.4
bird food diet	4.3	76.3	2302.3
baby bird food	2.1	33.1	94.3

Put another way, the user has to run a search of all the predefined keywords. For each keyword, the wordtracking application delivers a list of keywords that represent the most searched keywords during the past 30 days related to the keyword entered by the user. Each word shows a number that represents the amount of times it was entered in a search engine (e.g., Yahoo! or Google wordtracking system). It is very important to qualify the results of the reverse lookup and compare it with a typical result from any search engine (preferably the most popular) in order to identify the competitor scenario.

Let us suppose now that a marketer runs a reverse lookup for "fishing reel" in order to obtain a fair set of keywords for his Web site. The result provides the following list of monthly searches:

- Fishing reel, 10,711
- Fly fishing reel, 8,300
- Shimano fishing reel, 2,928
- Fishing rods and reel, 1,986

- Electric fishing reel, 1,840
- Antique fishing reel, 933
- Saltwater fishing reel, 602
- Fishing reel review, 543
- Ice fishing reel, 503
- Fishing accessories, 190
- Old fishing reel, 87
- Used fishing reel, 34
- Fly fishing rods and reels, 172

In order to qualify the results, the marketer needs to cross examine the keywords with the offering of the Web site. The list obtained from the reverse lookup application might not totally match the product to the market. For instance, it is obvious that "shimano fishing reel" represents a brand; for that reason, the marketer is unable to use that keyword, unless the Web site has the legal rights to promote (and eventually sell) that brand. For this reason, the list is now reduced to those keywords that match the product being offered:

- Fishing reel
- Fly fishing reel
- Fishing rods and reel
- Fishing reel review
- Ice fishing reel
- Fishing accessories
- Fly fishing rods and reels

Once this list has been filtered, the next step is to look for the keywords listed in a popular search engine in order to identify how many competitors are listed by those keywords. This process helps to recognize the level of attraction of these keywords and sometimes helps the marketer to identify different keyword variations. For instance, the keyword "fishing reel" is very general, and even if it is searched by online users, the result from Yahoo! shows more than 10 pages of diverse competitors, making it difficult to obtain a relevant place in a short period of time.

Tip	Never write your brand name in the keywords list.

Tip	Never repeat the same word or words more than three times in one meta-tag.

The final list of keywords might be very similar to the following:

- Quality fishing reel
- Fishing reel
- Fly fishing reel
- Fishing supplies
- Fishing accessories
- Fly fishing rods and reels

The meta-tags for the Web site will be similar to the following:

<meta name="keywords" content="fishing reel, fishing supplies, rods, fly fishing, quality reel" />

Figure 12.0

Overture Suggestions	Monthly Search Volume estimated	Google estimated(Overture)	Yahoo! estimated	MSN	Yahoo! Suggest	Wordtracker	KW Discovery	Goo Trei
media center	51,191	29,252	14,626	7,313	Y! Sugg	WT	KD	media
adaptec center control dual media remote tuner tv xp	189,574	108,328	54,164	27,082	Y! Sugg	WT	KD	adap center dual n remote tv x
20gb center dreameo enza media portable	121,380	69,360	34,680	17,340	Y! Sugg	WT	KD	20gb c drea enza r porta
linksys wireless media center extender wmce54ag	45,609	26,062	13,031	6,516	Y! Sugg	WT	KD	links wirel media exter wmce
window	41,713	23,836	11,918	5,959	Y! Sugg	WT	KD	wind

Keyword Suggestion Tool

Some wordtracking applications are called "keyword suggestion tools" or "keyword research tools." They provide the same service as the wordtracking applications, with the exception of generating reports with detailed information classified by the most popular search engines (see Figure 12.0). The user is then able to evaluate the differences (in the amount of searches) for each of the search engines that composed the report.

Figure 12.5

Chocolate Mint Italian style

style mint chocolate itallian

style itallian mint chocolate

style chocolate mint itallian

style mint itallian chocolate

itallian style mint chocolate

mint itallian style chocolate

itallian style chocolate mint

mint itallian chocolate style

itallian chocolate style mint

style itallian chocolate mint

mint chocolate itallian style

chocolate itallian style mint

chocolate style mint itallian

itallian chocolate mint style

style chocolate itallian mint

mint style chocolate itallian

mint style itallian chocolate

chocolate mint style itallian

mint chocolate style itallian

Combination

Obtaining several keywords is not enough. The combination of the keywords is an important technique that tries to create many other possibilities that the conventional suggestion tools might eventually miss. The combination involves a simple process of words permutation, considering all the possible combinations, with or without making sense in the reading; see Figure 12.5.

There is some software available to do the permutations, instead of doing it manually. Following are two of them:

- **http://www.5minutesite.com/local_keywords.php**

- **http://www.vicman.net/lib/by-keywords.htm**

Please note: It is important to obtain all possible keyword combinations. These will be used later when we discuss PPC activity in Chapter 7.

Typos

The typo or misspelling technique tries to anticipate in advance the potential (and common) mistakes or typos of the users in order to obtain a high ranking in a search engine's relevancy list. Most search engines offer an automatic typo corrector if a typo is detected (see Figure 12.8).

Figure 12.8

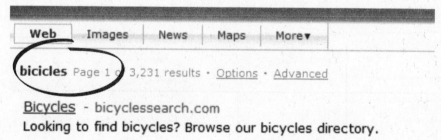

Although search engines provide an automatic suggestion to correct the typo, users tend to see and click on the first three links proposed by the search engine, if they correspond with the keyword entered. As a result, this principle makes marketers and developers rank the typos as conventional keywords, capitalizing on them and going over the results of them in relevancy and PPC lists. The user can obtain free online applications to generate typos:

- **http://www.selfseo.com/keyword_typo_generator.php**

- **http://tools.seobook.com/spelling/keywords-typos.cgi**

Keyword Matrix

The matrix helps to define the keyword strategy. Take your time while going through this topic. The keyword matrix is a very important technique that provides the set of keywords for the different campaigns of the Web site (we will learn about that in Chapter 7). The success of these campaigns depends of the keyword matrix and the strategy applied in designing and selecting the keywords (Figure 13.0 represents its basic structure).

Figure 13.0

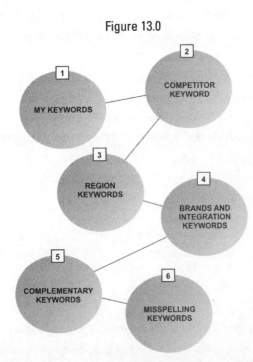

The six components of the matrix are:

1. **Basic keywords (also known as my keywords):** These represent the most significant keywords (browsing, association, and buying types), reviewed at the beginning of this chapter. These are the keywords that best represent the product or service of the Web site.

2. **Competitor keywords:** These are the keywords extracted from the competitor analysis explained earlier.

3. **Region keywords:** These keywords represent the geographical location that identifies the region of action of the Web site. If the offering is sold worldwide, this component of the matrix could be ignored.

4. **Brand and integration keywords:** This is a very important component of the structure. Depending on the product or offering, the user must identify the associative information that could bring a benefit by connection. For instance, if the Web site promotes sports shoes online and the company represents important brands that are well known, the keywords could potentially mention those brands, like Adidas, Puma, or Nike.

5. **Complementary keywords:** These try to capitalize on the need level of the users. For instance, in the recent example about sport shoes, the complementary keywords could include running, aerobic sports, and racing activities. These keywords require some degree of creativity from the developer, in order to combine situations and imagined searches of the users who will be potentially looking for the product in the future. The principle is simple — if somebody is looking for some particular activity that represents (or is linked to) a product, even if the search is not necessarily referring to the product, chances are, that user is going to be interested in the offering, considering he or she is part of the market.

6. Misspelled keywords: These represent the potential, common typos.

> **Tip** Although we have to, eventually, filter keywords in our strategy, there is no limit of keywords in the matrix; do not be afraid to add as many as you need.

Figure 13.5

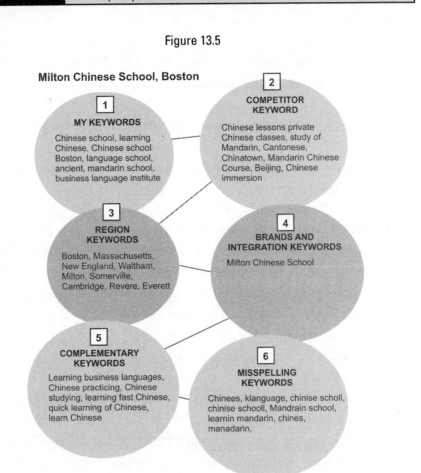

Let us analyze some examples to see the keyword matrix in action. Figure 13.5 represents a Web site example of the matrix developed for a Chinese language school in Boston. The user can clearly see the criteria and analysis applied. In this particular case, the region keywords are very important, considering that the market is highly defined by the geographical location of the potential customers. On the other hand, the brand and integration keywords are very limited, considering the school does not have to offer any special third party validations.

Figure 14.0 represents an example of a Web site for inkjet cartridges. For this particular business, the region keywords are irrelevant, since this business delivers the product worldwide. Another interesting fact, different from the last example, is that the brand and integration keywords are very important, considering the high level of validation people give to these brands.

Figure 14.0

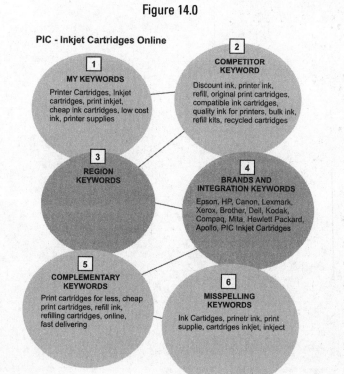

PIC - Inkjet Cartridges Online

1
MY KEYWORDS
Printer Cartridges, Inkjet cartridges, print inkjet, cheap ink cartridges, low cost ink, printer supplies

2
COMPETITOR KEYWORD
Discount ink, printer ink, refill, original print cartridges, compatible ink cartridges, quality ink for printers, bulk ink, refill kits, recycled cartridges

3
REGION KEYWORDS

4
BRANDS AND INTEGRATION KEYWORDS
Epson, HP, Canon, Lexmark, Xerox, Brother, Dell, Kodak, Compaq, Mita, Hewlett Packard, Apollo, PIC Inkjet Cartridges

5
COMPLEMENTARY KEYWORDS
Print cartridges for less, cheap print cartridges, refill ink, refilling cartridges, online, fast delivering

6
MISSPELLING KEYWORDS
Ink Cartridges, prinetr ink, print supplie, cartdriges inkjet, inkject

We will be working with the keyword matrix, studying different techniques overviewed in this book. For now, please ensure you understand the concept and the characteristics of each group.

4

Optimization of Web Pages

How to Optimize Your Web Pages

In the last chapter we learned how to identify the right (and more convenient) set of keywords for the Web site. Now it is time to start the optimization, as we overviewed in Chapter 2.

Optimizing your Web pages basically involves the following two steps:

- Optimizing the Web pages in coordination with the important keywords

- Ensuring the HTML code is error free

Optimizing Web pages according to the keywords ensures that the search engines will establish a high level of relevancy and content matching. Checking the HTML code of the Web pages ensures that search engines can identify and classify them with no problem. From now on, we will refer to this as valid HTML.

Top Ten Areas for Optimization

The following lists the 10 areas reviewed in this chapter:

1. Document title

2. Meta keywords and robot meta-tags

3. Meta description

4. Body text

5. URL

6. Headlines

7. Inbound hyperlink enhancement

8. Outbound links URL

9. Image ALT attributes

10. Footer

Two important considerations before starting are:

- Follow the list order

- Get the keywords of the Web site, applying the technique learned in Chapter 3

Document Title

The document title is one of the first components of the site detected by the spiders. It is important to consider the following set of rules. For reference purposes, Figure 15.0 shows the HTML code of the title tag.

Figure 15

```
<?xml version="1.0" encoding="iso-8859-1"?>
<!DOCTYPE html PUBLIC "-//W3C//DTD XHTML 1.0 Transit
<html xmlns="http://www.w3.org/1999/xhtml"><!-- Inst
<head>
<!-- InstanceBeginEditable name="doctitle" -->
<title>Real State Directory</title>
<!-- InstanceEndEditable -->
<!-- InstanceBeginEditable name="head" -->
<meta name="About the PageRank algorithm used in web
<meta name="keywords" content="PageRank, web searchi
<!-- InstanceEndEditable -->
<style type="text/css">
<!--
```

Rule 1: The title must not exceed 80 characters, including blank spaces.

Rule 2: Each single page in the site must have a representative title, reflecting as much as possible the content of the Web site. Read the page body text and, once you understand the concept, identify the most repetitive nouns and use them to build the title.

For instance, GEC Business Institute asked me to define the titles of their corporate Web site. The institute's main service is teaching high level English language for business people. On the home page, I defined the title, "Global English Language for Business and Executives — Advanced Training Institute." I used descriptive words that explained the type of activities engaged in by the Institute. I also avoided applying the brand, which is a waste of characters.

For another page of the Web site, the offering was the implementation of a very advanced system of online learning, accessing teachers of the institute through Web-classes. I defined the title, Online Web Conference English — US, Canada, Mexico, China. Figure 15.5 represents the process I went through to define the final title of the page.

Figure 15.5

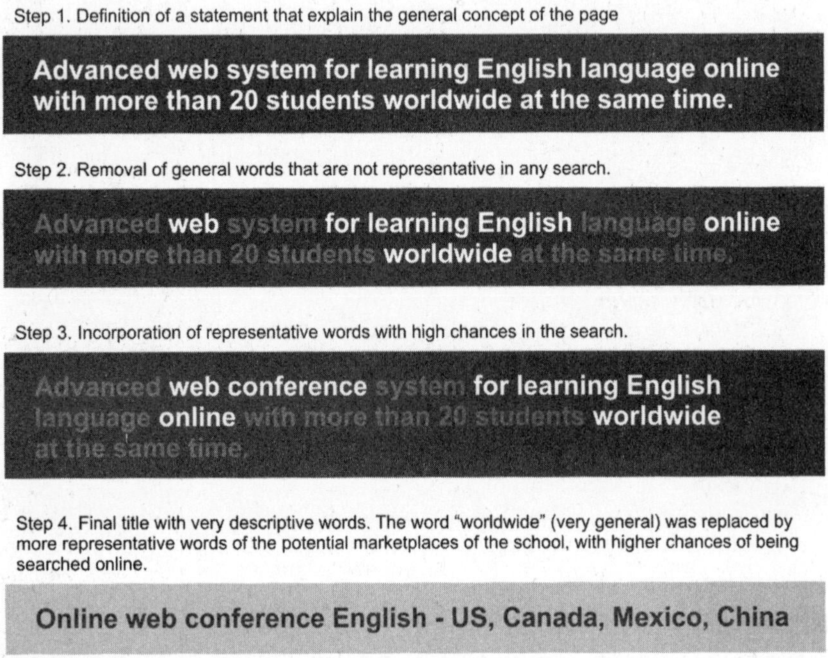

Step 1. Definition of a statement that explain the general concept of the page

Advanced web system for learning English language online with more than 20 students worldwide at the same time.

Step 2. Removal of general words that are not representative in any search.

Advanced **web** system **for learning English** language **online** with more than 20 students **worldwide** at the same time.

Step 3. Incorporation of representative words with high chances in the search.

Advanced **web conference** system **for learning English** language **online** with more than 20 students **worldwide** at the same time.

Step 4. Final title with very descriptive words. The word "worldwide" (very general) was replaced by more representative words of the potential marketplaces of the school, with higher chances of being searched online.

Online web conference English - US, Canada, Mexico, China

Rule 3: Never repeat the same word in the title, and do not use the brand.

The proper HTML code of a title is shown in the following example:

<title>Real Estate Directory</title>

Meta Keywords and Robot Meta-Tags

Meta keywords and robot meta-tags are important for allowing Web spiders to index the site properly. Conceptually, we identified some rules about meta-tag keywords in the last chapter, when we reviewed keyword definitions. Below are more rules for using meta keywords.

Rule 1: Never repeat the same keyword more than three times; coincidentally the most important keyword must be repeated exactly three times.

Rule 2: No more than 25 keywords per page. The ideal number is 20.

Rule 3: The relevancy level of the keyword is measured by considering the repetition of those words in the body text of the page. For instance, if you identify important keywords used by your competitors, the text of the HTML document must contain those words. This is extremely important for the relevancy qualification.

Rule 4: Do not use the brand as a keyword.

Meta-tag keyword code must be implemented in the following way:

<meta name="keywords" content="golden watches, men watches, silver watches, metal watches" />

Robot meta-tags are pieces of code that make the Web site "spider friendly." The code must be applied exactly as follows:

<meta name="robots" content="index, follow" />

Robot meta-tags have directives oriented to tell the robots an action for indexing the page. Using the following syntax <meta name="robots" content="noindex, nofollow" /> stop the spider analysis of the page. The set of directives for the robot meta-tags are:

<meta name="robots" content="index,follow"> (default syntax that say to the spider to index the page and follow the links - Recommended)
<meta name="robots" content="noindex,follow"> (no index the page but follow links

<meta name="robots" content="index,nofollow"> (index page but not follow links)

<meta name="robots" content="noindex,nofollow"> (do nothing with this page)

<meta name="robots" content="all"> (equivalent to index, follow)

<meta name="robots" content="none"> (equivalent to noindex,nofollow)

Figure 16.0 shows the code view of the meta-tags and robot meta-tags just learned.

Figure 16

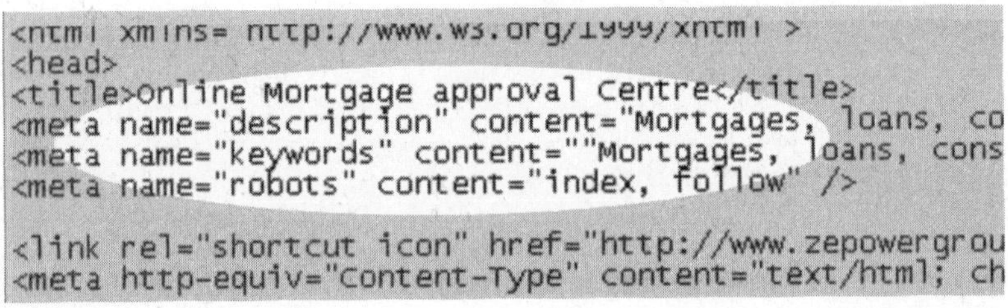

```
<html xmlns="http://www.w3.org/1999/xhtml">
<head>
<title>Online Mortgage approval Centre</title>
<meta name="description" content="Mortgages, loans, co
<meta name="keywords" content=""Mortgages, loans, cons
<meta name="robots" content="index, follow" />

<link rel="shortcut icon" href="http://www.zepowergrou
<meta http-equiv="Content-Type" content="text/html; ch
```

Meta Description

Meta descriptions explain, in more detail, what the Web site is about. They do not directly direct the ranking of the page, but express some level of relevancy and are used by the search engines to list the site and provide referential text underneath the link (see Figure 16.5).

Figure 16.5

Free MP3 music **downloads** - Free Music **Downloads** - MP3 Do
Download.com Music is your source for legal and free MP3 downloads. Dow
from thousands of artists.
music.download.com/ - 114k - Cached - Similar pages - Note this

MP3 Music **Downloads** - Buy MP3 Music Online - Digital Music C
MP3 Music Downloads - MP3.com offers links to legal digital music downloa
variety of services. Buy MP3 music online from your favorite artists

Rule 1: Take some time to select carefully the first 20 words of the text, considering that the search engine will show no more than 25 (depending of the company, some show 14 or less).

Rule 2: Do not repeat important words too many times.

Body Text

Only the hypertext of the pages is considered body text; the rest of the words, in images, flash objects, or other locations, are not detected by the Web spiders.

Rule 1: The most relevant rule to consider, in this category, is the usage of the predefined keywords in the body text. As explained before, the relevancy analysis of the search engines will evaluate intelligently all the words by repetition and cross-examine them with the meta-tag keywords.

Rule 2: Try to place the meta-tags keyword at the beginning of the body text.

Rule 3: The ideal level of keyword density by page is between 3 and 4 percent in the body text. It is important to keep this level as much as possible. Overuse of keywords in the body text irritate Web spiders and may disqualify the site.

Rule 4: The font attributes (size and color) of the body text are also important in the optimization process. In the past, many developers hid illegal keywords in the body text; for that reason, Web spiders analyze size and color of fonts with the intention of avoiding fraud.

Web site body text minimum size is 6 points; do not apply any size smaller than this. Concerning color, the rule is simple — never apply to the text the same or a very similar color to the background.

URL

The URL name represents considerable help for Web rankings, mainly when you and your competition have done a good job. If two Web sites are fighting for the first page, or the first place, the ranking position will depend of minor details, such as the relevancy of the URL name.

For instance, suppose that two accounting software Web sites have done a good SEO optimization job, and both qualify very high in the results list. Now the final ranking might be related to the relevancy of the keywords and the URL's name. For the keywords "accounting software," **accountingsoftware.com** will have more chances than **novoaccounting-systems.com**.

For this reason, many corporations buy different URL names, besides their own corporate Web site URL, with the intention of qualifying better in many search scenarios. If the name of the URL is formed by the potential search keywords, the Web site will come first in the relevancy list result, guaranteed. Even though the general rule is to get short and catchy names for URLs, do not underestimate the power of descriptive names as an alternative strategy for driving traffic to the site.

Note	This is a legal technique for SEO, but the IP address of the URL's name must be directed to the location of the Web server. If the developer redirects the page from the same or another server, with a typical HTML or JavaScript redirection code (window.location), the spider will classify this as a doorway, which is illegal.

Tip	If you are creating different URL names in order to increase chances of being detected by Web spiders, I recommend to also write the names with a "-"; for instance if you register **www.oldpopmusicmp3.com**, also try **www.old-pop-music-mp3.com**. Spiders sometimes get confused with long names.

Headlines

We define headlines to the titles of the body text. Please do not confuse them with the HTML document title, already reviewed. The size and other attributes of headlines are specially categorized by the Web spiders.

Rule 1: Consider the implementation of keywords in the headlines, it helps in the ranking, but take under consideration that headlines are also included in the keyword density analysis of the body text.

Rule 2: Never apply to the header the same color of the background or a very similar one, spiders may mistake this as an illegal attempt. Further in this chapter we will cover, in detail, the keyword density analysis technique.

Figure 16.7

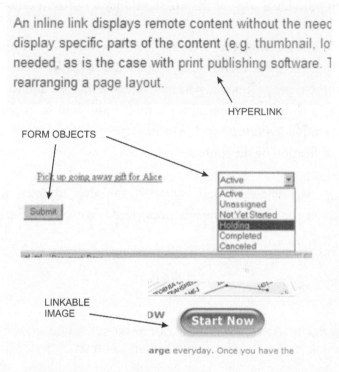

Inbound Hyperlink Enhancement

At this point, you know the importance of hyperlinks in the classification performed by Web spiders. There are numerous rules to consider for internal hyperlink optimization, all of them important. All the links that direct the visitor internally to other pages or documents of the same Web site are considered inbound links. Those links are relevant to facilitating the spiders' job.

Rule 1: Each page of the Web site has to include at least five links in the navigation menu, and six internal links outside the menu. My ideal number is 10 menu items and 12 other links in the body text or supplementary areas (minimum).

Rule 2: It is convenient for each page to have independent and customized links. For instance, if the home page has a particular group of inbound links, each individual page of the site should have different ones.

Rule 3: While making the Web site SEO friendly, it is important to consider that the most useful types of links are hyperlinks. We can easily identify three types of links; hyperlinks, linkable images, and form objects (Figure 16.7). It is best to optimize the most significant links of the site as plain and simple hypertext, as shown in Figure 16.8; this really facilitates the prequalification of the spiders.

Rule 4: As we examined in Chapter 2, the level of relevancy in the description of the link is extremely important. Figure 17.0 illustrates this case.

Figure 16.8

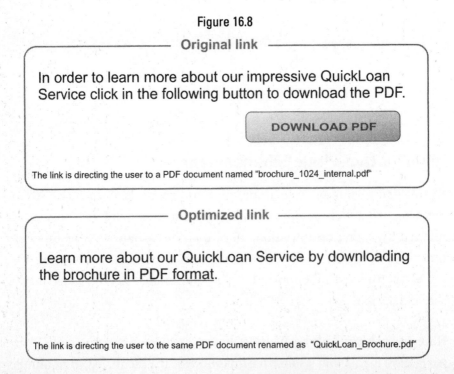

Original link

In order to learn more about our impressive QuickLoan Service click in the following button to download the PDF.

DOWNLOAD PDF

The link is directing the user to a PDF document named "brochure_1024_internal.pdf"

Optimized link

Learn more about our QuickLoan Service by downloading the brochure in PDF format.

The link is directing the user to the same PDF document renamed as "QuickLoan_Brochure.pdf"

Figure 17

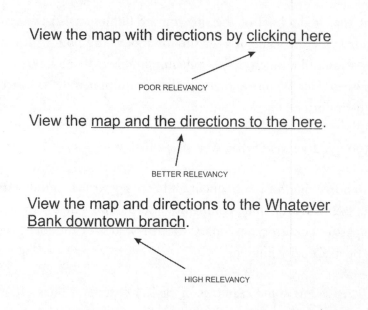

Rule 5: Flash objects' internal links are not detected by the Web spiders. Some developers make the entire embedded Flash object linkable instead in order to qualify for the spider (this is not always possible).

Rule 6: Try to identify a standard size and color for hyperlinks.

Rule 7: (For advanced developers) CSS is the easiest way to simplify Web designs, but do not overuse it for unnecessary developments.

Outbound Links URL

The outbound or external links are extremely important to raising the level of popularity of the site; the more links to high traffic Web sites, the better, and there are no limits. The general rule is to clearly identify the link, from images or hyperlinks, using the concept learned in the last topic (hyperlink enhancement), and avoid covering the link. Every time the site links to external Web sites your popularity level increases, following the logic on the following formula:

(0.03) X (popularity level of that Web site) / (4)

This means that if the level of the site you are linking is 12, the search engine will increase the value of your site for about 0.09 point. Although this does not look like much, it is a valuable number. If the linked Web site also links to your Web site, that number is multiplied by 4, which is considerably important:

[(0.03) X (popularity level of that Web site) / (4)] *4

Google search free plug-in is a frequent and easy way to add a link with a high-traffic, popular site. Some companies also publish other companies' logos from partners or associates, linked to their Web sites, in order to gain popularity by reciprocity linking.

Figure 17.3 represents some examples of typical outbound links on Web sites. The important rule to follow, for external links is the hyperlink text: the text must apply words that truly represent the target. If your site is linking to **www.automagazine.com**, the link may display: Click here to go to Auto Magazine Web site. This rule is not valid for linking images of course.

Figure 17.3

Images ALT Attributes

Alternative text, frequently known as ALT tags or ALT attributes, are used to present to the viewer when graphics are turned off, or the browser is not graphics capable. Also, ALT attributes have been extremely useful for the development of alternative computer displays, such as screen readers or Braille displays.

Spiders read the ALT attributes without considering part of the body text; this gives the developer a second option for improving keyword relevancy of the site without affecting the keyword density of the page.

Rule 1: Make the ALT attributes a textual equivalent of the images, not a description of the image. The ALT attribute should not be very long. For instance, if you are optimizing a travel agency Web site and have to define the ALT text for a beautiful image of a Hawaiian beach, the text "Hawaiian beach" or "Waikiki beach in Honolulu" might have a poor value. A better option would be "Travel with the best rates to the best beaches of Hawaii," "Hawaii," "Waikiki Beach," or "travel and book hotel online."

Rule 2: If the graphic is used as a link, then the ALT attributes should state that it is a link and where the link leads.

Rule 3: Use text in the ALT attributes that would make sense if read out loud.

The following example represents the correct syntax of the ALT attribute for images:

```
<img src="images/image6.jpg" border="1" alt="Hawaii, Waikiki Beach, travel and book hotel online." title="Hawaii Beach" width="650" height="362" />
```

Footer

Some developers are not aware of the importance of the footer to generating extra value for keyword density. Regardless of how much the marketers try, keyword density is a big challenge (typically for companies that offer many products or complex services). The connection of the body text with the keywords is not always easy or possible.

The footer of the page can compensate for those keywords missing in the body text.

If possible, I prefer to develop a footer for each page of the site (dynamically generated Web sites make this a bit more difficult. We will cover this topic at the end of the book).

There are few rules to consider when implementing a successful Web footer.

Rule 1: Because the footer objective is providing additional or secondary information (e.g., copyright information), the font's size is small. The minimum size font of the footer must be 6 points; otherwise, the Web spiders will ignore the text.

Rule 2: The footer can easily compensate the keyword relevancy by incorporating the missing keywords. For instance, if I recognize that a relevant keyword "homeopathic medicine" needs to be used at least two more times in a page, I would apply the footer, "Visit our stores at the most convenient location for you. You can also call us in advance to order any homeopathic medicine or herbal products, remember that all the products are prepared by order, and this might take a couple of hours. For our dedicated team of professionals the homeopathic medicine is an art; we love and respect alternative ways to consider people's health."

Figure 18.0 shows an example of a Web footer I developed for a holding company in the real estate business.

Figure 18

Important legal information - please read the disclaimer before proc
Products and services in these webpages may not be available for re
© UBSS-IT 1998-2007. All rights reserved.
Real Estate and Property Management services in New York and Ch
development. Wining of the Mason Hills award in 2002 and membe
Privacy Policy

Keyword Density Analysis

The keyword density factor is relevant because it transfers the value and importance to the meta-tag keywords. I would like you to pay special attention to this topic; the success of the site depends of it.

Figure 19

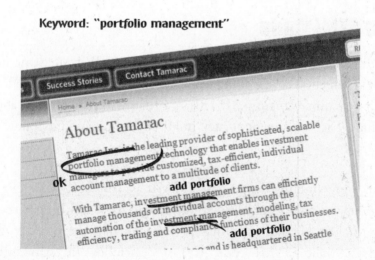

Keyword: "portfolio management"

For example, if the keyword is "parachute" and the text says "affordable parachute accessories and lessons," then one out of five is a keyword, so the keyword density in this case is 20 percent. It is not possible to automatically perform a keyword density analysis. It is a process of reading and applying creative adjustments on each Web page text. After I have finished defining the keywords of the meta-tags, I prefer to print the individual pages' content and highlight the keywords. To avoid confusion, I go keyword by keyword, establishing the density progressively (see Figure 19.0 for a better understanding of this).

Remember that the overall keyword density in each page must be around 3 percent; excessive appearance of keywords is penalized by search engines. Also do not forget that complex keywords (formed by more than one word) must be applied in exactly the same way to the body text.

Although software is available to perform the keyword density analysis, my advice is to go through the process manually, despite the time required to do it. It will be a good investment.

If you still want to rely on software to perform the keyword analysis, my recommendations follow.

Valid HTML Code

Many developers ignore a very important aspect of Web site structure — the validity of the HTML code. Most Web pages are written in HTML. As with any other language, HTML has its own grammar, vocabulary, and syntax. Each document written in HTML is supposed to follow these rules.

Like all programming languages, HTML is constantly changing. As HTML has become a relatively strong language, it has become easy to make mistakes. HTML code that is not following the official rules is defined as invalid HTML code. Web spiders follow the standards and identify the validity of the HTML code in order to find relevant content. If your HTML code contains errors, search engines might not be able to find everything on the page.

A Web page is indexed if it is compliant with the HTML standard. If there is a mistake in your code, the spiders might stop crawling your site and lose what they have collected so far. Although most major search engines can deal with minor errors in HTML code, a single missing character in your HTML code can be the reason your page does not appear in the result list of search engines.

You might find dozens of HTML validation tools online; I recommend the following list:

- **http://validator.w3.org/**

- **http://www.htmlvalidator.com/**

- **http://Webxact.watchfire.com/**

- **http://www.netmechanic.com/**

Web Site Structure

At some point, the structure of the Web site could facilitate the job of the Web spider. There is no golden rule for Web site design, but we can identify some important considerations that assist the indexing of the site.

A good Web site is a correct balance of three major components:

1. Creative concept (visually appealing)

2. Technical platform (e.g., php, javascript, or DHTML)

3. Optimization

A Web site that has not been designed following these three considerations might not achieve success. At this point, it is important to define what "success" is. Forrester Research estimated last year that the Internet had approximately 3.4 billion sites online. Morris & Money presented a report estimating that approximately 1,780 new Web sites join the Internet per day.

All the Web sites on the net are not aiming for the same objective, but we can be sure that 100 percent of the sites have a common objective — they want to be visited, they want traffic. Web designers, programmers, and marketers need to work together and coordinate their activities in order to generate a good final product.

The following list represents the most important concepts to consider for Web structure optimization:

- **Readability** — Text size and color must be easy to read. Avoid small text sizes.

- **Hidden text or hidden links** — Under any circumstances hide small text with the same color of the background.

- **Navigation** — The menu of the Web site is a key component of the structure optimization. The menu must be formed by hypertext; never use image buttons for the menu. The positioning of the menu is not crucial, but the most effective location is the vertical left side menu.

- **SSI** — The Server Side Included was very popular in the '90s, but is not longer an option for SEO optimization. Avoid any use of SSI on the site.

- **Text** — Search engines love text, do not be afraid of using as much text as you want. Between 70 and 80 percent of each page of the site must be hypertext.

- **Consistency** — The design and navigation of the entire Web site must be coherent. Do not change the design structure, navigation logic, or styles.

Figure 20.0 shows some examples of real Web sites designed under SEO optimization standards.

Figure 20.0

www.boatmotors.com
Designer: Roman Capalbo

www.godofgambling.com
Designer: Matterfore

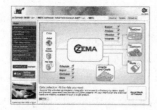

www.zemasuite.com
Designer: Miguel Todaro

www.golfio.com
Designer: Chris Lang

General Optimization Tips

Following are more tips for improving the ranking of your Web site.

Frames — Avoid using frames in your Web site. Search engines have difficulty crawling Web sites with frames. Sometimes frames are very efficient from the navigation standpoint, but they are not recommendable for SEO optimization. Frames do not fit in to the conceptual model of Web architecture (every page corresponds to a single URL).

Do not use frames on your Web site if you want to have high search engine rankings.

Flash — This is a very delicate topic. In the last couple of years, developers and programmers have been debating on the implementation of Flash in Web environments. Most search engines cannot index Flash pages. Flash is not transparent to the Web spiders, and all the text (even the dynamic text boxes) is not functional as hypertext, obstructing the Web spider's job.

I will cover this topic with more detailed information later, providing strategic data regarding Flash implementation. I always use Flash in my Web sites, but I never abuse it. There is a way to implement Flash project intelligently without affecting the SEO optimization. Some Flash Web developers have created impressive products that work very well with SEO, for instance, **2advanced.com** and **trump.com** (Donald Trump site). In these cases, the developers have worked ways around the conventional Flash implementation to secure their place in the search engines' result lists.

> **Tip** If you must use Flash on your Web site, make sure that you also offer hypertext for the search engines.

Splash pages — Welcome pages are a waste of time and resources. When the Web spider visits a typical "Welcome to our Web site" concept with a link to the actual site as the index page for the Web site, the spider might not follow that link.

Dynamic pages — The general advice in SEO optimization is to avoid dynamically created Web pages. Databases and dynamically generated pages are great tools to manage the contents of big Web (CMS) sites. Unfortunately, dynamically generated Web pages can be a nightmare for search engine spiders because the pages do not exist live in the server until they are requested. A search engine spider is not going to be able to select all necessary variables on the submit page.

Robots.txt and ror.xml — Make sure that you allow search engine robots to index your site.

There are two external files that need to be placed in the same root directory of the Web site, at the server: Robots.txt and ror.xml.

These two files are mandatory in order to tell the Web spider particular strategic, operational information. Their content and existence are relevant, and their location must be the same as the main html of the URL (usually named index.html).

The robots.txt indicates the level of permission for the Web spider on that particular URL. The Webmaster is able to identify particular areas of the Web sites that must not be indexed by the spider, for instance.

Robots.txt is a text file that can be created in any text processor. The file must follow the following basic syntax:

- User-agent: *

- Disallow:

This means that the site is able to be analyzed by any search engine, and with no restrictions. Some developers also recommend writing the file as follows:

- User-agent: *

- Disallow:

- Allow: /

The "/" means "all." For some reason, not all the spiders effectively interpret the "disallow" command.

If the desire of the Webmaster is to identify a particular search engine for the indexing and also disallow some directories with private information, or just operational programming data, they write the file as follows:

- User-agent: Googlebot

- Disallow: /cgi-bin/

- Disallow: /privatefiles/

You must add independent "disallow" commands for each directory you want to protect from the spiders. More information about robots.txt can be found at **www.robotstxt.org**.

The ror.xml (Resources of a Resource) is an XML format for describing the Web content, objects, and structure of Web sites in a generic mode so search engines can find and understand information more easily.

For example, if your Web site is selling watches, ror.xml enables you to document your product names, descriptions, prices, images, availability, affiliate programs, and other information. If your site provides information on a particular topic, it allows you to describe how this information is organized (e.g., sitemap, topics, categories, new information, or archive). It also provides terms for documenting objects, such as contacts, articles, newsletters, feeds, images, audio, links, reviews, privacy policy, and copyrights.

Adding such information to your Web site by adding a ror.xml file is simple. It is built on top of RDF, the W3 Resource Description Language (**http://www.w3.org/RDF**).

All objects are represented by a <Resource> tag, and can optionally have a <type> property to determine the type (or class) of the object (e.g., Product, Article, or Event). The other properties are typically determined by the type you choose. Here is a simple example of a product described in the ror.xml file:

```
<Resource>
<type>Product</type>
<title>My Product</title>
<desc>My great new product</desc>
<url>http://www.my-Web-site.com/my-product.htm</url>
<price>19.95</price>
<currency>USD</currency>
</Resource>
```

If you want to describe other objects, ror.xml provides other types, such as Contact, Article, Feed, and Event. You can find the current list of objects and their properties in the ROR Specification at **http://www.rorWeb.com/spec.htm**.

Let us examine how to assemble several objects together in a ROR file. In a ROR file, the meaning of information is determined by both the objects and the relationship between them. Depending on how an object is linked to another object, it will provide a different meaning. To link two objects together, the property "<resourceOf>" is used.

```
<Resource rdf:about="object-1">
 <title>Object 1</title>

</Resource>

<Resource>
 <title>Object 2</title>

 <resourceOf rdf:resource="object-1" />
</Resource>

<Resource>
 <title>Object 3</title>

 <resourceOf rdf:resource="object-1" />
</Resource>
```

The first object uses the "rdf:about" attribute to identify itself so it can be referenced elsewhere. The "<resourceOf>" property is then used to attach the second and third objects to the first. Attaching the two objects to the first one is a way to say that they contain information that relates to or further describes that object.

Now you can create a simple ror.xml file. Notice that the first object in this file has a type property set to Main. This designates it as the entry point into the data structure of the file.

```
<?xml version="1.0" ?>
<rdf:RDF
```

```
xmlns="http://rorWeb.com/0.1/"
xmlns:rdf="http://www.w3.org/1999/02/22-rdf-syntax-ns#">

<Resource rdf:about="mysite">
 <type>Main</type>
 <title>My Website</title>
 <url>http://www.my-Web-site.com</url>
 <desc>My great site with a ROR file to describe it</desc>
</Resource>

<Resource>
 <type>Contact</type>
 <name>Charles Steven</name>
 <phone>555 1212</phone>
 <fax>555 1213</fax>
 <mobile>555 1214</mobile>
 <resourceOf rdf:resource="mysite" />
</Resource>

<Resource rdf:about="products">
 <type>Product</type>
 <title>My Products</title>
 <url>http://www.my-Web-site.com/myproducts.htm</url>
 <currency>USD</currency>
 <resourceOf rdf:resource="mysite" />
</Resource>

<Resource>
 <type>Product</type>
 <title>Product 1</title>
 <url>http://www.my-Web-site.com/product1.htm</url>
 <image>http://www.my-Web-site.com/product1.gif</image>
 <price>19.95</price>
 <resourceOf rdf:resource="products" />
</Resource>
```

```
<Resource>
<type>Product</type>
<title>Product 2</title>
<url>http://www.my-Web-site.com/product2.htm</url>
<image>http://www.my-Web-site.com/product2.gif</image>
<price>29.95</price>
<resourceOf rdf:resource="products" />
</Resource>

<Resource rdf:about="myfeeds">
<type>Feed</type>
<title>My Feeds</title>
<resourceOf rdf:resource="mysite" />
</Resource>

<Resource>
<type>Feed</type>
<title>Daily News</title>
<url>http://www.my-Web-site.com/dailynews</url>
<updatePeriod>day</updatePeriod>
<resourceOf rdf:resource="myfeeds" />
</Resource>

<Resource>
<type>Feed</type>
<title>Weekly News</title>
<url>http://www.my-Web-site.com/weeklynews</url>
<updatePeriod>week</updatePeriod>
<resourceOf rdf:resource="myfeeds" />
</Resource>
</rdf:RDF>
```

You can create the file in any text processor, and then save it as "ror.txt," following the structure described in the last example. More information on ror.xml can be found at **www.rorWeb.com/**. You can also find several online sites with ror.xml generators, in order to simplify this task. Users may need to fill up forms and hit submit to generate the text for the ror.xml file, instead of writing all the code by themselves.

Flexible Web browsing — Considering the different Web browsers on the market (even though Microsoft Internet Explorer is the most popular), you must ensure that the Web site runs optimally in Web browsers such as Mozilla Firefox, Safari, Opera. Please consider that some programming components in JavaScript are not functional for all the browsers; also, some CSS styles do not perform in the same way for all of them.

Special Characters in the URL

Most search engines have problems indexing Web pages when their URLs contain special characters. The following list represents some of the special characters known as search engine spider stoppers:

- Ampersand (&)

- Dollar sign ($)

- Equals sign (=)

- Percent sign (%)

- Question mark (?)

Hosting — Choose a reliable, fast hosting service. Speed and service continuity are the most important elements to consider. If the Web service is down while the spider visits the site, you just lost an important opportunity of Web qualification. Even worse, if your Web site is already indexed and the search engine spider finds that your site is down, it might be removed from the search engine database. It is essential to host the Web site on trustworthy servers. Also, limit the size of the home page to less than 60K. Web loading speed is one of the performance issues analyzed by some spiders.

Submission

5

What You Will Learn About in the Following Chapter
• The principles of Web submission and its relationship with rankings
• Details about Web submission tools and an overview of applications and services
• Scheduling techniques
• Submission to search engines, directories, and other types of portals

The Logic Behind the Submission

We have learned the principles of SEO optimization and some of the secrets of aligning the sites for the best ranking on the relevancy lists. Now we will see the second (crucial) complement of the SEO optimization process — the submission.

Even if you do not take any specific action, if your site is online Web spiders will visit your site within one or two years. Search engines dispose a minimal amount of spiders for scraping the net randomly without following any specific criteria, but the majority of the spiders investigate the net following a list of URLs, also called the "list of seeds."

Those lists are complete catalogs of URL addresses created by the search engines from the voluntary submissions of people around the world. Submission is the only mechanism of telling the search engines that your Web site exists. Through the submission, search engines discover Web sites, their URL, description, type or line of business, category, and site details. The submission can be made by anyone, without any specific technical knowledge; the only requirement is to fill out the online form.

How to Submit Your Web Site

Search engine companies have specific URLs with forms designated to collect the Web sites' submissions. This is a process that must be performed manually and individually for each search engine. The process takes no more than three minutes, but could be problematic, considering the amount of existing search engines. Figure 21.0 shows a Google submission form, similar to the forms of the rest of the search engines.

Figure 21.0

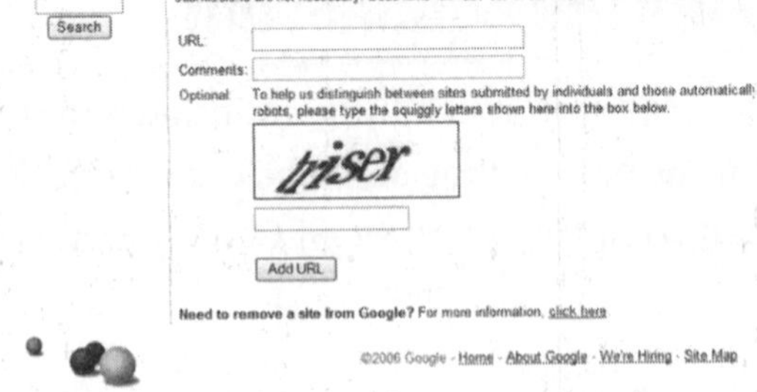

The information requested by search engines, in order to submit the URL, is simple — Web site URL, brief description, and probably the anti-spam security text.

The anti-spam textbox is a nonsense word formed by disarranged letters.

Online forms developed this system requiring the user to re-enter the word (in text format) to forbid bots or automated parsers from filling in the form instead of a human user (spam).

Submission Frequency

The URL submission has to be regular and must follow some important parameters in order to secure a correct submission.

Systematic submission — The recommendation of the search engines is to submit every three weeks. My advice is to submit once a month. Under any circumstances the submission regularity must not break the three weeks law. If the URL is submitted very often, the search engines will remove the URL from the seeds lists. Some companies have been banned for more than six months because of practicing weekly submissions. Very frequent submission does not secure better ranking at all. The reason for submitting regularly (once a month) is to allow spiders to identify the age of the site, and to update links and relevancies. Web site age is an important component of the qualification.

Analysis timing — After the URL has been submitted, it takes between 40 and 50 days for the search engine's spiders to visit your site. You will notice that your URL will not appear right away in the relevancy lists, or may not appear in the first five pages. Do not panic. Even if you have performed a correct SEO optimization of the site, it may take some time (four to five months) to appear in the first page. You will see that one day, the URL suddenly jumps to the first page in a relevant position.

Add-URL Form Pages

Search engines might not advertise the location of the online forms for submitting URLs. For that reason, the following list represents the location of the most important search engines on the market; any basic submission strategy cannot miss these:

North America:

- Yahoo!: **https://siteexplorer.search.yahoo.com/submit**

- Google: **http://www.google.com/addurl/**

- Alexa: **http://www.alexa.com/site/help/webmasters**

- Anoox: **http://www.anoox.com/add_for_indexing_free.jsp**

- AddURL-free: **http://www.addurl-free.com/submit.php**

- Best Search Online: **http://www.bestsearchonline.com/add_url. php?c=1**

- BigFinder: **http://www.bigfinder.com/submit/**

- E-sygoing: **http://www.e-sygoing.com/submit.html**

- Freekat: **http://www.freekatsearch.com/pre-release/add-site. html**

- FyberSearch: **http://www.fybersearch.com/add-url.php**

- Infotiger: **http://www.infotiger.com/addurl.html**

- JDGO: **http://www.jdgo.com/add.html**

- Meta   Web   Search: **http://www.metawebsearch.com/ site-submission.html**

- MSN: **http://search.msn.com.sg/docs/submit.aspx**

- NetSearch: **http://www.netsearch.org/addurl.html**

- OneKey: **http://www.onekey.com/kidsafe/newurl.htm**

- Scrub the web: **http://www.scrubtheweb.com/addurl.html**

- SearchIt: **http://www.searchit.com/addurl.htm**

- NetSearch: **http://www.netsearch.org/addurl.html**

- Walhello: **http://www.walhello.com/addlinkgl.html**

- Search-O-Rama: **http://search-o-rama.com/AddURL.asp**

- StopDog: **http://www.stopdog.com/add_a_page.htm**

- WhatUseek: **http://www.whatuseek.com/addurl.shtml**

- Walhello: **http://www.walhello.com/addlinkgl.html**

International Sites:

- Argentina: **http://www.caraygaray.com.ar**

- Argentina: **http://www.google.com.ar**

- Austria: **http://www.google.com.au**

- Austria: **http://www.atsearch.at**

- Belgium: **http://www.google.be**

- Brazil: **http://www.aonde.com**

- Canada: **http://www.google.ca**

- Canada: **http://www.bcwideweb.com**

- Holland: **http://www.google.nl**

- Holland: **http://www.vinden.nl**

- France: **http://www.antisearch.net**

- France: **http://www.google.fr**

- France: **http://www.caloga.com**

- Germany: **http://www.acoon.de**

- Germany: **http://www.fastbot.de**

- Germany: **http://www.google.de**

- Germany: **http://www.miko.de**

- Germany: **http://www.online-favoriten.de**

- Germany: **http://www.wolong.de**

- Greece: **http://www.google.com.gr**

- India: **http://www.google.co.in**

- Ireland: **http://www.gasta.ie**

- Ireland: **http://www.google.ie**

- Italy: **http://www.arianna.it**

- Italy: **http://www.google.it**

- Italy: **http://www.libero.it**

- Mexico: **http://www.google.com.mx**

- New Zeland: **http://www.google.co.nz**

- Spain: **http://www.caloga.es**

- Spain: **http://www.google.es**

- South African: **http://www.jonga.co.za**

- Swiss: **http://www.google.sh**

- Turkey: **http://www.google.com.tr**

- UK: **http://www.findonce.co.uk**

- UK: **http://www.foundya.co.uk**

- UK: **http://www.google.co.uk**

- UK: **http://www.mirago.co.uk**

Note Some international Web sites require additional descriptions in local language.

Directories

As we learned in Chapter 2, any site with a hyperlink to your Web site brings an enormous benefit (outbound link popularity). A good method is to list the URL in Internet directories.

Online directories are different from search engines for two major reasons:

- Web sites' URL submissions are reviewed by humans.

- The listing means a physical "link" that brings link popularity to your Web site. Keep in mind that being listed in the relevancy lists of search engines does not bring any link popularity.

Directories are usually subdivided into categories, and you have to submit your URL under the most appropriate heading. If you do not, it is very likely that your Web site will not be listed.

It is important to establish a strategy for directory submission in order to secure a big number of links from Web sites with two important advantages:

- Directories are well ranked for search engines, which means they could easily enhance your link popularity.

- In 95 percent of them, the submission is free.

The way to submit a URL to these directories is similar to the way to submit to search engines — filling out the online form, as shown in Figure 21.5. The new extra request is selecting a category, since directories are organized by categories (and sometimes sub-categories). Some directories also allow the user to add logos or small images of the site.

Figure 21.5

accept all sites, so please don't take it personally should your site not be accepted.

Category:	**Shopping: Clothing: Uniforms: Medical**

Head wear intended for use by medical professionals.

⚠️Are you sure this is the most descriptive category for your site? If you are unsure, pl find the most appropriate category.

Site URL:	http://

What type of link is this? ⦿ Regular ⃝ PDF ⃝ RSS ⃝ Atom

⚠️URL stands for Uniform Resource Locator, which means your site address. Exampl

- Do not add mirror sites.
- Do not submit an URL that contains only the same or similar content as other sit submissions of the same or related sites may result in the exclusion and/or deletic
- Do not disguise your submission and submit the same URL more than once.Exam http://www.dmoz.org/index.html.
- Do not submit any site with an address that redirects to another address.
- The Open Directory has a policy against the inclusion of sites with illegal content

Here are some rules for defining a good directory submission strategy:

Rule 1: Be sure you submit your site to the most important directory on the net, the Open Directory Project, by going to **www.dmoz.org**.

Rule 2: Submit the URL to all the general interest directories. Following, you will find a complete list of them:

- 01webdirectory: **http://www.01webdirectory.com/content_ submit.asp**

- AA Trax: **http://aatrax.com/addurl.htm**

- Abilogic: **http://www.abilogic.com/how-to-suggest-a-site.php**

- Add-your-site-free-submit: **http://www.addyoursitefreesubmit. com/add_premium_listing//**

- Anthony Parsons: **http://www.anthonyparsons.com/submitsite/**

- Apexoo: **http://www.apexoo.com/recommend_now**

- A-Web-Directory: **http://www.a-web-directory.com/**

- E-commerce Directory: **http://ecommerce-directory.org/add_ choose.php?cat=**

- Exchange Links: **http://www.exchangelinks.biz/submitlink/**

- Exchange-Links: **http://www.exchange-links.biz/submit.php**

- Gloose: **http://www.gloose.org/cgi-bin/GlooseDir/addurl.cgi**

- Go Guides: **http://www.goguides.org/info/addurl.htm**

- Illumirate: **http://www.illumirate.com/add_your_site_exp.cfm**

- IMarvel: **http://www.imarvel.com/goodidea.htm**

- Info Listings: **http http://www.info-listings.com/**

- Kingdom Search: **http://www.kingdomsearch.co.uk/submiturl. htm**

- Land of Links: **http://www.landoflinks.com/docs/help/addtop. html**

- Linkopedia: **http://www.linkopedia.com**

- Mavicanet: **http://www.mavicanet.com/**

- NetInsert: **http://www.netinsert.com/en/insert.html**

- One Big Directory: **http://www.onebigdirectory.com/cgi-bin/ dir/addurl.cgi**

- Search Systems: **http://www.searchsystems.net/submit.php**

- SicCode: **http://www.siccode.com/register.php**

- Top online shopping: **http://www.toponlineshopping.com/ register.php**

- Yahoo Directory: **https://ecom.yahoo.com/dir/submit/intro/**

- Yeandi: **http://www.yeandi.com/add-url.asp**

Rule 3: Search for local directories. If your business has markets in particular geographic locations, you might find good results by submitting your URL to directories of those regions. The following list shows some local directories by country:

- Australia: **http://www.directoryaustralia.com**

- Austria: **http://www.dmoz.at/**

- Austria: **http://www.austriaseek.at/**

- Canada: **http://www.cdnbusinessdirectory.com/**

- Denmark: **http://www.add2me.dk/**

- France: **http://www.francite.com/**

- Germany: **http://www.findigo.de/**

- Germany: **http://www.dmoz.de/**

- Germany: **http://www.limeo.de/**

- Germany: **http://www.web.de/**

- Italy: **http://www.yahoo.it**

- Spain: **http://www.ya.com**

- Swiss: **http://www.sharelook.com**

- UK: **http://applegate.co.uk/**

- UK: **http://www.searchuno.co.uk/**

- UK: **http://www.lifestyle.co.uk/**

- UK: **http://www.yahoo.co.uk/**

Rule 4: Identifying specialized directories by particular industry or business niche may help in the link popularity rankings, and could bring some direct customers. In many cases, you will find different directories focused by industry; the amount of dedicated directories online is surprising.

Associations or professional organizations may publish their directories with their members' information, but you probably need to become a member to appear in their lists.

The majority of the specific directories are independent business; for that reason, the submission to those sites is not free. The following list shows some examples of specialized directories by industry:

- Kids: **http://www.directorykids.com/**

- Kids: **http://www.ukchildrensdirectory.com/**

- Golf: **http://www.ultimategolfdirectory.com/**

- Lawyers: **http://www.directorylawyer.com/**

- Basketball: **http://www.internationalbasketball.com/categories. html**

- Photography: **http://www.photographydirectory.org/**

- Musical instruments: **http://www.musicalroll.com/**

- Car accessories: **http://linkcentre.com/cars/Car-Accessories/**

- Pets: **http://www.yourpetdirectory.co.uk/**

- Power boats: **http://www.boatinglinks.com/**

- Medical equipment: **http http://www.esurgicals.com/**

- Bicycles: **http://www.totalbike.com/**

- Trucks: **http://www.truckguide.net/**

- Boxing: **http://www.directoryboxing.com/**

- Beers: **http://www.beers-of-the-world.com/links/beer_directories.html**

There is a directory for every single industry or human activity on this planet; no matter how strange it may seem. You just need to invest time and effort in finding them, as the people interested in that industry will do.

Submission Services

Web site submission is a repetitive task that demands much time to be executed properly. If you developed a good SEO strategy for your site, you might be facing the submission of the site itself plus the complementary verticals URLs, which means many sites to submit.

A couple of years ago, with the proliferation of search engines and directories, a new type of Internet service began — SEO submission companies. These companies offer the submission of your URL to an enormous number of search engines and directories, managing this tedious task for you.

I prefer to manage my own Web submission, but I have confirmed many times that the submission companies offer an acceptable service; they usually charge between $20 and $80 for submitting to more than 500 search engines periodically (monthly). You can use any online search engine to find the company that suits your budget and expectations; you will discover hundreds of them.

There are also some software companies that developed interesting applications for the management of the SEO submission:

- IBP (Internet Business Promoter) is one of my favorite SEO applications that also offer other significant optimization tools — **http://www.ibusinesspromoter.com/**

- WebPosition Gold is very reliable and popular software for SEO submission and optimization — **http://www.webpositiongoldpro. com/**

- Web CEO is an acceptable application that offers the submission, web analysis, performance and SEO optimization, and PPC management — **http://www.webceo.com**

- Trellian SEO Toolkit offers a complete set of optimization tools for a very competitive price — **http://www.trellian.com/seotoolkit/**

- All-In-One Submission was reviewed positively last year, ranking as one of the most wanted SEO applications on the market — **http:// www.sharewarist.com/share/order.htm**

- SEO Effect is a web-based SEO optimization tool with excellent reviews in the last year — **http://www.seoeffect.com/**

6

Link Popularity & SEO Rankings

What You Will Learn About in the Following Chapter

- The fundamentals of link popularity and its influence on Web rankings

- Techniques and secrets for increasing link popularity

- Considerations about Web partners and link generation

- Page ranking

What Is Link Popularity?

Link popularity is the number of other Web sites that link to your Web site. The more other Web sites link to your Web site, the higher your search engine rankings will be. The concept is that search engines evaluate Web sites based on the number of referring links to them — a Web site must be important if many other sites link to it.

Of course, the number of links alone is not enough to improve search engine rankings; it is also important that the other Web sites are related to yours. Links from unrelated Web sites will not do your site much good. If the links to your Web site include your important keywords in the link text, the effect on your search engine rankings will be much higher.

Figure 22

www.hosting.com	30687	472	11100	1680
www.electroniccottage.com	81739	264	23900	23500
www.artquest.com	90763	329	27300	26900
www.micex.com	112227	764	35600	35600
www.bnn.nl	119605	721	34100	28700
www.jobpilot.de	260388	3530	80500	77200
www.manchesteronline.co.uk	504360	11000	157000	156000
www.bmw.com	567152	2420	161000	157000
www.realestateabc.com	1384422	6570	356000	359000
www.hotscripts.com	3810428	35900	1210000	1180000
www.msn.com	**18619000**	982000	5720000	5740000
www.microsoft.com	23623983	142000	7060000	6700000
www.mysql.com	24621979	159000	6710000	6310000
www.apache.org	26519175	113000	5120000	4800000
www.yahoo.com	90027159	585000	29500000	25900000
www.google.com	222041606	2920000	66400000	59400000

If you want to be found for the search term "English Tea," then it is much better to get links like:

<a href="http://www.example.com">English Tea</a>

than links like:

<a href="http://www.example.com">Andersen Tea Inc.</a>

If the link to your site includes your search term, search engines think that your Web site must be significant for this search term, and then the ranking of the site in that particular keyword increases considerably.

High link popularity alone will not bring you high search engine rankings, of course; your Web site content must also be optimized for search engines. It does not make sense to get many incoming links if your Web site does not have much content. If search engines find that the links to a particular Web site and the content on that Web site does not match, they will not give the site high search engine rankings for its topic.

Search engines use the following to determine the rank of your Web site:

- **Content** — The content of the Web site, considering that the Web site has been optimized for search engines while being attractive to human visitors. You will be surprised by spiders' ability to detect Web components. In many cases, the spiders are smart bots capable of capturing some design elements with the purpose of identifying whether the site is a real site or a code generated page, designed to attract spiders for ranking purposes.

- **Quality** — Links must have valuable keywords that match the referred Web site's keywords. A combination of optimized Web page content and good link popularity leads to high search engine rankings, guaranteed. Your Web site must have both if you want to get good results.

- **Consistency** — It is difficult to get high search engine rankings for a Web page with good link popularity that does not have optimized content.

Increasing Popularity

Incoming links are an important factor for search engine rankings. It is important to have a reliable instrument for identifying how good your link popularity is, and compare it with your competitors.

There are hundreds of online tools that analyze link relevancy of Web sites; the following list represents links to the most popular free, Web-based link popularity analysis tools:

- **http://www.marketleap.com/publinkpop/**

- **http://www.linkpopularity.com/**

- **http://www.widexl.com/remote/link-popularity/index.html**

- **http://www.submitexpress.com/linkpop/**

- **http://www.seochat.com/seo-tools/link-popularity/**

- **http://www.iWebtool.com/link_popularity**

Some of these tools allow the user also to identify competitors' URLs in order to compare popularity with them. These tools use the results of the major search engines to identify the amount of external links (links coming from different URLs) to your site.

You will also find reliable desktop software for link popularity check. This depends of the developer's preferences. I tested both, and the results obtained are very similar.

Some licensed software is able to identify the URL's links in the result page; this is a very interesting feature considering you can run an analysis on your competitors' sites and obtain potential sites that may link to yours.

Link popularity check is essential in the SEO optimization activity. You will be able to evaluate your site popularity and, once you get the result, describe a strategy around it.

Very good (and recommendable) link popularity is between 300 and 600 links, above 1000 links is the optimal popularity desired by all SEO experts, but it is not easy to get.

The definition of a link popularity strategy begins by evaluating the current level of popularity of your site (also two competitors for comparison purposes) using one of the Web-based tools mentioned before (see Figure 22.5).

Figure 22.5

www.okey.com	34
www.gamenow.com	46
www.faith.net	49
www.cookies_example.com	**55**
www.consideration.com	126

Figure 22.5

www.honesty.com	132
www.competitor1.com	**147**
www.movie_now.com	231
www.automotive.com	398
www.competitor2.com	**315**
www.other.com	321
www.association.org	420
www.thenet.biz	452

If the site is new, and this is its first time for developing a link popularity strategy, the results will probably be low. This is the most common scenario all Web sites will face from their beginning stages.

The next step is to build the strategy to generate a new (higher) number of link popularity. The following list represents a set of actions for achieving that goal:

Directory submission — Researching the most popular and specific directories for submitting the Web site URL.

Bonus sites — This is a technique developed by the online gambling industry in 2005. It worked well and is a perfectly legal action. The idea is to develop a simple Web site of no more than three or four pages with the intention of carefully elaborating an article (or a few) related to the topic of the Web site. The key element of the action is to publish the site in a totally independent URL address.

Figure 22.7

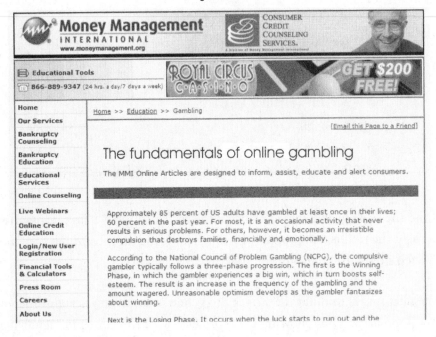

The bonus HTML sites (Figure 22.7) implement all the SEO optimization techniques learned before (e.g. meta-tag's keywords and content management), allowing the spiders to rank it very high in the relevancy lists of search engines. The site establishes ads and different links to the "main" Web site, in order to promote it and give external link relevancy.

I use this technique often, with excellent results. Bonus sites need to be submitted to search engines and directories in the same way we do with the main site. The article content allows me to redefine weak keywords of the main Web site, and increase the link relevancy. Figure 23.0 represents the "bonus site" technique. In my opinion, there is no limit of bonus Web sites; I usually create at least 10. The important factor to consider is that all of them have to be unique in design content in order to properly support the main Web site. The bonus Web site also needs to incorporate other external links to popular sites (besides the inbound links to the other pages); otherwise, the spiders will reject the site.

Figure 23.0

Marketing and promoting a natural product for Arthritis' treatment.

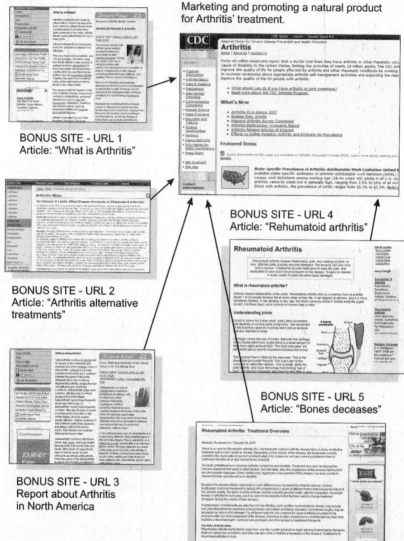

BONUS SITE - URL 1
Article: "What is Arthritis"

BONUS SITE - URL 2
Article: "Arthritis alternative treatments"

BONUS SITE - URL 3
Report about Arthritis in North America

BONUS SITE - URL 4
Article: "Rehumatoid arthritis"

BONUS SITE - URL 5
Article: "Bones deceases"

Figure 23.5

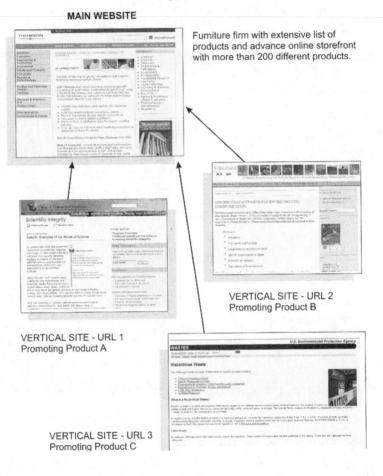

MAIN WEBSITE

Furniture firm with extensive list of products and advance online storefront with more than 200 different products.

VERTICAL SITE - URL 1
Promoting Product A

VERTICAL SITE - URL 2
Promoting Product B

VERTICAL SITE - URL 3
Promoting Product C

Support HTML gates — Conceptually, the support HTML gates are similar to bonus sites. The difference is that instead of an article, the content is an extension (or expansion) that promotes a particular offering of the main site (Figure 23.5).

These mini-sites are also called "portal Web sites." We will see this topic in more detail later. For now, it is important to remember that these gates will bring the same result of bonus sites, with a particular characteristic — sometimes vertical portals qualify better than the main site.

Affiliation programs — The affiliate system, also known as "rewarding marketing," is based on exchange of traffic in a basic agent/referral fee sales channel concept. After 2000, many e-commerce projects started to apply affiliate marketing techniques, obtaining impressive results. A good example is **Amazon.com**, one of the first sites that implemented the online affiliate program, which has currently almost 1 million affiliate sites.

Affiliation with big Web sites does not necessarily increase the link popularity of the site, unless the affiliation is mutual. Many e-commerce Web sites offer double-way link, in which case the link relevancy increases for both sites simultaneously.

Associated URLs — If there is no conflict of market, you can also initiate your own affiliate program with friends' or associates' Web sites, obtaining mutual benefits from the linking.

Online ads — This action has not been created to increase link relevancy, but eventually, if you engage an advertisement campaign online, it will enhance link popularity level, since the ads have a hyperlink directly to your Web site's URL, as learned before.

Google PageRank

As we mentioned, Google uses a PageRank system to calculate the ranking of Web sites. The official PageRank number that can be seen in the Google toolbar is more a marketing instrument for Google than the real ranking. Some professionals believe they can choose their partners (for link popularity strategy) based on the information displayed in the bar (see Figure 24.0).

Figure 24.0

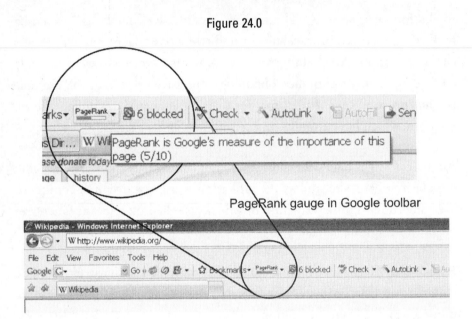

PageRank gauge in Google toolbar

Trading links with potential partners is a strategic move more complex than a simple analysis of ranking numbers. An important point is the concordance between the two linked sites. If the potential linking Web site is related to your site (somehow), it makes sense that visitors of that site be interested in your site; even if the level of popularity of the site is not high yet, it eventually might climb.

Ranking Check

There is not a concrete method to identify the real value of a Web site's page. The search engines ranking system is similar, but not identical. Some SEO professionals believe that Google has the best ranking calculation in the market, but since the algorithm has never been fully disclosed, there is no real evidence of the full evaluation procedure. All we can do is guess about that formula.

I have studied "The Anatomy of a Large-Scale Hypertextual Web Search Engine" from Sergey Brin and Lawrence Page, an extraordinary document that acutely analyzes the "behind the scenes" world of Web ranking. I have not found any practical element that could help a developer to better understand the secrets of page ranking from the SEO optimization perspective, only a group of formulas and calculations that search engines use to calculate ranking, and a possible combination of them, considering the variables of each particular Web site. I do not believe there is any point in knowing, in detail, those components of the ranking evaluation. I think we need to know what the fundamentals are that influence that ranking, and learn how to manipulate those elements according to our interest.

So far, all we have learned in the past chapters about optimization provides enough helpful indications and advice to make your Web site qualify among the first positions in the search engines' relevancy list. It is important to consider also that the algorithm is dynamic and changing almost every quarter. For that reason, there is no fixed rule. SEO news can be found at **sempo.org**; I also recommend signing up for any SEO newsletter online, to be frequently updated in SEO news.

7

Introduction to PPC Campaigns

What Is Pay Per Click (PPC)?

In 2004, I was working for a big real estate project in Seattle. The company decided to implement an Internet marketing strategy in order to promote the business to business side of the project. I created a complex Web structure with the objective of promoting the building and providing sensitive information about the shopping mall area and the office space that was open for leasing.

Considering the short age of the site, my best bet was the sponsored results in Yahoo! and Google. The project manager was concerned about the efficiency of this PPC characteristic of the plan; his argument — valid to some extent — was his own experience as a user of search engines. He rarely paid attention to or clicked on sponsored links. People often find it hard to believe that users do click and visit the sponsored results list.

After I planned and implemented the PPC campaign for the project, we obtained an impressive response — in the first six weeks, the Web site received more than half a million visitors, which brought 40 good new customers over a total investment of 7 million dollars. Many people click on the sponsored results; I have proven this fact several times in the last couple of years, obtaining satisfactory results.

In Chapter 1, we reviewed the beginning and evolution of PPC (traditional marketing versus digital marketing). Now it is time for you to understand its fundamentals and know how to implement a PPC campaign that brings results.

Figure 25.0

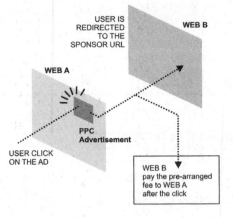

PPC is a type of advertisement model used on search engines and Web sites where advertisers only pay when a user clicks on an ad and is redirected to the advertiser's Web site URL. PPC is a model that might be applied to search engines' sponsored results or traditional online graphic ads; Figure 25.0 and Figure 25.3 represent the concept.

Figure 25.3

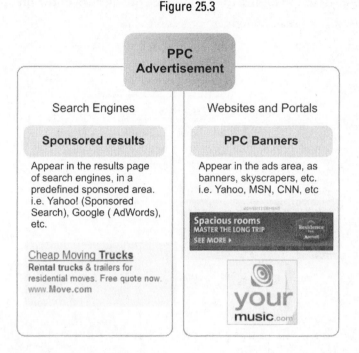

Search Engines PPC

Advertisers bid on keywords to define priority on the position. When a user types a keyword that matches one of the advertiser's keywords, a predefined ad is shown. These ads are called "sponsored links" or "sponsored ads" and appear next to, and sometimes above, the relevancy list results on the search engine.

PPC ads may also appear on content network Web sites. In this case, ad networks, such as Google AdSense and Yahoo! Publisher Network, attempt to provide ads that are relevant to the content of the page where they appear, and no search function is involved.

Although the ideal objective of promoting a Web site is to be listed in the relevancy list of search engines, sometimes it is not possible in the short term for many reasons, such as short age of the Web site, continued development of SEO optimization, or being in a competitive market niche with many companies fighting for the first place. In that case, PPC is the second best option to ensure the appearance of your site in the first page of the results page of search engines.

Figure 25.5

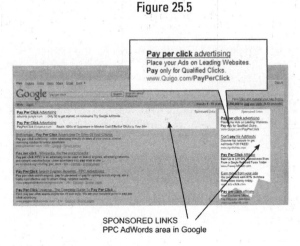

SPONSORED LINKS
PPC AdWords area in Google

Figure 25.5 shows the results page of Google; you can see the highlighted area where the AdWords (PPC) are placed. The structure of the sponsored results is usually similar to the relevancy results, as shown in Figure 25.7.

Figure 25.7

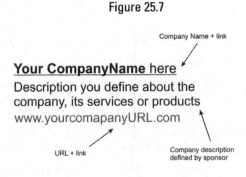

Web Sites or Portals PPC

Many Web sites and Web portals offer a PPC advertisement system to attract sponsors with a valid, interesting ROI formula. Very popular Web sites and networks offer advertisement space with PPC management, allowing advertisers to access a new level of benefits, absent in traditional advertisement models, Figure 26.0 shows some examples of PPC ads.

Figure 26.0

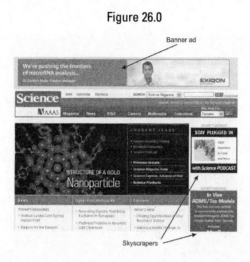

Any Web site that offers online advertisement space shares sensitive information about potential performance of the ad once published. Those reports, with intelligence about traffic, audience segmentation, and more, are called the "media package."

Figure 26.3

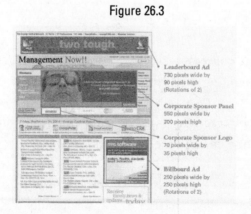

The media package delivers statistical information that presents a referential scenario for the advertiser, in order to define the type of ad, location, cost, and to estimate potential results. Figure 26.3 and Figure 26.4 show a real media package for a specialized online magazine, outlining type of ads with its respective sizes and traffic segmentation facts.

Figure 26.4

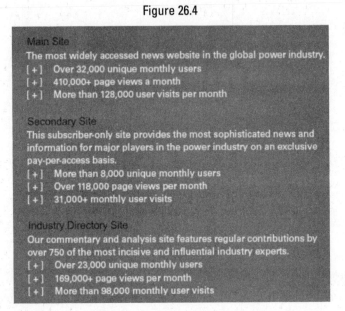

Main Site
The most widely accessed news website in the global power industry.
[+]   Over 32,000 unique monthly users
[+]   410,000+ page views a month
[+]   More than 128,000 user visits per month

Secondary Site
This subscriber-only site provides the most sophisticated news and information for major players in the power industry on an exclusive pay-per-access basis.
[+]   More than 8,000 unique monthly users
[+]   Over 118,000 page views per month
[+]   31,000+ monthly user visits

Industry Directory Site
Our commentary and analysis site features regular contributions by over 750 of the most incisive and influential industry experts.
[+]   Over 23,000 unique monthly users
[+]   169,000+ page views per month
[+]   More than 98,000 monthly user visits

General Characteristics of PPC Ads

The three major characteristics of the PPC model are:

- **Investment control** — Payment only for the clicks of interested visitors, obtaining excellent ROI.

- **Practical interactivity** — Engaging the visitor and redirecting potential customers to the advertiser's URL.

- **Tracking users** —Analysis of visitors' actions and responses after the click, allowing the advertiser to measure results and (occasionally) capture strategic information.

For these reasons, online advertisement has become very popular and effective in the last seven years. Companies finally gained control of their campaigns' performance, progress, and results. PPC ads outlined the beginning of a new type of promotion, inexpensive and able to:

- Better identify ROI

- Engage a proactive approach

- Extrapolate intelligence information about potential customers

- Analyze effectiveness of the message

- Engage the user with interaction

There is no other media channel with the level of sophistication of this type of ad. Later, we will overview several professional samples of real ads and you will be amazed about their possibilities (from the creative and marketing standpoint) and results.

How PPC AdWords/Sponsored Results Work

The principles of PPC AdWords are simple:

1. A user visits the search engine and types a particular keyword, such as "mp3 music."

2. The search engine displays the results page. Ads that match "mp3 music" are positioned in the right column or at the top of the page, identified as "sponsored results." Some companies also place a light gray background in the area of sponsored links.

3. The user can freely click on one of these results, and he will be immediately directed to the link target, usually the sponsor's Web page. At the same time, for that click, the client is charged by the search engine company with an amount pre-arranged (more than one cent) in the "bid system" (this will be fully explained further in Chapter 11).

Yahoo! and Google are currently the leaders of PPC sponsored results, since they are the major search engines in the market. The following list represents the fundamentals of the operation of PPC of search engines:

- **Keywords** — The keywords are the functional logic of the PPC sponsored results, the advertiser can identify maximum cost-per-click (CPC) for individual terms (keywords).

- **Cost** — How much the advertiser pays is exactly determined by the type of auction process and how many advertisers are interested in that particular keyword (bidding or auction process).

- **Positioning** — There are eight positions available, and the order is related to the value established by the advertiser. The uppermost cost more than the lowest.

- **Management** — The advertiser has access to a control panel to create and manage the PPC campaigns.

Optimization for PPC

As we discussed, PPC of search engines defines positioning based on the cost of the ad for each keyword (established by the advertiser). However, the ad's positioning is also influenced by the SEO optimization of the Web site. This is known as "ad quality value."

As described in Figure 26.5, the quality value of the ad is determined by the relation between the cost-per-click (CPC) of the keyword and the relevancy of the site. In other words, Yahoo! or Google will establish the position of the ad by a combination of the maximum CPC and the relevancy ranking obtained from the spiders' work (e.g., keyword density, link popularity level, and page ranking).

Figure 26.5

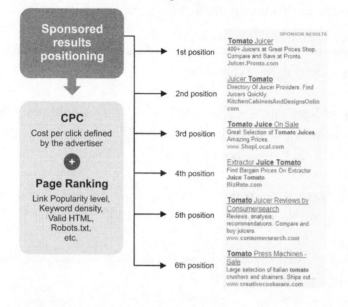

Search Engine PPC Versus Traditional Advertisement

We have already overviewed, in past chapters, conceptual advantages of search engines versus traditional promotional channels, in terms of reaching potential customers. Following is a list of tangible advantages of the search engine PPC system:

- **Account opening** — Very low activation fee; Google charges $5 and Yahoo! charges $30.

- **Budget control** — You determine how much you want to pay per click, from $0.01 to $100; this is called the CPC factor. You only pay when someone clicks on your ad, establishing a daily budget you specify limits in your investment.

- **Monitoring** — The system enables you to track the campaign process at any time. You are able to generate detailed reports, and you can deactivate ads or an entire campaign in seconds.

- **Multi-campaign management** — An account is able to manage as many campaigns as you want.

- **No obligations** — There is no monthly minimum spending commitment and no contract length. The account is settled only after the clicks have been received.

- **Full creative control** — You determine the text of your ad and specify the keywords for which your ad will be displayed.

- **Edits** — You can easily change the text of your ads at any time with no additional cost.

- **Internet expansion** — The ads can also reach Internet users on numerous partner sites.

- **International reach** — Your ad reaches Internet users from over 250 countries in more than a dozen languages.

- **Cross appearance** — The same ad can appear for several keywords.

- **Implementation** — The ads are up and running in just minutes.

- **24/7** — The ads are online all the time, with no exceptions.

Alisa Marfield initiated an online empire, selling underwear in her 25 different Internet storefronts. In 2002, during the first year of operation of the sites, she collected $800,000 dollars in sales, out of a total investment of $12,000 dollars in SEO and PPC advertisement. Many experts at that time were skeptical about the success of this enterprise.

The Partner Sites' Advantage

Sponsored results ads are also entitled to participate in the partner's network of Google and Yahoo! Your PPC ads might appear in any of the sites that participate in the network of partners because Google AdSense and Yahoo! Publisher Network are similar programs oriented to generate an enhanced business mesh that allows sponsored results to display their ads in relevant search listings.

Some partners of the network for Yahoo! are HP, USA Today, eBay, Salon, MTV, AlltheWeb, Infospace, Move, National Geographic, NetZero, United, and iVillage.

Some partners of the Google network are AOL, AT&T Worldnet, Business.com, CompuServe, HowStuffWorks.com, Netscape, Shopping.com, The New York Times, and Weather.com.

You can learn more about this topic at the following links:

- **http://searchmarketing.yahoo.com/srch/network.php**

- **https://www.google.com/adsense/login/en_US/**

Considerations Before Starting

The optimization of PPC ads for sponsored results is an obligatory step, if you want to succeed. New advertisers are continually joining the sponsored results programs, and your competition frequently updates its offers. You have to regularly check and optimize your ads. Some fine tuning to your ads can make the difference between an ineffective and a successful campaign.

The optimization of ads (Figure 26.7) is detailed in the following points:

- **Keywords** — The success of your campaigns depends on whether you advertise for the right keywords. After you identify all the keywords that represent your product or offering, and your competitors' keywords, you may prioritize them in order to get a list that will be essential for the definition of the campaigns.

- **Ad text or content** — If you do not strike the right tone and use the correct (convincing) text, your campaigns will not be effective. In the next chapters, we will discuss tips for writing successful ads.

- **Price strategy** — Which position is right for you, how much is the maximum cost of the ad, and how much should your daily budget be? These are questions we have to answer at the time of the campaign definition.

- **Destination pages** — The content of the landing pages your target group sees when they click on your ad is a vital factor in the success of your advertising campaign.

- **Product** — Your products must have a competitive advantage in comparison to similar products and be offered at a competitive price.

Figure 26.7

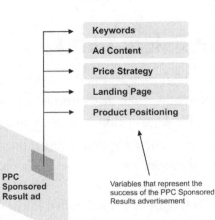

8

First Stage of Sponsored Results

What You Will Learn About in the Following Chapter

- Beginning of search engine's PPC

- PPC planning and details of ads

- Defining campaigns

- Ads management and control

Opening an Account

For the beginner, there are some initial difficulties; the Web interface of sponsored results might be complex and unfriendly. I will walk you through the whole process, with the intention of providing all the instruction you need to become an expert.

Conceptually, Yahoo! and Google offer a very similar, easy step-by-step process for opening the account. In just minutes, any user can register a new account.

Conceptually, Yahoo! and Google offer a very similar, easy step-by-step process for opening the account. In just minutes, any user can register a new account.

The first step is directing your Web browser to the following:

- Yahoo!: **http://searchmarketing.yahoo.com/**

- Google: **https://adwords.google.com/select/Login**

Yahoo! Search Marketing

The next step is to identify the type of account and setup. I recommend "self serve."

Then, define the language and region of influence of the account; you may identify the countries you will be interested in promoting your ads to. Next, you will be asked to define the keywords. Do not be so precise about this part; you will have the opportunity to edit them anytime after the creation of the account. Remember to implement the whole set of keywords extracted, using the techniques learned in Chapter 3.

In the next step, you will be asked about the limit of the budget, to control the investment and to avoid spending excessive money. You should be able to establish the daily budget and the maximum bid. Since this data can be edited anytime, I usually enter $50 for daily budget and $0.12 for bids, as initial values.

Once you are done with this process, the next step will be the ad creation. This is important, but again, the information can be edited anytime after the account is created and running. The interface offers to enter the content for the title, the description, and the URL (landing page). There should be a preview of the ad, to check the look of it in the result page. The last step is to review the entered information and activate the account. The interface asks the user to identify user name, password, and billing information.

Google AdWords

The first step is to identify the type of account and setup. I recommend "Standard Edition." The next step is to define the language and region of influence of the account; you may identify the countries you will be interested in promote your ads to. Next, you will define your ad's content. This section involves entering the title, description, (line 1 and 2), and URL.

The next step is about defining the keywords for the campaign, and they can be edited any time. The interface also offers checking the keywords with a wordtracking tool.

Next step, the user is asked to fill in financial options —currency selection, maximum budget per day, and default CPC bid (the maximum you are willing to pay per click).

Finally, the site offers the review of the data entered and the final sign-in. If you do not have any other product from Google (i.e., Gmail) the site asks you to fill out a form with the e-mail address and password, and these become the user login information.

Campaign Structure

Once the account is created, the user is able to login anytime and access the control panel of the PPC ads. This interface, called "Campaign Management," offers complete control of the campaign and full functionality divided into three sections (Figure 28.0) — campaign management, reports, and detailed account information. The interface sometimes looks complex, but you will see that there is no big secret to defining the campaigns.

Figure 28.0

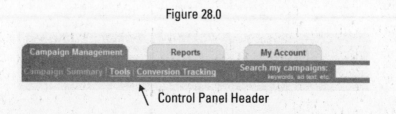

Control Panel Header

It helps to understand the characteristics of the campaign's structure, and the relationship between all the campaign components.

Let us learn the way that PPC ads organize their data and represent their operational structure. It is necessary to understand this:

- **Campaigns** — Each account is able to have many campaigns.

- **Group** — Each campaign is able to have different groups.

- **Ads** — Each group is able to have many ads.

- **Keywords** — Each ad may contain one or more keywords.

For better comprehension, Figure 28.5 represents the logic of PPC ad structure. This organizational model allows search engines to offer a very flexible advertisement system, with almost any imaginable combination.

Figure 28.5

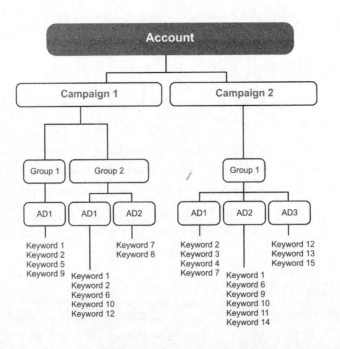

Let us visualize this in the following example. Imagine you are in charge of the PPC strategy for an art supplies store online. We can identify two important market segments: students of fine arts and professionals. The students buy a specific set of low-priced materials, and the professionals buy another type of expensive supplies.

In this case, we can design a PPC strategy that differentiates the two groups in the following way:

- **Group students** — With a set of different ads that appeals to the students, using keywords of the material they usually buy

- **Group professionals** — Offering exclusively the type of products that the professionals usually acquire

Although the sponsor is the same store, the segmentation has been set by two different ad groups under the same campaign. Each ad is able to group its own set of keywords.

Campaigns are usually targeting the same category of customers. For instance, if we analyze the last example, we can see that both segments (students and professionals) are interested in the same type of products. If the same site also sells furniture (which is a different kind of product than art supplies) it may require creating a new campaign with the intention of directing at potential customers for that type of product instead.

Campaigns also allow for differentiating markets according to geographic location. For instance, a company might offer the same set of products for India, Italy, and Greece. In that case, you might define one campaign for each location, with a specific set of groups and ads for each type of language by location.

The general schema of any campaign must be outlined before starting. The schema is a very simple representation that expresses the general idea of the strategy (Figure 29.0), before taking any action. I usually sketch out the schema with the intention of symbolizing the campaign and adjusting details. Once the schema is finished, I begin to think in the ads content, then I start using the campaign manager.

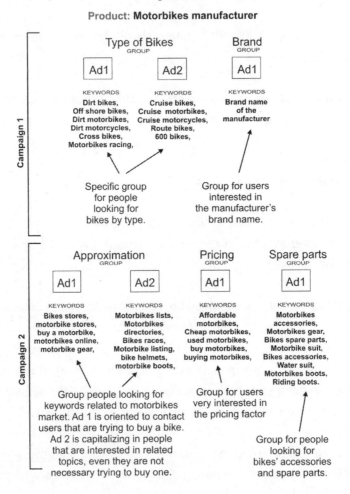

Figure 29.0

Product: **Motorbikes manufacturer**

Tips for Managing Your Account

Following are tips to consider to get the most out of PPC campaigns.

- **Group quantity** — If your campaign has too many groups (i.e., more than 20), create a new campaign, in order to facilitate the overview and management.

- **Results organization** —You may consider organizing groups according to the success of specific keywords. You could have campaigns with a high budget for very successful ads and other campaigns grouping less successful ads, with a lower budget, in order to optimize in the future.

- **Daily budgets** — The system allows setting daily budget by campaign; this is extremely useful for controlling costs and identify the daily limit by campaign.

- **Content targeting** — This is an option you will see in Google's control panel of your account. It means that your advertisement is also published in Google's partner sites, instead of the search site only. We will talk more about this option later.

9

Keywords for PPC Campaigns

What You Will Learn About in the Following Chapter

- Keyword creation for Search Engine's PPC

- Secrets and tips about successful PPC keywords

- Defining PPC keywords

- How to select the best PPC keywords for your site

Difference Between SEO and PPC Keywords

There is no difference between SEO and PPC keywords, except for the important element of control. SEO keywords are evaluated by search engines to qualify the site, while PPC keywords are evaluated by the advertiser to qualify the site.

In Chapter 3, I advised you to create the keyword matrix with all the keywords you could find about each of the keyword types: basic keywords, competitor keywords, region keywords, brand and integration keywords, complementary keywords, and misspelled keywords. I also advised you to identify the maximum amount of keywords that best represent your product or service.

SEO has a limitation for keyword usage and PPC does not. You control the keywords and apply them to particular ads, according to your own criteria. Some SEO experts also create ads with keywords that name their competitors or services. This practice is legal in PPC. Toyota, for instance, has significantly invested in ads for keywords such as Ford, BMW, Audi, and GMC.

> **Note**
>
> Yahoo! has a reviewing policy that analyzes every keyword you add to your account. Sometimes, they dismiss some of the keywords if they consider that there is no consistency with the industry of the advertiser.

There is no limitation for PPC keywords. You can define an unlimited amount of campaigns, groups, ads, keywords, and even accounts.

The keywords matrix is an important procedure you need to perform seriously, not only for the definition of the SEO optimization keywords, but also for the PPC ads' keywords.

Keywords Matching

The content or keywords matching is an option that allows you to define more precisely the type of search that will show your ad. This function permits the ad to be shown for entered keywords that do not necessarily match the keywords listed for that ad.

Negative Keywords

Search engine PPC offers a very useful function — negative keywords. These are keywords that, in conjunction with your keywords, make your ad not displayable. The objective is to save appearances of your ad from searches that are visibly not promising for you. The most popular negative keyword is the word "free." If your keyword is "data management software," the search for "free data management software" will not show your ad, since the user is looking for your category but not willing to pay, which dismisses the user as a potential lead.

Negative keywords protect the advertiser from confusing searches. Any user looking for "books of real estate" is not interested in your services of "real estate." If you apply keyword matching for your ads, you must define a negative keywords list for avoiding wrong appearances.

Following is a standard set of negative keywords you may consider incorporating into your campaigns.

- **Computer program seeker exclusion** — download, downloads, software, demo, freeware, computer program, computer programs, game, programs, program, shareware, windows

- **Service seeker exclusion** (if not offering a service) — consultant, consult, agency, help, error, problem, expert, return, repair, service provider, yellow pages, specialist, service, warranty, technical expert, support, customer service, customer care, consultation

- **Erotic seeker exclusion** — jpeg, jpg, erotic, porn, naked, sex, sexy, nude, lust, intimate

- **Earn money with computer seeker exclusion** — affiliate, affiliates, partner, home industry, earn, partner programs

- **Free seeker exclusion** — costless, free, complimentary, gift, gratis, no charge, exempt, no cost

- **Blog seeker** — blog, blogs, RSS, article, Weblog

- **Bargain seeker exemption** — auction, opportunity, classified ad, cheap, coupon, deal, discount, eBay, economical, bargain, direct sale, reduced, save, samples, sample, low cost, trial, sale

Magnitude Limitation

Search engines propose some limits in the amount of keywords, ads, and campaigns in order to facilitate the management of the account online and the efficiency of the system in general.

Google, for instance, recommends the following:

- **Campaigns** — maximum of 25 per account

- **Ad groups** — maximum of 100 per campaign

- **Keywords** — maximum of 750 per ad, 2,000 per campaign, and 50,000 per account

Keyword Profitability

The most common mistake in PPC ads for search engines is bidding for the wrong keywords. The success of your ad depends on selecting the right keywords. The following paragraphs represent a set of valuable techniques to ensure you are on the right track.

Specific Keywords

Specific keywords attract qualified visitors to your Web site (Figure 29.5). Let us analyze the following example. You run an office in Wisconsin providing insurance services specializing in farms. The evident keywords are insurance farm, farms protection, farms insurance services, farmhouse insurance, and harvest insurance.

Figure 29.5

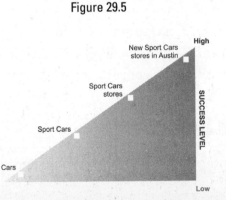

From the profit perspective, these keywords are not very recommendable. Without clear information about location (Wisconsin), the ad will be displayed for any single search matching those keywords. A farmer from California or Texas would click on the ad, and the advertiser would have to pay for that click, without gaining a potential customer.

Keywords are profitable if they are precise; only specific keywords bring qualified visitors. A better keyword for the example presented would be "insurance farm Wisconsin." In this case, a farmer from that location who types that keyword will be a potential customer.

Note	People look for specifics; this is the secret of PPC ads for search engines.

Some aggressive SEO professionals recommend bidding for generalized keywords and being very specific in the title or description of the ad. For instance, you could bid for the keyword "Farm insurance" and describe "Farm insurance Wisconsin" in the headline of the ad.

Keywords Phrases

Keywords composed by more than one word are a must. The objective of any SEO and PPC campaign is to anticipate potential search of users that could become customers. People usually enter complex keywords, never isolated words. Think in the context, put yourself in the position of the user and imagine all the options. Figure 30.0 shows data about users' behavior at the moment of using search engines; as you may appreciate, more than two-thirds of the users online use complex keyword phrases for their searches.

Unusual Keywords

Using the keywords suggestion tools and your own judgment, you may identify different sets of keywords that are very specific, but also very unique.

Figure 30.0

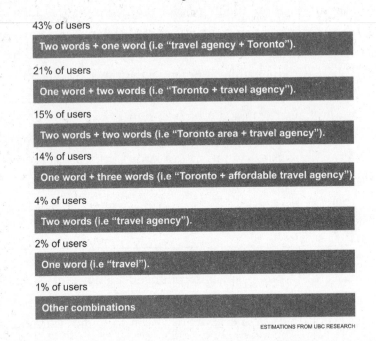

43% of users
Two words + one word (i.e "travel agency + Toronto").

21% of users
One word + two words (i.e "Toronto + travel agency").

15% of users
Two words + two words (i.e "Toronto area + travel agency").

14% of users
One word + three words (i.e "Toronto + affordable travel agency").

4% of users
Two words (i.e "travel agency").

2% of users
One word (i.e "travel").

1% of users
Other combinations

ESTIMATIONS FROM UBC RESEARCH

For instance, "Marine power boats engine diesel Miami" is a complex and unusual keyword. Many SEO experts define entire campaigns for those types of keywords, for cheap bids ($0.01 to $0.05) considering there is no competition for them.

The first keywords you often think of are also the ones your competition is using or thinking. If you are promoting a competitive product, you are forced to contend for high bids in common keywords.

Let us imagine you are promoting a notebook product. Other than the brand name of the manufacturer, the rest of the keywords you might think of are the same as your competitors, probably with more history than you and, consequently, with expensive bids.

Proactive Keywords

This is an interesting option. Usually, proactive keywords generate the most unexpected positive results, demanding intensive creative thinking. A couple of years ago, I had been hired to participated in the PPC strategy of an important hotel in London. This hotel also organizes and promotes tourist trips to London, offering extraordinary packages for competitive prices.

Figure 30.3

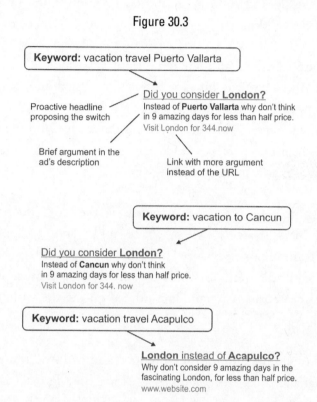

I created four different campaigns with 600 keywords — a branding campaign, a competitive campaign, a relational campaign, and, finally, a proactive campaign. The proactive campaign had several groups with specific keywords for people who were not necessarily looking for a trip to London, but planning for a vacation. I created groups for each important tourist destination in the world. For example, a Mexico group had one ad for each particular city — Cancun, Acapulco, Yucatan, Puerto Vallarta, and others.

The structure of the ads for each city is represented in Figure 30.3. The objective of the ads was offering intriguing options for people who entered keywords for those cities, motivating the switch. I realized that several users were looking online for holiday options without having decided the destinations of their vacation. These were my target: people open to receiving advising and good price options for vacationing in an exciting new tourist destination.

These ads are called AI ads. These types of ads simulate an intelligence response to the keywords hit. The user is intrigued and, for a second, wonders how the ad recognized his original intention and offered an option. The response to this campaign was impressive, and the conversion rate was superior to 4 percent, which was the best conversion rate from all the campaigns that formed the strategy.

Another example of proactive keywords is the PPC development of recognized SEO strategist Milan Prata, for a sports supplies online mega-storefront. Prata specialized in proactive keyword generation and identified 3,400 different keywords organized in 70 campaigns with the objective of promoting each product offered on the site with a high level of detail.

He created one campaign for each product, and defined groups of ads for specific characteristics. For example, the category "Puma" contained ad groups for each product of the brand, such as "shoes," "backpacks," and "jackets." Each group was formed by numerous ads promoting each single item (one by one) of the category. In this case, the strategy is aimed at displaying ads for each possible related specific search, considering that customers of sports products are very specific in their searches — they know what they are looking for.

These types of users usually enter keywords such as "Puma King Exec Trainer" instead of simple searches like "soccer shoes" or "puma sneakers." Figure 30.5 represents the organization schema of Prata's strategy.

Figure 30.5

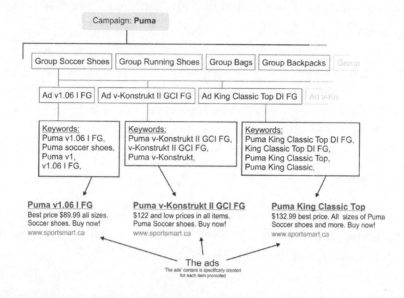

Finding More Keywords

Finding more keywords is a constant objective for SEO and PPC promotion, since it is impossible to anticipate all the potential combinations of words that users may apply.

The following paragraphs show some alternatives for finding and adding more keywords to your campaigns.

Spelling Variations and Errors

Applying variations of existing keywords provides very interesting results. Suppose you are bidding for the keyword "car rental." You can enlarge the keyword's list by applying some of the following techniques:

- **Plural** — This is the first easy variation usually recommended for keyword expansion. You could add "cars rental" to the list.

- **Hyphens** — Many users apply hyphens to their keywords' search, for instance, "car-rentals."

- **Word transposing** — This is a very popular technique you have to practice. If you are bidding for "car rental" you may try "rental car."

- **Spelling errors** — As we have seen before, spelling errors or typos are a good option for finding new keywords; some options for the current examples might be "car rentel," carrental," car rentl," "car renatl" and "car ental."

Synonyms

You can find different ways to express any idea. The usage of synonyms is very common for keyword expansion. The idea is to define a list of potential words that, somehow, represent the same thing.

If you are bidding for the keyword "building," you may consider adding other keywords such as "edifice," "house," "construction," "structure," and "residence." I use the thesaurus sub-site found through **www.dictionary. com** to collect new variations of my main keywords.

Auxiliary Keywords

These are words that usually combine very well with almost any predefined keyword, with the objective of creating a new variation in order to anticipate potential searches.

Auxiliary keywords qualify your ad for popular searches, separate from the product you are promoting. For example, if you are selling pool tables online, auxiliary keywords such as "article" or "advise" in conjunction with your keyword will link your ad to potential customers, even if you are not necessarily selling articles about pool tables.

The following lists represent some of the most recommendable auxiliary keywords:

acquire
active
adequate
advise
affordable
article
attractive
beginner
better
brand-new
best
catalog
cheap
classic
clear
collection
combination
comfortable
common
compare
consult
correct
data
official
online
operating
on-time
organization
overview
perfect
percent
plan
planning
popular
price cut
price reduction
price markdown
procedure
professional
program
purchase
quality

describe
design
detail
detailed
economical
efficient
excellent
experience
expert
expertise
explain
facts
fast
fee
final price
functions
general
good
grand
handy
help
ideal
important
rebate
recognized
reduced
regular
relaxing
reliable
replace
sample
second-hand
second hand
secret
selection
service
services
setup
simple
small
sophisticated
special

impressive
improve
improved
index
info
information
inquiry
installation
intensive
interesting
Internet
Know-how
large
list
list-price
luxury
manual
market
meticulous
new
news
normal
offer
specialist
standard
summary
system
table
techniques
test
tip
tips
toll
trial
try
tutorial
understand
unique
use
used
Web

Popular Keywords

All the keyword tools overviewed in Chapter 3 are also useful for finding PPC keywords. You know, at this time, how to use them effectively. PPC keywords are more proactive; their objective is not to qualify for the search engines' evaluation, but to make the ad appear in front of potential customers as much as possible.

Your objective is to be present, all the time, with ads that match potential customers' expectations. Popular keywords are not enough; you must consider their combination and implementation of creative keywords with the objective of your ad.

Seasonal Keywords

Many products and services have relation with calendar events or periods. Many ads may find suitable appearance for users that are looking for your keywords in combination with these typical seasonal words.

The following lists represent the most important seasonal keywords, according to the calendar:

January:	February:	March:	April:
• New Year's Day	• Valentine's Day	• St. Patrick's Day	• April Fools' Day
• Epiphany	• Presidents' Day	• Start of spring	
• Martin Luther King's Day	• Carnival	• Easter	
May:	**June:**	**July:**	**August:**
• May Day	• Father's Day	• Independence Day	• School enrollment
• Cinco de Mayo	• Start of summer		
• Mother's Day	• Vacation season (June/September)		
• Memorial Day			
• Pentecost (May/June)			

September:	October:	November:	December:
• Start of fall	• Thanksgiving	• All Saints' Day	• Start of winter
• Labor Day	• Halloween	• Veterans' Day	• Christmas Eve
	• Columbus Day	• Martin's Day	• Christmas
		• Day of Repentance and Prayer	• Kwanzaa
		• Thanksgiving Day	
		• Advent Days (November/ December)	

10

Writing Profitable PPC Ads

The Ad Needs to Be Successful

The real attraction of a PPC campaign is the ad. If your ad is not right, your campaign will fail — no matter how good your keyword and bidding techniques are. The user needs to be attracted, invited, convinced, and, occasionally, induced to click on the PPC ad.

The information in this chapter provides enough directions to create successful ads, based on proven rules of PPC advertisement that every SEO strategist must manipulate daily. It is important to understand the ad content is part of the PPC strategy, in coordination with keywords definition and pricing strategy.

Ad Content Structure

PPC ads are simple and easy to read, which is part of their success.

Figure 31.0

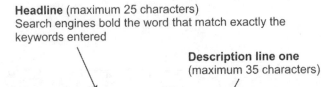

Figure 31.0 represents the basic ad structure of a PPC ad. Each ad is formed by the following components:

- **Headline** — This is the first line of the ad text, with a maximum of 25 characters (including empty spaces). The only punctuation permitted is the question mark.

- **Description lines** — The next two text lines have a maximum of 35 characters (including empty spaces), and they must be edited separately in the control panel of the ad campaign.

- **URL** — This is the last text line (maximum of 35 characters, including empty spaces) with a link to the landing page. The link text must be edited in the control panel (maximum of 1024 characters).

Writing Headlines

The most visible and important component of the ad is the headline. This is the first text that the users read. If the headline does not capture the user's attention, he is not going to continue reading the ad.

Figure 31.5

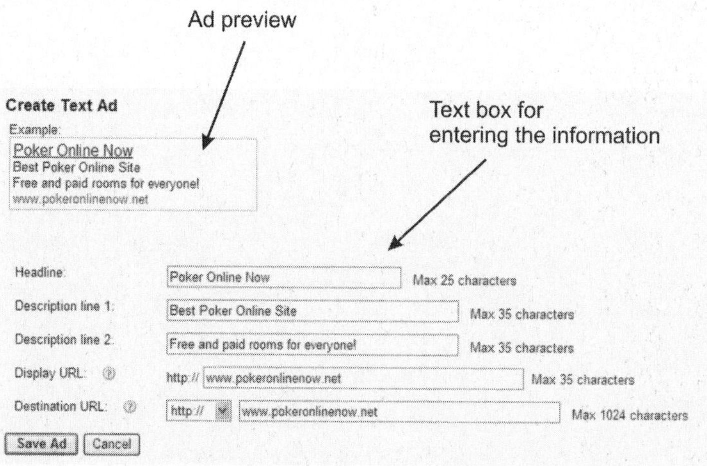

The most important advice SEO experts provide is to use the keywords in your headline (Figure 31.5). This is because users have a natural tendency of identifying the headlines with the entered keywords faster. It has been proven that by matching exactly the keywords entered by the user, the advertiser will notice a natural increasing in the click-through rates of the ads. Also, Yahoo! and Google both display in bold font the words that match the keywords entered in the search, which means your ad's headline will be bold and more visible.

Dynamic Keyword Headlines

PPC ads offer dynamic headlines, which is an option that consists in the automatic appearance of the keyword entered in your headline's ad. To accomplish this, the user simply needs to write a piece of code in the headline textbox:

{Keyword:alternative keyword}

This displays the keywords from the search in the headlines. If the keyword entered is longer than 25 characters, the ad will display the alternative keyword. For example, let us imagine your ad is using {Keyword:Poker Online} for keywords such as "poker online," "online poker," "gambling online," "free poker online," and "poker online rooms" (Figure 32.0).

Figure 32.0

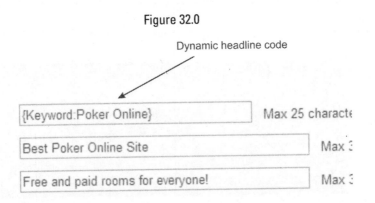

If someone is looking for "poker online" or "gambling online," the ad will adapt the headline to one of those keywords. If the user enters a very long keyword, such as "Internet poker online rooms and Web sites for free," the ad will display the "Poker Online" headline. Unfortunately, the alternative keyword cannot be longer than 15 characters, including empty spaces.

Since most of the advertisers use dynamic headlines for their ads, the sponsored results display very repetitive headlines. I personally prefer to create headlines with some variations instead, and attract users with some new, proactive titles. The following paragraph teaches some important techniques for writing powerful headlines.

Writing Great Headlines

Take your time writing the headline; the ad's success depends of the efficacy of it.

Sometimes, the elaboration of the title is a slow process and requires applying ingenious combinations in order to grab an Internet seeker's attention. Following is a list of headline writing techniques. Do not forget that the headline maximum amount of characters is only 25.

- **Interrogate the user** — This is a very useful technique that may intrigue the potential customer. "Want to travel?," "Depressed and bored?," and "Still with the same car?," are examples.

- **Instruct the user** — Users react very well to dominating statements. "Download freeware now," "Learn Real Estate," or "Keep car battery forever," for example.

- **Tell stories** — This is not one of my favorites, but depending of the product, it may work well in some ads. "How to deal with lawyers," "I made 25K in two days," and "I always won poker," are examples of this technique.

- **Disclose data** — People feel attracted to "secrets" revealed. "Egyptian mystery exposed," "NASA files here," and "What IT people hide," for example.

- **Unbelievable statements** — Never underestimate the power of the impossible, this has always been a powerful techniques for titles. "Make $3,275 per week," "Lose weight without diet," and "Fly tickets for free," are examples.

- **Trust factor** — Provide reliable atmosphere. "Recommended by doctors," "50,000 pleased students," "Never broken," "20 years of experience," and "Dentists favorite," for example.

- **Offer comparison** — Contrast helps to identify value. "Brighter than the sun," "Better than before," and "Bigger than a car," for example.

- **Superlatives expressions** — Avoid using super positive exclamations, such as "Fastest car on market," "Greatest seafood," or "Cheapest wine."

- **Repetitive punctuation** — Double punctuation marks ("??") are not recommended or permitted by search engines.

Successful Ad Text

SEO experts say that the headline objective is to attract the user and the description aim is to motivate action. The user must be convinced that the ad has a real value and that there is something (exciting) waiting behind the link. The click must be motivated.

Before Starting

You may consider the following set of tips before beginning to write the description text for the ads.

- **Analysis** — I recommend generating a list of functions and characteristics of your product or service. This helps you visualize and comprehend the product. Think in terms of benefits for the user, instead of feature descriptions.

- **Benefits** — Sometimes it is not easy to identify benefits. Transferring features into benefits is a process that requires imagining users' needs and potential interests.

  For example, business intelligence applications are very sophisticated tools, but the real value is determined by the enormous amount of time and the data management efficiency that the user obtains using these types of software.

- **Positioning** — All advertisers need, eventually, to place their products against the competition; this is called "product positioning." What does your product offer that your competitor's product does not? Identifying the added value helps you to write characteristics of your product that the competition cannot.

- **Target** — Before writing a single word of your ad, it is important to know to whom the ad is intended (i.e., gender, age, social segment and characteristics, and other demographics). The knowledge of your public will define the ad's language and message. Marketing is about target understanding and anticipation. Know your target segmentation before anything else.

Writing the Ad Text

- **Motivation** — Your number one objective is to motivate the user to click on the link. Do not try to achieve anything else; just make the public go to the next step by going to the landing page. The ad's objective is not selling a product or service, but convincing the user to click and redirect the browser to the link.

- **Benefits** — Many ads list features or product characteristics. People are looking for convincing arguments and direct benefits; they want to know why they should believe in the ad's argument. You may persuade users just with one word, if is the correct one. Mention benefits instead of features. For instance, instead of writing "advanced energy drink" try "feel energetic and vigorous all the time."

- **Low-value words** — Every single word-space in the ad is essential. Go directly to the point. Avoid unnecessary vocabulary; remember that users have less than a second to identify words. Instead of "Gardening and organic supplies including compost" write "Organic compost and supplies."

- **Specific language** — Users value direct messages; be specific in the way you create the text. "Shoes" is not as effective as "leather Italian shoes." Specific content will ensure that the concept comes across effectively.

- **Targeting** — The whole idea of identifying the audience segment is to generate a text that really makes contact with them. If your audience is price-conscious, they will react better to descriptions such as "good deals" or "lowest price in market" than "unmatchable quality" or "high level."

- **Simple words** — The most effective formula is simple wording in short sentences. The ad has to be easy to read. Users' eyes scan the search engine's result page in milliseconds, and immediately filter the content. The most direct ads have the highest chances of succeeding. Look for the simplest way to express concepts. Instead of writing "Delivery free of charge" try "Free delivery," or replace "Obtain immense benefits" with "Great benefits."

- **Facts** — Statements of real details are beneficial for audiences that are looking for validation of the advertiser. The ad's content is all you have to convince the users. For example, "hundreds of engineers on the floor" or "millions of customers online right now" are oriented to express a certain level of credibility by revealing real data. Be honest; do not invent facts that you cannot support.

Promotional Expressions

There are several powerful expressions you may use in your ads. These are typical selling terms already tested after all these years of PPC ad implementation:

10 reasons to…	Free delivery…	Open 24 hours…
10 top…	Free to the door…	Opportunity…
10 tip to…	From experts…	Original…

Access now...

All models...

All sizes...

Ask us...

Available now...

Bargain price...

Best quality...

Big selection...

Brand new...

Buy now...

Click here...

Compare...

Cool price...

Create your own...

Do you need? ...

Everything...

Facts...

Fast...

Finally...

Flexible...

For lovers...

Free...

Greater selection...

Good...

Half prices...

Hot price...

Ideal for...

Immediate...

Important...

Improving...

In minutes...

Including...

In stock...

Increase...

It works...

Last week...

Low prices...

Money-back guarantee...

New...

Now only...

Offer...

Once in a lifetime...

Only until...

Free catalog...

Perfect...

Price breaker...

Price guarantee...

Quick & easy...

Ready...

Recommended by...

Reduced...

Save...

Save money...

Save now...

Say yes...

Sample...

Special offer...

Special price...

Step-by-step...

Today only...

Try if free...

Try it now...

Unlimited...

Why pay more...

Works every time...

Your chance...

Learning from Competitors

All the players of a particular market must watch their competitors and monitor their activities. PPC strategy requires you to constantly investigate ways to improve results and determine evolution of current campaigns. Many SEO experts use the following process to keep their campaigns updated and functional.

Look for your keyword in any search engine (e.g., "golf supplies"). Take notes of the sponsored results ads. Imagine seven ads were displayed. Now repeat the search, only this time, add the keywords "free" (e.g., "free golf supplies").

The sponsored results now are different. If some of the ads from the previous search are now also listed in this search, those are not smart competitors, considering they have not filtered negative keywords (Chapter 9). Remove these competitors from your notes.

Now repeat the original search, only this time, add a fake word (e.g., "golf supplies ftcyrfg"). The ads that are still on the list are either from large corporations (usually they make huge investments, qualifying even for nonsense keywords) or very small competitors with mediocre PPC work.

At this point, you may exclude these ads from your notes, and focus on the ads left. Those are the competitors that are performing a good PPC campaign strategy. Analyze their ads and Web sites, learn how to identify your strength, and keep them in mind for the bidding war you will learn about in further paragraphs.

Advertising the Price

This is a contradictory topic. Some experts do not recommend mentioning the product price in the ad; however, I have obtained impressive results publishing and making the price information available in the first line of the description. Certainly, not all ads are suitable to this technique. Only a price-conscious audience reacts positively to this type of message.

If you advertise your product's price, you must ensure your price is the best. If the price you are promoting is not competitive, the results could be catastrophic. Even if your price is competitive and users react positively to it, you must monitor this type of campaign almost constantly (sometimes hourly), considering that your competitors may launch a new ad with lower prices, just to establish a winning factor between the ads. This could hurt the objective of your campaign.

I love aggressive techniques, such as price exposure campaigns, but I know that I have to be ready to react fast (and sometimes be ready to drastically change the ad) if the market conditions adjust negatively.

Note	If you use price as the main argument of your ad, take into consideration a basic rule of search engines for PPC campaigns. The advertised price must be also present in the destination Web site, within one or two clicks; otherwise, the search engine may dismiss your ad.

PPC Pricing System

We have learned already that pricing is one of the important components of the PPC strategy, in conjunction with the optimization of the Web site, the keywords definition, and the ad concept. Now we will learn how to identify the correct value of the ad, and how to win the bidding competition.

Every time the search engine displays an ad, this is called "impression." If the user clicks on the displayed ad, this is called "click." An impression does not necessarily mean that the user has seen your ad, but a click does, and also demonstrates interest in its content.

The click-through rate (CRT) is a calculation between the clicks and the impressions of the ad, represented in Figure 32.5. If the ad has been clicked 3 times out of 100 impressions, the CRT is 3 percent (3 * 100 divided by 100 impressions); if the ad has been clicked 8 times in the last 250 impressions, the CRT is 3.2 percent (8 * 100 divided by 250 impressions).

CPC Logic

The PPC strategy is completed when the advertiser identifies the real cost per click. Since the whole system is based on cost per every single click on the ad, not the impression, the definition of that cost is essential. Figure 32.7 represents the logic behind the pricing strategy. As you can see, advertisers propose maximum cost for keywords; the highest determines the position in the sponsored result list.

Figure 32.7

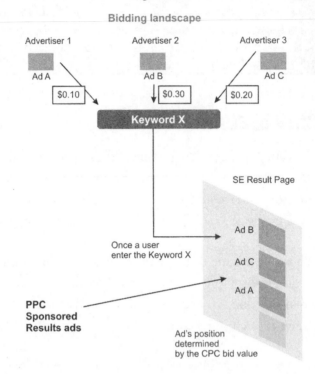

Using the control panel of the campaign manager, you will visualize all the options regarding your ads and the maximum cost per keyword (Figure 33.0). The control panel allows you to control the CPC and also the ad's position in the sponsored results list.

Figure 33.0

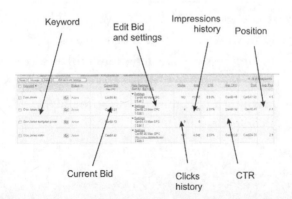

Maximum CPC Calculation (CPC)

Nobody can establish the maximum CPC for you. You are responsible for determining that value, according to different parameters.

Let us imagine, for example, your competitor defines a maximum CPC of 40 cents and you set your maximum at 66 cents. If nobody else is bidding for that keyword, SE will recognize your bid as the highest and they have a mechanism (you must submit to them, for instance, Google Discounter system) to determine your original bid from 66 cents to 41cents.

Although the maximum CPC is set to 66 cents, you will par 41 cents, until other advertisers raise that maximum to some other value higher than 66 cents.

SE also offers auto-bidder functionality, which automatically increases your maximum CPC to one cent higher than the current highest bid. This is not recommended.

How to Calculate the Maximum CPC

There is a simple calculation for determining the maximum CPC of your ad.

Figure 33.5

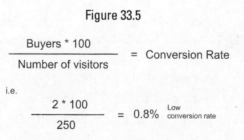

Remember that in Chapter 2, we learned how to calculate the conversion rate in order to identify how many visitors became customers. For example, four users in three hundred by your product; then your conversion rate is 1.3 percent (4 X 100 divided by 300) as shown in Figure 33.5.

Figure 33.7

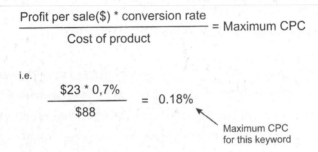

The maximum CPC formula establishes the relationship between the conversion rate, the profitability, and the product cost (Figure 33.7). Let us suppose, for example, your site is selling a product for $30, your profit is about $5, and your conversion rate is 1.2 percent. In this case, your maximum bid for the ad must be established in $0.2 (5 * 3.2 divided by 30).

You do not want to drive people to your Web site with a negative ROI. This is the logic behind the CPC calculation, defining the limit in which your ad became a cost instead of an investment, called the break even point. Perhaps you will see that the bidding scenario for some keywords is below your maximum CPC. This means that your position is comfortable for that bid and there is plenty of room for you to raise the CPC later.

Daily Budget

At the end of 2005, SE established a daily budget system to help advertisers control their monthly investment in PPC campaigns. This daily budget system is defined by campaign. Before the implementation of this system, some companies had bad experiences in controlling daily costs of the campaigns. Many advertisers commonly made the mistake of starting the daily budget very low, which does not help the expansion of the campaigns.

I follow a simple strategy that never fails. Once I have finished defining the ad strategy, the ad groups, and all the keywords, I set a high value for the daily budget of a couple of hundred dollars. The value is unrealistic, but it helps to define the final budget by observing the progress of the PPC campaign during the first days, with the objective of discovering the natural limit.

For example, I managed a campaign where the maximum the client could afford per day was $500. I obtained much better performance out of the campaign after I set the daily budget at $1,000. The money spent was usually around $400 to $500, fitting perfectly within the range of what the client was willing to invest. I examined the account throughout the day to make sure we were not going over budget (successful PPC ad users have a finger on the pulse of their account activity on a daily basis). Finally, after the first months, the daily budget was adjusted to $700, but the daily spent was still around $400 to $500.

Setting a higher daily budget will not only result in additional impressions, but will also provide you with the meaningful data you need to accurately project costs versus sales, and ultimately, to determine your daily profit.

Pricing Strategies from the Best

The PPC pricing strategies have been defined over the course of time as a result of different specialists' experiences and experimental combinations:

- Top positioning strategy

- Competition mirroring strategy

- Minimum bidding strategy

Top Positioning Strategy

This option requires a large budget. It is the strategy implemented by big corporations with big advertisement budgets. The objective of this strategy is to be at the top of the results list, no matter the cost. Sometimes this strategy generates unrealistic CPCs; this makes the system vulnerable, considering that once that the CPC is too high, nobody is able to drop it down.

This strategy is very risky, but it also may bring the best results. CMC Research presented in a report, last year, that the first position of PPT ads receives 10 times more traffic than the tenth position. In his study about PPT ads, Steward Lehman has proven that the first position of the PPC ads has 40 percent more probability of being clicked than the second position. This is very important, considering you may not reach 40 percent of your potential customers if you are not listed in first place.

If you have the right product and price, a top positioning strategy might bring the fastest result for you, but it is important to consider that the cost of the first place, for popular keywords, will be very expensive. Top positioning strategy makes your ad an easy target of the competitor, who has established a similar strategy. In that case, chances are you will eventually face a bidding war.

Competition Mirroring Strategy

This strategy consists of putting your ad's price always below the ad price of your immediate competitor. You sacrifice position, but you avoid a bidding war. In this case, your skills for creating powerful headlines and content are essential.

I usually apply this strategy if the audience is price-conscious and I know I am able to publish a competitive price. For example, if you and your competitor sell notebooks and you beat them in price, you would use this strategy to take the second immediate position with an aggressive ad, like "Notebooks from $549" or "Best portable computers half-price."

Advertisers with very popular products may chose this strategy, hoping to make the difference with their shocking price argument. Products or services with niche markets do not fit with this strategy.

Minimum Bidding Strategy

This strategy does not drive too much traffic to the sites, but may accommodate tight budgets and still provide some good results. If you implement this strategy, you need to identify (as much as possible) very specific keywords that match your product. In this case, you increase the chances of publishing your ad in many searches, where your competition may not be present.

The Best Strategy

The best advice about pricing strategy might be to alternate between the three strategies. The best way to optimize budgets and obtain a satisfactory result is to optimize the campaign between all the components we have learned. Defining the CPC is a slow process that you will adjust once the audience reaction starts providing signals. Nobody can anticipate this.

Bidding Wars

Every time you raise your bid on a particular keyword to beat your competitor, you may initiate a bidding war. Many times, advertisers that have seriously invested in PPT campaigns keep outbidding constantly for higher positions, even the first place.

If this mechanism does not stop, the keyword cost will go far away from the realistic CPC, and will remain unreachable for all competitors. I have seen many competitors ruin keywords, making them unavailable for the rest. Epson and Canon, which pay enormous amounts of money for particular keywords, made some agreements in the past to balance the cost of some high priced keywords they were competing for.

Sometimes it is recommended to resign the first place for some particular keywords, but to gain the first place in critical keywords your competitors may not appear. If you analyze the situation carefully, you will find the right balance.

Click Potential

In 2005, Nancy Frisch from *Internet World* published a study about PPC SE advertising. She reveals the positioning importance of the PPT ads in search engines; she states that the click potential "is the percentage of probabilities of clicking on the ad."

Following, you can find an extraction of the information revealed in the document, created from statistical information from a test performed on 1,700 users interested in the same product.

- 68 percent of the users preferred the result of relevancy lists (non-sponsored results)

- The 32 percent left (544 users) selected the PPT ads (sponsored results)

- 73 percent of click potential for position number 1 of PPT ad (394)

- 60 percent of click potential for position number 2 of PPT ad (327 clicks)

- 27 percent of click potential for position number 3 of PPT ad (152 clicks)

- 17 percent of click potential for position number 4 of PPT ad (96 clicks)

- 9 percent of click potential for position number 5 of PPT ad (49 clicks)

- 5 percent of click potential for position number 6 of PPT ad (29 clicks)

- 2 percent of click potential for position number 7 of PPT ad (12 clicks)

- 0.7 percent of click potential for position number 8 of PPT ad (4 clicks)

The most interesting concept of the click potential analysis presented by Frisch is the big gap between positions two and three. That difference seems to continue as a pattern for the rest of the positions. I have conducted my own experiments regarding the click potential of PPT ads, according to their position, and this study information is incredibly accurate.

Conclusion: The value of the first two positions in the list of PPT ads is significant; appearing in one of these two places is imperative to facilitate making contact with your potential customers.

PPC Ad Optimization

Landing Page

After all this development, it is necessary to consider a couple of last details to secure success. The landing page is one of them. In the industry, the people refer to the URL destination page where the ad links as the landing page. The ad convinces the user about the existence of some particular value, the destination page persuades the potential customer to buy the product or service, and the landing page will introduce the credentials of the site and try to match the expectations generated by the ad.

Remember that the user is "looking for something;" for that reason, the landing page must give them what they are looking for. Every time I am defining the landing page of an ad, I ask myself the following question: Am I delivering in three seconds the promise of the ad? The answer to this question is essential to define the level of possible success of the ad. Many marketers do not value the landing page factor, and they simply direct the user to the home page. This is incorrect.

Last year I conducted a study about the level of relevancy of landing pages of Web sites from diverse industries (300 Web sites advertised through PPT ads). The results: 65 percent of the home pages did not directly address the topic of the ad; in many cases, the user needed to click three times to locate the information required in the search. If the user does not access the information at least in the first three seconds after arriving to the link, that user is gone.

Let us imagine, for instance, a particular user looking for model cars at Yahoo!; he enters "replica model + porsche." In this case, like many others, the user knows what he wants.

Figure 34.0

Porsche Replica Model
Best replica of Porsche models,
Free shipping, immediate delivery.
www.planet-replica.biz

The first ad of the sponsored results is represented in Figure 34.0, which is a good ad for the entered keywords. Once the user clicks on the link, there are two possibilities:

1. The ad opens a home page of the storefront with a welcome paragraph, promotional ads, pictures, and information about all the replica models of cars, planes, trains, and boats. The user is unable to identify where the Porsche model car is located. After looking around for a while, he decides to press the back button and find another supplier.

2. The ads open a sub-page of the Web site with images and information about all the models of Porsche's car replicas. He is able to locate the precise model he is looking for and, without clicking on any link, he finds characteristics of the product, price, delivery options, and more.

Remember to create a special and separate landing page for each PPT ad.

Characteristics of the Landing Page

The following list represents some important elements to consider while designing the destination page:

Navigation — It must be easy to navigate; avoid complex navigation menus.

First level information— Try to keep the user on the page, without making him click on links to access to more information. This is also called "first level navigation" or "one-click navigation." Additional clicks discourage users; more than 40 percent of the visitors leave the destination page if they have to click more than one time.

Objective — Never forget the purpose of the landing page. That page needs to be branded in order to be consistent with the main site, but its objective is to provide all the necessary information regarding the product or service promoted in the ad.

Menu — Many developers make the mistake of replicating the same menu of the Web site's home page in the destination page. It is preferable to offer a back button and send the user to the home page instead. The landing page needs to remain clear and focus on the product and its characteristics.

Benefits — Think about the ad, and imagine the expectation of the users after reading the ad. Create the landing page with those expectations in mind. The landing page must offer an important value to catch the user's attention and convince him that he is in the right place. Think in terms of benefits for the user, not in terms of product features.

Identify unique value proposition (UVP) — The page must state the UVP from the beginning. Headlines, images, and text must be applied in order to differentiate the product from the competitor.

Answer the following questions to incorporate this concept into the destination page:

- Is the product any better or less expensive than the competition? Why?

- Is the company able to make a commitment for promotional reasons (e.g., extended guarantees or special discounts)?

- Does the product offer features that the competitor's product does not?

- Is the company the largest in the market?

- Is the company the smallest in the market?

Reliability — The page must communicate a reliable message that generates value and trust. Nobody logs in at **Amazon.com** and, after making the decision to buy a product, hesitates to purchase because the site does not provide enough guarantee. The worst thing that could happen to an e-commerce site is to make people wary about the purchasing, credit card validation, customer information, spyware, security penetration, delivering processes, or other such issues.

Although your Web site is not an e-commerce site, you need to manage the trust factor very seriously; down the road, your Web site is going to "sell" something and the user must be comfortable with the Web site proposition.

Read the following set of tips for making your site more reliable:

- Provide references that the users can verify easily. The visitors appreciate proof and evidence.

- Provide extensive contact information that makes you real and reachable, such as real phone numbers and street addresses. Make the "contact us" section of the site easy to find and to fill out.

- Show the people involved in the company behind the Web site with pictures, names, and testimonials. The Web site must appear as the "device" that allows the user to reach "people" who will take care of them.

- Money transaction validations are key components of e-commerce sites. You must offer (sometimes up front) the information of the company that manages the validation of the credit card transactions or any financial operation.

- Show that the Web site is regularly updated. Some developers identify the last update in the home page. Provide the feeling of constant work behind the scenes.

- Hire a professional developer or designer to make the Web site (if you are not one).

- Errors are big enemies of Web sites. Users get disappointed with all kinds of errors (no matter how big or small they are), such as typos, missing images, and dead links.

- Money back guarantee is a very convincing argument for e-commerce sites, it helps to offer this type of financial protection for potential customers.

- Proactive message — The destination page must engage the user. Remember that this visitor is not just a curious surfer who arrives to your site just by chance, this is a "potential customer" (if you have done a good PPT strategy of course) and it is valid to invite him to take an action. Anything you can recommend will help them to act; for example, "Order now!," "download the demo now!," "fill out the form to get a free sample," "get the brochure," "get the newsletter," or "click here!"

- Capture interest in the headline — Repeating the keyword in the headline is important for the success of the landing page. I have created more than 10 different similar html destination pages, and my only change was the headline, edited specially to represent the keyword ad. People tend to read the body text if the keywords entered (or some of them) are repeated in the headline.

- Web site performance — You must test the functionality level of the site. Some developers do not take this topic seriously. The Web site must load fast (and easily) and must not require any extra plug-in or special download to appear and be accessible for any type of browser (e.g., IE, Firefox, or Opera).

- SEO the landing page — I recommend developing a simple html page with basic design components (headline, two or three images, body text, and footer), publishing it in the server, and submitting it individually, in the same way as was done with the Web site. This also increases the chances of being indexed by the spiders and appearing in the relevancy list of the SE.

Examination of the PPT Campaign

Developers, marketers, or companies always decide to initiate a PPT ad campaign with a tangible economical expectation. All the work involved in the execution of the campaigns and the development of the complementary activities is not an insignificant exercise. At this point, you may conclude how complex and time consuming the process is.

The ROI is the component that visualizes the level of efficiency of the ad's campaigns. Sometimes the components of the campaigns are correct, the ads are correct, and the landing pages are correct, but the visitors do not click on the ads. This does not mean necessarily that the campaign is wrong; many times some elements need to be adjusted to make the campaign work as expected and obtain a positive ROI. Testing is the only reasonable way to identify those components that need to be adjusted.

In past chapters, we learned about conversion rate and ROI. In this chapter, we will cover this topic in detail. We know that the conversion rate is the percentage of visitors that become customers. Say you receive 150 visitors and 12 turn into customers; subsequently your conversion rate is 8 percent (12 * 100 divided by 150).

The most problematic situation is the keyword rebound, where keywords attract many users to the site, but the ROI is very low (almost inexistent). If this happens to you, you are paying for clicks with no return at all; in other words, you are paying for free clicks.

The best way to test this is to perform small tests with changes in the components of the ad and the landing page. Never do a total optimization, you may lose a valid learning process; the idea is to recognize the element(s) that are working wrong.

Escalating ROI

If you are able to increase ROI, your site will make more money. The only solid process to achieve ROI escalation, as we mentioned, is testing. First, you need to be clear about the components to evaluate, such as number of visitors, subscribers, sales, or newsletter requests. Once you have a clear goal for measuring results, you may begin to test the ads by reviewing (one at a time) the number of clicks. Wait until your ad has achieved 250 clicks, as a minor number could provide wrong conclusions.

Select the ad you believe is not getting enough click (or unsatisfactory return) and add an extra ad with adjustments in the headline or the description (see Figure 34.7).

Figure 34.7

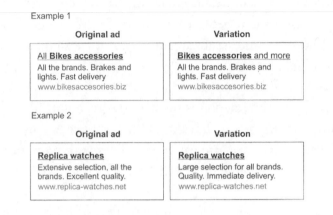

Search engines PPT system automatically displays one and then the next (if you have more than one ad for your keyword). By doing that, SEO developers are able to compare results between ads and evaluate the one that is obtaining better outcome.

This test model allows continuous evaluation and substantially improves the performance of the ads; simultaneously, this also teaches about the best punching lines or tricks that work effectively for that particular market.

Remember all the elements to adjust in the ads, as reviewed in the last chapter. The destination page also needs to be tested. Sometimes the ads are obtaining a good number of clicks, but the landing page is not matching visitors' expectations. Review all the page components and adjust them to evaluate the results. I have been surprised many times about the results of small adjustments in ads or landing pages.

The price is a major factor you should test as well. Depending of the market (some are very competitive and price sensitive), the cost of the product and the way to advertise it might be important factors to analyze. If the price is good, and you believe it is not the problem, you may consider a second, but significant, component of any e-commerce site — the payment system. Part of the optimization of any e-commerce site is the options and security of the payment section; later, we will review this important topic in detail.

Campaign Test Tips

Following is a set of tips for optimizing the evaluation of the campaign's components.

- **Secondary destination page** — In the same way you create an alternative ad for testing purposes, you can design a second landing page and perform tests about an audience's reaction to different destination page designs, headlines, images, and more. The secondary landing page might be linked to the additional ad.

- **Patience** — It is important to wait before reaching any conclusion about campaign performance. You need to have between 200 and 300 clicks before beginning any evaluation.

- **Optimization** – Search engines PPT ads offer, by default, an optimization option (for instance, Google AdWords' "automatic optimization"). This function must be deactivated during the testing period.

- **Partner sites** — Turn off the option of publishing the ads in the partner sites (for instance, Google Partner Network), as this may produce an unreal number of clicks.

- **Seeds list exclusion** — During the testing period of landing pages (two or more), it is best to exclude them from the SE robots indexation. This ensures that the results obtained are coming from the PPC ads.

To avoid spiders' indexation, you must add the following tag in the html code of the page:

<meta name= "robots" content="noindex,nofollow">

You may add this tag just before the keyword meta-tag, as a temporary action, until you finish the test. Once you define the final destination page, you need to completely remove the tag.

<table>
<tr><td>**Note**</td><td>Administration of the PPC campaigns is an ongoing process. Every day you need to watch the PPC control panel and review the status of your campaigns. You need to identify which keywords are successful and which ones are not.</td></tr>
</table>

Click Fraud

The PPC advertising servers have an IP address filter that recognizes the IP address of the user computer. The objective of such a system is to count just one click per day on the ad, for each individual IP address detected. Many competitors or malicious users tried, in the past, to manually click hundreds of times on an ad, with the objective of making the advertiser pay money for nothing. The IP address filters protect advertisers from this type of fraud.

Since early 2006, more sophisticated Internet crime organizations have attacked PPC advertising. Automated scripts or computer programs may imitate a legitimate user of a Web browser clicking on an ad for the purpose of generating a charge per click without having actual interest in the target of the ad's link. Use of a computer to commit this type of Internet fraud is a felony in many jurisdictions in North America. There have been arrests relating to click fraud with regard to malicious clicking in order to deplete a competitor's advertising budget.

Click Farms

As this industry evolved, a number of advertising networks developed that acted as middlemen between publishers and advertisers. Each time a (believed to be) valid Web user clicks on an ad, the advertiser pays the advertising network, who in turn pays the publisher a share of this money. This revenue sharing system is seen as an incentive for click fraud.

Click farms are automated and organized crime networks that perform numerous amounts of clicks with sophisticated functionality that allows them to regenerate IP fake addresses, confusing the PPT security filters.

Google's AdWords/AdSense and Yahoo! Search Marketing act in a dual role, since they are also publishers themselves (on their search engines). This complex relationship may create a conflict of interest. For instance, Google loses money to undetected click fraud when it pays out to the publisher, but it makes more money when it collects fees from the advertiser. Because of the spread between what Google collects and what it pays out, click fraud directly and invisibly profits Google.

You may visit the following links to learn more about protection systems against click farms and different types of PPC fraud:

- **http://www.clicktracks.com/click_fraud_offer.php**

- **http://www.ppcassurance.enquisite.com**

- **http://www.hitslink.com**

- **http://www.adwatcher.com/**

Some SEO service companies offer, in their promotional ads, an impressive amount of clicks driven directly to your site. They do not explain their techniques so do not trust this type of approach; these are usually click farm systems that try to steal money.

I hired this type of service for an e-commerce company, as an experiment, a couple of years ago. I was able to identify the visitors coming from their "system;" they drove (as promised in the ad) 10,000 visitors in three weeks, and none bought a single item. Meanwhile, from my SEO campaign, I obtained a conversion rate of 2.3 percent in one month, proving that the site offered a competitive (and sellable) product.

Ad Appearance

Occasionally (it happened to me few times) your ad does not appear in the sponsored results list. If this is happening to you, it is important to check the daily budget of the campaign. You must increase the daily budget; probably the amount of money invested per day is not enough for that keyword, and your ad stops displaying for that search for the first couple of hundred seekers. If the keyword is very popular, your CPC is $0.85 (which is a high CPC), and your daily budget is $80, then your ad will not be displayed after the first 94 clicks.

Premium Position

Also called "bonus positions," these are sponsored results that appear on top of the relevancy list results, behind a light yellow or sky blue background, as shown in Figure 35.0. It happens from time to time if there are few (or no) advertisers competing for that keyword at that particular time. There is no way to force the advertisement to appear in that position, but the best advice is to define a large set of distinctive keywords with a low rate of competitors; this usually increases the chances of being listed in the premium area.

Figure 35

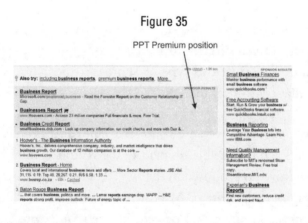

Running Out of Keywords

Sometimes you have applied all your creativity to develop an extensive set of keywords, and you cannot find more, even using the systems suggested in Chapter 3. If you face this situation, make sure you check all the following subjects:

- **Plural** — Did you consider the plural and singular forms of all the keywords?

- **Synonyms** — Did you consider all the synonyms of the keywords?

- **Typos** — Did you consider all the possible misspellings?

- **Words order** — Did you alternate the position of the words in the keyword phrase?

- **Abbreviations** — Did you add all the possible abbreviations?

- **Competitors** —Did you analyze competitors' keywords?

- **Tools** — Did you use keyword generation applications?

Custom 404 Pages

A custom 404 or custom error page is a feature of most Web server software that allows you to replace the default error messages with ones you create. The default error messages are generic html pages that notify the user that the page cannot be loaded.

These pages are not user-friendly, so making custom messages for a site is highly recommended for increasing the retention of users in case that particular page of your site is broken for any reason.

You can make them look more like the rest of a site, and provide better recovery navigation. The Not Found (404) error is the one users are most likely to encounter, so it is the most likely to be customized; Figure 35.3 shows the default error page.

Figure 35.3

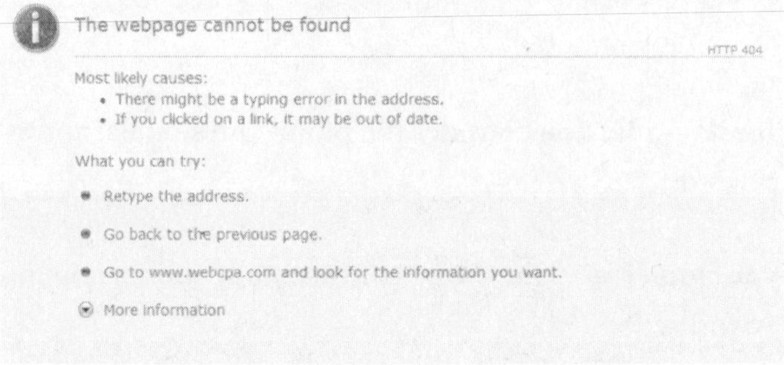

In order to create your own 404 page, you need to know the type of server OS your Web site is published with — Apache or Microsoft IIS. If you run a Web server using the Apache HTTP Server software, you can easily specify custom error pages through server configuration files, such as httpd.conf or .htaccess. You can specify custom error pages using the ErrorDocument directive. It is used as follows:

*   ## File paths are relative to the Document Root (/)

*   # '404 Not Found' error

*   ErrorDocument 404 /404.htm

*   # '403 Forbidden' error

*   ErrorDocument 403 /my.htm

*   # '401 Unauthorized' error

*   ErrorDocument 401 /401.htm

*   # Or..

*   # ErrorDocument 401 "The Web server could not authorise you for content access.

This may be put in an .htaccess file, which can be created using any text editor. Everything defined in an .htaccess file will only take effect for the directory it is located in and its child directories. In the example above, "404.htm," "my.htm," or "401.htm" are the custom HTML pages you designed; the user will be redirected to those pages in case of one of those errors take place.

If your site is running on a Microsoft IIS system, you need to have access to the server operating system and follow these steps:

Use a text editor or an HTML editor to create your custom page on your server.

From your server's desktop, launch the Internet Services Manager (usually located at Start->Programs->Administrative Tools->Internet Services Manager).

Click the [+] to the left of the server name.

Right-click on "Default Web Server" (or any other name you changed in the past), and click on "Properties."

Click on the "Custom Errors" tab.

Click on the number of the HTTP Error you want to make the custom message for, then click "Edit Properties."

Use the "Browse" button to locate the custom HTML file you created and click "OK." Keep clicking "OK" to dismiss the windows, then close the IIS window.

In Figure 35.4, you may see one customized error page, in which case the developer is apologizing about the missing information and at the same time, providing a fully interactive page to motivate the user with more navigation options.

Figure 35.4

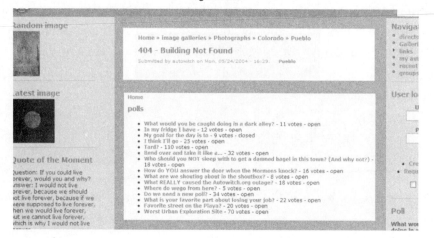

Case Study

The purpose of this section is to apply all the PPC SE ads learned in a semi-real case, from scratch. I will walk you through the following example in the same way an SEO specialist is consulted in order to elaborate an SEO strategy and its implementation.

The need

The fictional client is a company called Echo CarRental, a car rental company with headquarters in Washington and branches in New York, Boston, and Chicago. The Web site offers rates, discounts (promotions), vehicle guides, reservations online, and more.

Starting point

The SEO strategist designed a keyword matrix, as discussed in Chapter 3, to define the set of complete keywords to use in the SEO optimization (analyzing competitor keywords and using the available keyword tools). Now he will apply the same matrix to define the PPC keywords. Figure 35.5 shows the keyword matrix of this project.

Case Study

Figure 35.5

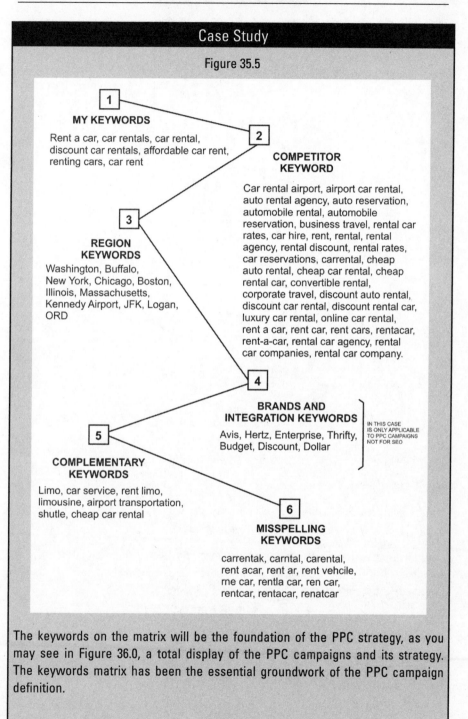

1 MY KEYWORDS

Rent a car, car rentals, car rental, discount car rentals, affordable car rent, renting cars, car rent

2 COMPETITOR KEYWORD

Car rental airport, airport car rental, auto rental agency, auto reservation, automobile rental, automobile reservation, business travel, rental car rates, car hire, rent, rental, rental agency, rental discount, rental rates, car reservations, carrental, cheap auto rental, cheap car rental, cheap rental car, convertible rental, corporate travel, discount auto rental, discount car rental, discount rental car, luxury car rental, online car rental, rent a car, rent car, rent cars, rentacar, rent-a-car, rental car agency, rental car companies, rental car company.

3 REGION KEYWORDS

Washington, Buffalo, New York, Chicago, Boston, Illinois, Massachusetts, Kennedy Airport, JFK, Logan, ORD

4 BRANDS AND INTEGRATION KEYWORDS

Avis, Hertz, Enterprise, Thrifty, Budget, Discount, Dollar

IN THIS CASE IS ONLY APPLICABLE TO PPC CAMPAIGNS NOT FOR SEO

5 COMPLEMENTARY KEYWORDS

Limo, car service, rent limo, limousine, airport transportation, shuttle, cheap car rental

6 MISSPELLING KEYWORDS

carrentak, carntal, carental, rent acar, rent ar, rent vehcile, rne car, rentla car, ren car, rentcar, rentacar, renatcar

The keywords on the matrix will be the foundation of the PPC strategy, as you may see in Figure 36.0, a total display of the PPC campaigns and its strategy. The keywords matrix has been the essential groundwork of the PPC campaign definition.

Case Study

Figure 36.0

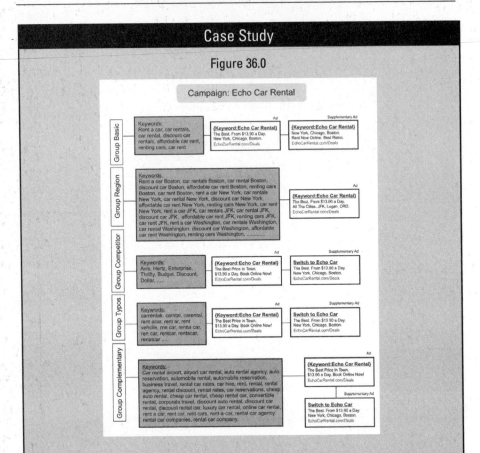

Observation

Now let us examine the case.

Dynamic keywords – The entire campaign works with dynamic keywords, in order to provide a direct match with the keywords entered.

Capitalization – The first letter of each word has been typed in uppercase, for example, "The Best Price In Town." This technique is recommended for obtaining better click-through rates.

URL secret – The URL name does not show the "www" prefix, in order to be more specific displaying the name of the site.

Linking – The links are consistent, always showing the same URL, but each of them sends the user to different destination pages.

Specific factor – The whole campaign uses specific terms, avoiding general words. The more specific the word, the higher the conversion rate of the traffic will be.

12

Newsletters

What You Will Learn About in the Following Chapter

- History and evolution of newsletters

- Principles of a good newsletter

- Successful secrets and real examples

- News and the categorization of the market

The Electronic Newsletter Effect

An electronic or online newsletter is a frequently distributed virtual publication, generally about one main topic that is of interest to its subscribers. Many newsletters are published by organizations, societies, associations, and companies to provide information of interest to their members, employees, or visitors. General attributes of newsletters include news and upcoming events of the related organization, as well as contact information for general inquiries.

At some point in 2004, many users were inundated by all types of newsletters, overwhelming the market and exhausting the users across the world. As a result, people stopped paying attention to newsletters. In the last year, the market has begun to make better use of this type of publication, by adding real value for their current and potential customers.

At this point, it is important to make a good distinction. There are three types of newsletters:

- Promotional newsletters

- Active newsletters

- Subscribed newsletters

Figure 37.0

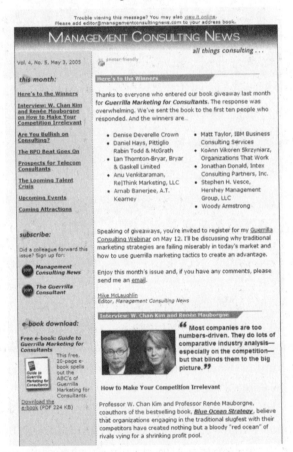

The promotional newsletter, also called the "trashy newsletter," is a false promotional instrument. Its content does not present a real value proposition, and the only goal is to promote or generate a covered marketing activity. People generally detect this type of promotional material and dismiss it instantly.

The active newsletter also has a promotional objective, but from a different perspective. Many companies distributed interesting material through active online newsletters, such as opinionated articles, useful data, relevant industry news, and tips or tricks (see Figure 37.0).

Subscribed newsletters are the most effective, since they are distributed among users who requested them. Web sites may offer simple forms to encourage visitors to subscribe (see Figure 37.5). The users of these types of newsletters are really interested, for some reason, in the company or the products, in which case, the value of the information published is very high.

Figure 37.5

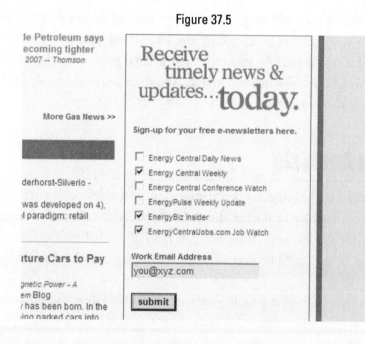

It is important to differentiate the active from the subscribed newsletters. They might be similar, but the subscribed information must have an extra value that makes the newsletter somehow more specific and less promotional. Subscribers are not expecting advertising; they expect useful data.

Figure 38.0

The initiation of a newsletter project is a big task, and must be considered very seriously. Figure 38.0 represents the basic (and generic) operational structure of a newsletter. As you can see, the final product is the result of an evolution of steps — market analysis, product analysis and definition, design, and delivery method.

Market Analysis

The evaluation of the target market is important to the development process. That may be the first challenge the developer/marketer faces before even starting the whole process. Who are you talking to? What is that market waiting for? What could be naturally interesting for them?

Newsletters must interest people. Internet marketer Elliot Buckanan says, "If I am creating a newsletter for restaurant owners, a market that I serve very frequently, I define a main topic such as 'Learn about the new trends of European restaurants' or 'See the new main dishes of New York cuisine for the coming year.' I am thinking always in related topics that make any owner feel obligated to read in order to be on top of the last important market's news. Once I capture the visitor's interest, I show some ads here and there, but never sell the product upfront in a newsletter."

It is also important to differentiate the customer's newsletter from the potential customer's newsletter. They may have some similarity, but the language and approach is slightly different. Customers usually are willing to receive information from the company, and want to learn more about products and such. Potential customers are not interested necessarily in the company yet, and they have no desire of knowing more about the company or its products.

Product Analysis

The newsletter is the product. Forget about the company or services you want to promote; the newsletter that reveals this clearly usually fails. Think of the challenge of a journalist who tries to come across with a clear message, without selling anything but the idea of the article. The most effective newsletters I have seen are the ones that engage the user with industry articles; these newsletters seem like sections of newspapers with little promotional elements.

Design and Content

The content and design must be easy to read and navigate. Later in this chapter, you will find an expensive set of tips for improving content and design.

Distribution

This is a complex topic. The distribution of the newsletter is the final step that must be managed carefully in order to achieve success. The whole project might fail in this stage, no matter how well the newsletter has been created.

Newsletters Produce Sales

Many Internet marketers do not consider the real potential of newsletters, and as a result, they do not create these types of products. Newsletter development is not a minor topic, it is a complex process of evaluation, market analysis, and product definition. In fact, I could write an entire book about newsletters exclusively, and outline the many secrets of its promotional power. Next, I will outline the most important elements in the creation of effective newsletters, and provide essential tools for their development, from the concept to the final stage.

Charles L. Cristobaldi has developed impressive newsletter concepts in the last 10 years, with extraordinary sales results. He has managed the balance between the objective and the look. Everybody knows that the objective of the newsletter is basically promoting services or products, but the users are not willing to go through the newsletter just to read a piece of covered advertising material. They want much more than that.

Cristobaldi excels at creating an interactive platform to engage users' curiosity and participation. He produces newsletters based on micro-Web site templates, fully navigational (Figure 38.3) and offering independent content from the main company Web site. This approach requires a good deal of effort, time, and additional investment, but it is worth it.

Figure 38.3

I usually take a considerable amount of time to develop a programming Content Management System (CMS) platform specially designed as a template to let the company produce their own newsletter by filling the content out in a more friendly environment, and without any special developmental knowledge.

The Basic Recommendations

A newsletter is a powerful sales channel, but you need to consider the following set of tips in order to succeed:

- **Give it personality** — Think of the newsletter as an individual product. The newsletter must represent the company and the products, but must also be unique and have its own personality. Users must recognize the newsletter as an individual (and valuable) piece of information carefully designed by a company to provide information to the market.

- **Forget sales** — You need to entirely remove the sales concept from your mind. Think that you have become a newspaper editor and your assignment is to make the people interested in your material.

- **Brand** — Branding is an important balance to master. Developing an effective newsletter requires you to accommodate the company branding and the newsletter's own style in an articulated way, with no conflicts or negative impact.

- **Break the mold** — A newsletter gives you the opportunity to be creative and distinctive. Do not miss the chance to do something different.

- **Generate interesting topics** — Nobody will read a newsletter that just tells information about the company. The best approach is to talk about related and general topics, with a certain level of excellence. For instance, I designed a series of newsletters for Seiko

Watch Corporation, relating the history of wristwatches and its evolution since 1891 until today. The newsletter linked the data with historical episodes in an original way, showing the participation of wristwatches in critical moments of history. The response of the market was impressive, with high promotional value; remarkably, the newsletter did not have one single mention of Seiko's products or any type of ads.

- **Mini-site** — The best newsletter is the one that is being developed as a micro Web site with menus, links (external and internal), images, and all the optimization. The newsletter is not necessarily a site, but must be conceived as one, creating a formal folder structure and navigational logic.

Electronic newsletters propose an interesting angle for the promotion of products and services; they are not necessarily proactive, they work slowly and in different layers than PPC advertising or SEO promotion. Users reflexively learn from these types of products, obtaining information that eventually may convince them about benefits, suitability, and other characteristics of the product/service offered.

Layout Components, Structure, and Content

In the following paragraph, you will find referential information about newsletter production and finishing tips.

The Layout

From the design perspective, there are some key layout components you must know:

- **Space optimization** — The first 300 pixels (height) of the newsletter are the most critical and vital. The attraction factor of the newsletter is there. The user basically defines, in less than 10 seconds, his interest for the newsletter's content. Those 300 pixels play a decisive part in the user's retention aspect.

- **Size** — The total area-size of the newsletter is the first element to consider in the layout creation. My favorite size is 750 pixels (width) x 3200 pixels (height). Some developers do not indicate any limit for the height, considering that there is no negative value in the vertical size of the page.

- **Header** — The newsletter header is essential and may be your only opportunity to show the company brand. Never develop a header more than 80 pixels tall.

- **Headlines** — Identify the headlines very clearly. Use a bold font that is easy to read, but do not apply a very big size; remember the space optimization.

Figure 38.5

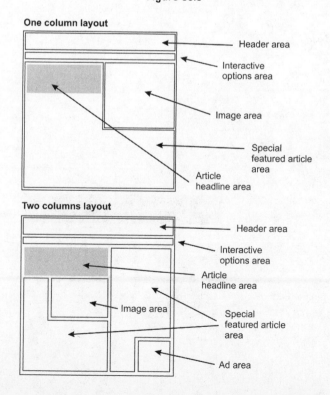

- **Columns** — It is up to the designer whether to create a layout with one, two, or more columns. It may depend on the amount of information to display and the visual style of the layout. The most recommended layout is the two-column design.

- **Navigation** — I usually recommend creating a simple menu for the newsletter, and a set of buttons that allows the user to navigate through different HTML pages easily and fast is important. The user must be comfortable and able to find anything he needs.

Please review Figures 38.5 and 38.7, for a better understanding of the structural components of the e-newsletters.

Figure 38.7

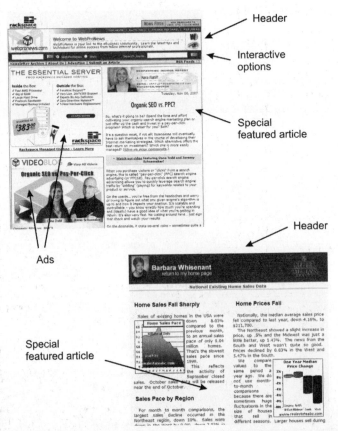

The Content

From a content perspective, there are some relevant components and tips to consider:

Headlines — The most important component of the newsletter is the headline. On average, five times as many people read the headline as the body. David Ogilvy says, "when you have written your headline, you have spent 80 cents out of the dollar."

The headline must appeal to the user's self-interest and promise a benefit. For instance, I wrote a headline for a Golf Academy electronic newsletter: "How men over 45 can master golf in 3 months." I segmented the audience and intrigued them with a beneficial statement. If you like golf, you have not mastered it, and you are over 45 years old, you will read the content.

Do not be afraid of using long headlines. Short titles are not always catchier. Long headlines are more effective; between eight to 12 words is perfectly acceptable.

Avoid using negative concepts in your headlines. You may change "The down side of power boats" to "Do you know everything about power boats?" engaging people's curiosity with the absence of negative assumptions.

Body text — The content has to be direct and clear, avoiding promotional superlatives, generalizations, and platitudes. The text must be always fascinating, regardless of how boring or simple the main topic. The length of the text has to be long enough to promise value. Short body text is not effective, but neither is very long text; both usually disengage readers. Keep the text between 800 and 1,400 words.

Ads — I try to be discreet in the use of ads. I usually make the ad appear as a part of the editorial component. The concept is to recreate the ad with absence of promotional style. Typical ads in newsletters are usually rejected by users.

FAQ — Users like to see their own questions or inquiries reflected in the content of the newsletter. A "Frequently Asked Questions" section is always an interesting added value.

Tips and tricks — The audience is always attracted to advice and good recommendations. Many newsletters dedicate sections with the objective of sharing smart advice. Aston Martin Lagonda Ltd. initiated in 2005 a successful newsletter campaign teaching driving techniques from experienced racing pilots. For each new issue, a different pilot covered a new topic, providing tips and driving techniques. The newsletter obtained 643,200 new subscribers worldwide in a period of 14 months, and the impact on sales was calculated as 6,800 new customers in Europe.

Distribution Is the Key

The distribution of the newsletter is a big task. There are three types of effective newsletter distribution:

- E-mail newsletter

- Online newsletter

- PDF newsletter

All of them are powerful. Developers may consider creating the same newsletter for all three versions, in order to cover different approaches to the market.

1. E-mail Newsletter

This type of newsletter is delivered by e-mail, and the design is embedded in the e-mail body using HTML language; these are the most popular types of newsletters.

A study from Forrester Research published on 2007, shows that more than

190,000 models of electronic newsletters are sent daily to e-mail inboxes around the world. These electronic newsletters are sent to a total of 39 million users.

E-mail is the biggest distribution method for newsletters. There is no better system to deliver newsletters effectively to a big number customers and potential customers.

In the last couple of years, e-mail spam abuse forced the creation of new regulations that somehow complicated the distribution activity. Today, for example, the user must be asked to be removed from the distribution list in order to avoid a serious complaint from the e-mail receiver.

Anti spam systems sometimes filter the user's inbox, stopping the e-mail newsletter from reaching the recipient. The best recommendation to improve the delivery is to use an e-mail blaster application with a high ranking in anti-spam delivery. At the end of this chapter, you will find several recommended tools regarding this specialized topic.

The e-mail newsletter implants HTML language in the e-mail body. The best way to do that is to develop the design in a common HTML editor, adjusting all the visual elements and components, and move the HTML code to the e-mail. Any e-mail composer program, like Outlook for instance, gives the option of composing the e-mail in HTML format. The only important consideration is the embedded images; there are two ways to place images in e-mail newsletters:

URL linked — This is the most popular way to link images into the e-mail body. The images must be stored in the Web server and the HTML code must refer to that location, as shown in the following example:

<img alt="TechSoup.org" height="102" width="359" src= "http://www. isonet.com/images/TSlogo.jpg"/>

Notice that the path to the location in the attribute "src" is the complete path to the URL location at the server, where the image file is located. Usually POP e-mail applications block the display of the images for security reasons (virus and spyware), giving users the option of downloading the images at their own risk. Figure 40.0 shows an e-mail newsletter before the images are blocked and after the user accepted downloading the pictures.

Figure 40.0

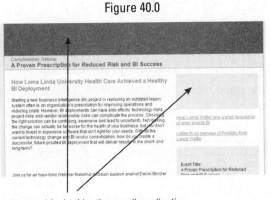

Images blocked by the email application

Images downloaded once the user confirmed

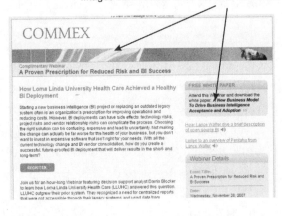

Attached images — This is my favorite option. The secret is to develop the HTML code and point the location of the images at some particular place in the local computer where the design is being generated. In this case, the images are assumed as attachments, and the e-mail application will show them with no other considerations or questions to the user.

2. Online Newsletter

The online newsletter is posted as a Web site. The designer develops a Web site concept with the newsletter content and publishes it in a URL address. The user is typically redirected to that address from the e-mail text. Figure 40.5 shows the same newsletter delivered in two formats, the typical e-mail newsletter and the online version.

Figure 40.5

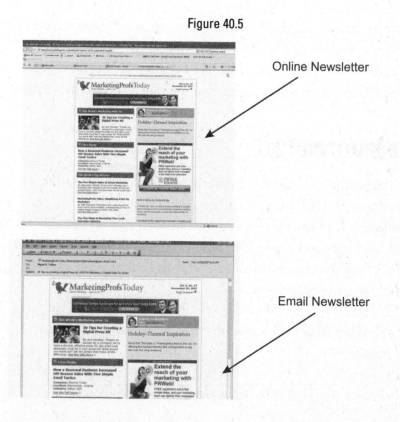

Online Newsletter

Email Newsletter

3. PDF Newsletter

There is also a third option: the PDF newsletter. These are very convenient and secure. Once the newsletter has been created, it is attached to the e-mail for a more comfortable delivery. These types of newsletters are more graphical, and the information is static.

Images: The Nightmare of E-mail Newsletters

This issue is one that marketers and developers have been trying to resolve in the last two years. The security layers and firewall systems avoid the downloading of images in an e-mail body formatted in HTML language. For that reason, many images are not available until the user accepts downloading the images in order to see them.

If you want to override this limitation, I recommend following the advice I provided a couple of paragraphs above, allocating the images in the local drive at the moment of designing the HTML. In this case, the e-mail editor assumed the images as attachments, and they are displayed by default.

Newsletter and SEO

Once the electronic newsletter is finished and distributed, I publish it online in a very specific URL location, in a different domain than the main site. The objective is to use the newsletter as an SEO complementary activity, for link relevancy and application of new keywords. If the newsletter is a micro-site, as I recommended already, it must be developed with the same guidelines we already reviewed.

- Develop a set of keywords that represent the content of the newsletter

- Include the keywords in the headlines and body text

- Make sure the HTML title and description are relevant to all keywords

- Make sure the newsletter complies with the SEO optimization guidelines

The idea is to optimize and submit the newsletter to the search engines, in the same way you do with the main Web site and any additional sites.

Critical Component

The most critical component of any newsletter activity is the distribution list, also known as the strategic contact database. The developer and marketer have different options for obtaining this database that will provide the basic list of contacts for the distribution:

- Buying a pre-existing database created by industry

- Collecting data from organic research online

- Subscribing to some of the available directories online

- Gathering information from the "subscribing forms" and "contact us" pages of the site

The accuracy of the data and the clarity of the information stored in the database is essential to securing a positive result of the newsletter activity. The whole newsletter action is based on the distribution list; without a reliable database, the activity will be poor and weak.

Newsletter Tools Guide

There are an extensive amount of resources and tools online for supporting newsletter creation and distribution. The first set of links represents different resource Web sites with valuable information regarding newsletter development.

E-mail Newsletter Templates

http://www.mailchimp.com/resources/templates/

Spam Evaluator

http://spamcheck.sitesell.com/

Articles

http://www.thesitewizard.com/archive/newsletter.shtml

http://www.idealware.org/articles/fgt_e-mail_newsletter_tools.php

http://www.techsoup.org/learningcenter/Internet/page5935.cfm

The e-mail distribution must be automated and managed by an application specially designed to achieve that task. These applications may be called "bulk e-mail software." The following list provides links to some of those tools:

- http://www.kmailer.com/

- http://www.sendblaster.com

- http://search.constantcontact.com

- http://www.xellsoft.com/TurboMailer.html

See the following chapter for a detailed report about types of bulk e-mail software.

13
Direct E-Mail Marketing

The New Direct E-mail Marketing

In the '80s, direct mail techniques were the only alternative to engage the most effective direct marketing strategy (rather than cold calls). Millions of pamphlets and promotional brochures and letters were sent monthly around the world. As a result, people got tired of receiving these types of direct advertising and the term "junk mail" became popular. The effectiveness of this marketing technique decreased significantly.

By the mid '90s, another option had entered the market, proposing new rules for direct marketing — direct e-mail marketing. Once every business contact had an e-mail address, millions of promotional e-mails overflowed users inboxes, promoting all kind of services and products. By 2004, the overuse of direct e-mail marketing almost killed the efficiency of this strategy, making it difficult to use this method as an alternative for promotions.

Terms like spam, e-mail filters, ad e-mails, and anti-spam have become popular in the last couple of years. In my experience, the use of e-mail marketing techniques provides extraordinary results, but I make sure I take care of several details in order to make this system of promotion effective and produce a positive reaction from the market, instead of upsetting potential customers.

The best advantages of e-mail marketing are the low cost of the distribution and the instant factor (people receive the e-mail in seconds). On the other hand, we have to consider the CAN-SPAM act of 2003, signed by President George Bush into law that December. The law establishes the United States' first national standards for sending commercial e-mails and requires the Federal Trade Commission (FTC) to enforce its provisions. The acronym "CAN-SPAM" derives from the bill's full name: Controlling the Assault of Non-Solicited Pornography and Marketing Act of 2003. This is also a play on the usual term for unsolicited e-mail of this type — spam.

On December 20, 2005, a detailed report to Congress on the effectiveness of the act indicated that the volume of spam had begun to level off, and due to enhanced anti-spam technologies, less is reaching consumer inboxes. A significant decrease in sexually explicit e-mail was also reported. The CAN-SPAM Act is commonly referred to as the YOU-CAN-SPAM Act because the bill was backed by lobbyists for spammers and preempts stronger state anti-spam measures. The bill permits e-mail marketers to send unsolicited commercial e-mail, as long as it adheres to three basic types of compliance defined in the CAN-SPAM Act:

1. **Unsubscribe Compliance** — A visible and operable unsubscribe mechanism must be present in all e-mails.

2. **Content Compliance** — Accurate from lines (including "friendly froms"), relevant subject lines (relative to offer in body content and not deceptive), a legitimate physical address of the publisher and/or advertiser, and, finally, a label present if the content is adult.

3. **Sending Behavior Compliance** — A message cannot be sent through an open relay, and the message cannot contain a false header. Note that falsifying header information is a serious violation of the CAN-SPAM Act and generally is an indicator of criminal or malicious intent, which can bring the attention of other law enforcement agencies besides the FTC, including but not limited to the FBI, DOJ, and US Postal Inspectors.

The content is exempt if it consists of religious messages, political messages, content that broadly complies with the marketing mechanisms specified in the law, or national security messages. There are no restrictions against a company e-mailing its existing customers or anyone who has inquired about its products or services, as this constitutes a "prior relationship" under CAN-SPAM.

Your e-mail campaign must always be under the regulations of the CAN-SPAM act. In 2006, more than 540 companies were penalized in many ways for spamming (according to SEC Research Institute study) and 32,000 people were investigated by the FBI for pornography and adult content e-mail marketing spamming.

The Direct E-mail Campaign

In order to design an effective e-mail campaign, you have to follow precise stages:

Target definition — The first element to consider is the distribution list of the direct campaign. You need to select the correct audience according with the characteristics of the service or product you are promoting. You can use your own CRM database; look for published e-mail in Web sites or by acquiring e-mail lists from researchers and associations that facilitate this type of information.

Figure 41.0

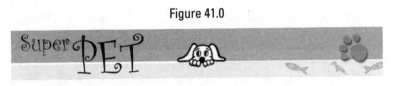

Definitive dog odor remover shampoo

Awarded Michael's Bell Pets shampoo is the most effective and convenient pet odor remover, according to 300 users survey, promoted by Pets products Magazine, last month.
We proudly advertise this product online, 100% money back guaranteed, in

People get very upset about receiving unsolicited e-mails with unrelated messages; your biggest chances are with markets of potential customers that really need (or eventually qualify for) your product. Research effectively before designing any strategy.

Campaign concept — The best results I ever obtained were with concise messages. Instead of promoting generalities or benefits of the product or service, identify one specific advantage and qualify that as the main topic of the e-mail. If you are promoting a dog shampoo, select one of the best characteristics of the products and articulate an e-mail considering that (see Figure 41.0).

Branding — This is the big dilemma amongst Internet marketers. Some experts believe that the most effective marketing e-mails are the simple text message ones, with no branding whatsoever. Others are more familiar with the branding concept, identifying the sender in a header on the e-mail body, and sometimes in the footer as well. I usually prefer this last option (Figure 41.5), but I know that both generate good results independently. The best way to apply images (i.e., headers or footers) is the same as the one we overviewed in the last chapter for the newsletters (HTML attached images).

Figure 41.5

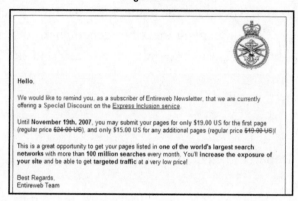

Hello,

We would like to remind you, as a subscriber of Entireweb Newsletter, that we are currently offering a Special Discount on the Express Inclusion service.

Until **November 19th, 2007**, you may submit your pages for only $19.00 US for the first page (regular price $24.00 US), and only $15.00 US for any additional pages (regular price $19.00 US)!

This is a great opportunity to get your pages listed in **one of the world's largest search networks** with more than **100 million searches** every month. You'll **increase the exposure of your site** and be able to get **targeted traffic** at a very low price!

Best Regards,
Entireweb Team

Subject creation — The e-mail subject is a critical component of promotional e-mails. Users decide, by reading the subject, whether they are interested in going through the e-mail. The title must be balanced. Do not write very short or very long titles; the best length is around six words. This allows the writer to elaborate a concept and intrigue the audience at the same time. Long titles do not even appear completely in the e-mail application; consider this carefully (Figure 41.7). Never use lousy techniques like applying "RE:" in the title, simulating a reply to a user's inbox; people react very negatively to these types of tricks.

Figure 41.7

Reminder: Enbridge Γ/U   Thu 11/15/
midPhase/SingleHop Notification for midPhase Dedicated Clients   Thu 11/15/
AnooX News: Free Web chat for your web site, Lower cost of Advertising, a...   Thu 11/15/
Reminder: PR job openings   Thu 11/15/

Several years ago, Alfredo Torre, one of the best title creators I ever met, gave me excellent advice: "Whatever you decide to write the title, make sure of two things. First, try to create one single word that represents or describes the idea of the ad. Second, use that word in the first three words of the title." This is an amazing technique. For example, if you are promoting a new mp3 player device and you decide that the best describing word is "mp3," then your title could be "The mp3 experience you deserve" or "A new mp3 technology has arrived."

E-mail sender — The sender information is also an important factor for stimulating the user. Never fake the sender information as a person's name. Use the name of the company or identify a generic need that supports the subject. For example, I created the following sender and title for a phone service company:

Title: "Telephone service"

Subject: "Important: Savings of 30 percent announced"

Consider that 74 percent of e-mail users read the sender name before anything else, according to a study of Marcos Widergrehem from Baylor University.

Compliance verification — Before sending any e-mail, you need to verify that the e-mail is under the specification of the CAN-SPAM law, overviewed at the beginning of this chapter.

Scheduling the Campaign

The effectiveness of one single e-mail is very low. The need for a campaign is to generate a synchronized promotional effect in a segment of time, sometimes one month, other times one year. There are no formulas; you need to evaluate the timing and frequency according to the product and market characteristics.

Never send weekly e-mails. That usually disengages users. I usually elaborate a diagram to identify the best timing to send the e-mails and frequency. My approach considers the following elements in order to plan an effective e-mail schedule:

Seasonal factors — I consider calendar holidays in order to avoid sending e-mails around that time; people get very distracted and less responsive right before and after a holiday.

Market characteristics — If I am promoting kids' school products, I can define my campaign for middle of summer, for instance.

Product considerations — Consider the applicability of the product. Do not promote motorbikes at the beginning of winter.

The best days — Never on Monday or Friday. Choose the sending days carefully, securing the best user reaction.

Personalization — Some bulk sending programs allow you to personalize the e-mails with the user name and last name in the body of the e-mail (i.e., Dear $name will produce Dear John Drenet in the final e-mail); the objective of this is generating a feeling of familiarity and a direct message to the user. Users usually perceive this approach as more friendly than the typical promotion.

The Best E-mail Marketing Ever

I have seen extraordinary direct e-mail campaigns. The fact is that no matter how good you are in developing this type of promotion, you will never be able to anticipate market reaction.

Case 1

E-mails written as press releases and corporate announcements are usually an effective technique to wake up people's interest. These types of messages are very well received by the audience, since the content does not apply typical promotional language. At the end of this chapter, you will find extensive information about press releases and online press campaigns.

Case 2

Advising messages are extremely valuable. If you are able to create a message that advises potential customers about some of their problems or issues, you have a great argument.

Case 3

The third type of campaign is the typical, action-oriented e-mail. "Transform your store into a beacon for buyers." These e-mails attack the point in the first three words, with no confusion or noise. This approach filters right away interested potential customers from uninterested ones.

Case 4

The personal style text is the fourth type. Usually these e-mails look like they are coming from a contact person; they are written in a simple text format (no images or HTML at all) and sound like any other e-mail. It is the "Dear Mr. Roberts" idea. My best advice for this type of e-mail is to apply a real e-mail account of a real employee in the company, providing the feeling of a personal message. You can still use any automated system to send the e-mail, but the nature of the e-mail must give the feeling of a personal message.

Case 5

This is the series of lessons concept, ideal for subscribers to newsletters or people who requested to be contacted from the "contact us" form at the site. The idea is to elaborate a course, organized into different lessons and distributed by e-mail every two weeks (or so). I have seen extraordinary results from applying this technique. An energy drink company developed a course of 25 lessons about healthy tips for improving every day energy levels in people; the market response was impressive.

The 10 Rules of E-mail Marketing

1. Never send an e-mail you would not like to receive.

2. Highlight the benefits.

3. Use no more than 15 text lines in the body of the e-mail.

4. Links in the e-mail body are highly recommended.

5. Propose an action to the user in the subject of the e-mail.

6. Bullet points help to understand concepts.

7. Do not mention the brand in the subject, unless it is very popular.

8. Do not mislead the audience with tricks.

9. Surprise the audience with a sign-up bonus.

10. Testimonials are always positive.

Sending E-mail

The list of e-mail bulk systems provided in the last chapter is adaptable either for newsletters or e-mail campaigns. I recommend that you adopt one of them and test it to analyze the results. The following list represents the most important components of the e-mail bulk system that need to be considered for a professional evaluation:

- **Template library** — These applications provide pre-built newsletters and e-mail templates for use by the user.

- **Contact management** — This internal function is a replication of the contact list used, typically in an encrypted format of the application.

- **Scripting function** — Many bulk e-mail programs offer some scripting functionality that allows implementation of some interesting games, for instance, replacing part of the e-mail's text with the company name or the name of the contact. The scripting functionality may look like this: Dear %name% %lastname% but will show as Dear John Smith in the final text of the e-mail. This personalization function is popular for promotional e-mails that try to pretend being a personal message.

- **Integration** — It is interesting if the application is able to interconnect with other common applications, such as Access and Outlook. This integration allows extending the functionality in other levels of operations.

- **Scheduling** — The scheduler is a function that allows the automation of the sending of e-mails in a particular schedule. This is very useful for international markets with significant time differences or to balance the weekly strategy. For instance, many marketers identify the best day of the week to send particular messages, according to their markets. Monday is the worst day for sending promotional e-mails.

- **Tracking and reporting** — Probably one of the most important functions of these types of applications. Without this functionality, the marketers loose an extremely important measure of the evaluation of the campaign. The tracking system must provide the number of successful e-mails sent, number of undeliverable e-mails (and analysis of the reasons if possible), detailed information regarding contacts that opened e-mails, detailed URL information regarding contacts that click any links, and unsubscribed contacts. The tracking function may be attached to the reporting feature, which generates a detailed and exportable report for presentation and analysis purposes.

- **HTML and plain text features** — The applications must be able to manage the creation of HTML and plain text templates. The HTML option is the way to develop e-mails with some visual additions, such as images, headers, and font attributes. The plain text option is, by default, simple text e-mails that any single application offers. You must ensure the application is able to offer both options.

- **Campaign management** — This is a neat feature that helps to organize and administrate different campaigns by categories, such as target characteristics, products promoted, and more.

- **Anti-spam filtering** — Advanced bulk e-mail applications are intelligent in order to trick the anti-spam systems of the targeted contacts. This is a very critical feature, considering that the anti-spam filters are always dynamically evolving and improving. For that reason, a professional application usually maintains frequent updates of that component. Even if the software meets the CAN-SPAM requirements, the anti-spam filters may block e-mails coming from these types of applications. The anti-spam filters look for technical elements, not necessarily related to the compliance rules, such as open mail relays, open proxy servers, and SMTP and ISPs authentication.

- **Archiving** — The results analysis is a vital part of the e-mail strategy. The application must be able to archive and store the past e-mails sent.

- **Unsubscribed contacts management** — This is a very important feature that must be present in any solution you choose. The CAN-SPAM standard outlines that a professional bulk e-mail system has to provide the unsubscribe function for all those contacts that request being unsubscribed from the sending list. This feature may track the e-mail and contact name of the un-subscriber and keep record of that for future sending, in order to avoid delivering e-mails to that particular contact.

- **IP switching** — Some systems regenerate or alternate IP addresses in order to avoid being identified for firewalls blockers or anti-spam filters.

There are two categories of e-mail bulk systems on the current market:

1. Application based

2. Services based

The application based solution is stand alone software that the user installs and runs from any computer. This option offers more independence to the user and the big advantage is that usually there is no limit on the number of e-mails sent. The service based option is the most popular and consists of an online account that allows the user to login to the provider server in order to use its system to manage the e-mail blasting. Internet marketers recommend this option for the following reasons:

- **Server limitations** — Companies usually offer a very reliable hardware (e-mail server) specially configured for blasting e-mails. The service is 100 percent guaranteed and minimizes any possible system down.

- **Spam** — The anti-spam filters are always up-to-date.

- **Rigorous tracking** — The tracking systems of these services are very accurate and detailed.

- **Amount limitations of e-mail sent** — If the user sends a big number of e-mails per month, the subscription may become expensive. These services may charge per amount of e-mails sent.

- **More flexibility** — More offering of templates and WYSWYG interfaces.

- **Reliability** — The information integrity is secured. If the user's system collapses or is down, the loss of information is critical.

I prefer an application that can be installed and run from the office, instead of relying in an outsourcing service, but I have observed extensive advantages (and improvements) of these types of options in the last couple of years.

14
Powerful Press Campaigns

What You Will Learn About in the Following Chapter

- Classification of press releases

- Marketing value of press releases

- Press release strategy

- Propagation and additional SEO value

What Is a Press Release?

Press releases or announcements are written pronouncements that seek to draw media attention to a specific event, product launch, or news. From a practical, press releases are "free promotion." Journalists and editors receive press releases in their inbox, in order to evaluate their publication.

Press releases provide useful topics for different media channels (including online media of course), as a result of a mutually beneficial relationship. Editors need news and marketers need promotion. Of course, there are some rules we must follow in order to obtain the expected promotional results, and also to get the green light from the editor. This chapter will reveal the details of this important complementary activity.

The Power of Press Campaigns

I have obtained the most impressive results with this strategy. People are more receptive to news than to promotional messages. A press campaign is a sequence of predefined actions for promoting company news or its products or services, in a conventional press release format.

The benefits of online press campaigns are basically two:

1. **Hidden promotion** — Image propagation and high external exposure as a result of being mentioned in major traffic online channels, such as online magazines, association portals or news portals.

2. **SEO link relevancy** — Online magazines or online media products are usually very well ranked by the search engines; the link relevancy of the site increases substantially by publishing the news on them.

Let us summarize the basic process for developing and implementing a press campaign by defining the following priority list:

1. Press classification

2. Media contacts information list

3. List of potential topics

4. Template design

5. Content management

6. Outsourcing to newswire companies

7. Delivering plan (CRM, potentials and media contacts)

Step 1: Press Classification

This is the first step. Identify the type of media or press that might be interested in your product or service publication. Forget about the promotion for a while and think about the additional concepts that your product or service is associated with.

For instance, if your Web site is trying to promote sunglasses, list all the associated items (motivations) that could make the general public (including your potential customers) curious about the product. The audience is always thinking in secondary effects that might be missing for the marketer at the first look. The following list may represent a decent group of motivations for people looking for sunglasses:

- Fashion reasons

- Prescription reasons

- Dependency reasons (people used to wearing sunglasses)

- Comfort reasons

- Seasonal reasons

Now let us take the first item and think about the potential subcategories of one of the reason:

Fashion reasons:

- Looking younger

- Looking cool

- Looking modern

- Very popular these days

- Showing power (money) by branding recognition

- Making the face more classy

- Providing sense of elegance

The next step is to identify the age segment of your market, depending on the characteristics of the product. Teenagers, young people, ages 30 to 50 years old, and ages over 50, for example. The data obtained so far will allow the marketer to immediately look for the range of online media offerings that might become interested in publishing articles related to those categories. Without having a single word written yet, we would be able to research all the potential targeted media sites.

Please note that I am not referring to any commercial portal; only magazines or news portals that might be interested in publishing an article regarding some of the topics defined above. Usually the marketer asks himself about the suitability of the potential articles in the media, considering the following criteria:

- Popular media (e.g., newspapers online)

- Some categories or sections of popular online newspapers or magazines (e.g., the health section and the fashion section)

- Specialized media (online magazines or publications)

> **Note**   If you are looking for specialized media, it is always useful looking for organizations or associations related to the topic; they usually publish a magazine for their members and subscribers. For instance, for the sunglass example, the marketer might look for any related association or group of fans of sunglasses.

Step 2: Media Contacts List

After finishing the first step, research contact information for each media. They may provide the e-mail address (or at least the basic contact information) of the editor responsible or the journalist in charge of that section.

The media contacts list is a database with all the gathered contact information organized by magazine or publication name. Most organized media sites have a specific press release inbox section to receive releases for evaluation and potential publishing.

Step 3: List of Potential Topics

The list of generic motivations of the audience (designed in step one) provides important data for the creation of topics for news and articles.

For example, let us suppose that our site sells life insurance and we already profiled the customer's motivations. The following list shows some of them:

- Stress as a result of insecure feelings

- Popular among social group

- Demonstration of long-term vision to family members

- Investing reason

Think about the list as a topic generator. Any person with good writing skills and product knowledge is able to identify at least ten different titles from each item on the list. Start creating a good title that fully expresses the concept of the release. Do not try to develop the content yet, work on the title for a while.

For example, we could take the first item of the list above, "Stress as a result of insecure feelings," and try to create some attractive titles that you may find in any newspaper (press style):

Title 1: "Insecurity: Is it possible to end the stress?"

Title 2: "Financial freedom is no longer an option"

Title 3: "Financial stress cure announced"

Title 4: "Converting worries into opportunities to seize the future"

The titles above are not promoting, but are enunciating. The reader must have the feeling that he will find nothing but useful information with some additional value. The title is promising enough to experiment with potential styles or ideas.

Step 4: Template Design

There are some codes that the press release must follow in order to qualify. The media company usually dismisses right away any piece that does not follow the standard criteria.

The following template shows a typical press release:

Sample Press Release 1

For Release

CompanyName Inc. Shareholders Approve Acquisition by OtherCompany Inc.

CHICAGO, IL April 04, 2007 — CompanyName Inc® today announced that CompanyName shareholders have approved the previously announced arrangement whereby OtherCompany Inc, through an indirect subsidiary, will acquire all of the outstanding common shares of Company Name for US $6.40 in cash for each CompanyName common share. The arrangement was approved by approximately 99 percent of the votes cast by shareholders present in person or represented by proxy at the CompanyName special meeting.

The arrangement is subject to final approval of the Chicago Superior Court of Justice which is expected to be sought on May 12, 2007, in Chicago. Provided that final approval of the Court is obtained, and that all other conditions to completion of the arrangement are satisfied or waived, the arrangement is expected to close during the last calendar quarter of 2007.

Sample Press Release 1

About CompanyName Inc

CompanyName (NASDAQ: CCCO) is the world's largest enterprise software company. For more information about CompanyName, please visit our Web site at **http://www.company.com**.

CONTACT:

John Donaldson
johndonald@company.com
Marketing Manager
CompanyName Inc.
234-122-7156

Let us see now the components and some additional information on the following case:

Sample Press Release 2

For Immediate Release: (usually this is a conventional intro for any press release)

Eclipse, Inc. Announces Widget to Maximize Customer Response Rate

This headline is one of the most important components of the press release as it needs to capture editors' attention. It should be in bold type and preferably in a bigger font size than the body text. Preferred type fonts are Arial, Times New Roman, or Verdana. Keep the headline to 100 to 125 characters maximum. It is a standard rule to capitalize every word with the exception of "a," "the," "an," or any word that is three characters or less.

<City>, <State>, <Date> — Your first paragraph of the release should be written in a concise manner. The opening sentence contains the most important information; keep it to 25 words or less. Never take for granted that the reader has read your headline. It must contain information that will "attract" the reader. Avoid using any sales language.

The body of the press release must be not longer than 500 words, using a consistent language and direct message. Say what you need to; do not provide excessive details. Also, you need to include at least three links to different URLs in order to acquire link relevancy from the sites where the announcement is published.

About <Company> (usually in bold, but the same font size of the press release body text)

Sample Press Release 2

Include a brief description of your company, along with the products and services it provides. This explanation may end with the Web site address.

CONTACT:

Contact Person
Company Name
Voice Phone Number
FAX Number
E-mail Address
Web site URL

The following is another example of a typical press announcement:

Sample Press Release 3

GlobalView expands Skyper services across Europe

Houston, TX, June 2007 — European conference call provider GlobalView, is extending its partnership with Skyper to provide the first ever link up of its kind across Europe. This week Skyper services will become available across Holland, Germany, and France for the first time, with even more coverage to follow over the coming months.

Skyper is a free VoIP (voice over Internet protocol) solution which facilitates free telephone calls across the Internet. GlobalView is the only conference call provider to offer Skyper Y3 dial in into its conference calls, thus opening up worldwide access to conference calls for hugely reduced costs.

Robert Dimitri, director of GlobalView comments: "This is a great opportunity for all European GlobalView users. They are able to benefit from our lower dial-in rate and are now able to access this service from wherever they are in the world. We are excited to be the first European voice conferencing company to offer this unique service to our customers, achieving our goals to provide the lowest rate possible to users, in the simplest, most effective way possible."

The service is now available for Open Access, Enhanced Access, and Gold Access customers. GlobalView's innovative service centers around a simple dial-up where each invited participant calls a number and, using a PIN, joins the private voice conference. There are no bills for organizers, no contracts and each participant simply pays for their own call. The conference service is immediate, with no need to book, no registration and no conference service charge. More information could be found at **www.globalviewnowip.com**.

Sample Press Release 3

About GlobalView

Established in 1996, GlobalView Systems offers a wide array of superior business tools to help you grow your business. In addition to GlobalView, our products include virtual office solutions, online faxing products and lead generation, call capture systems for real estate. All are packed with robust features that help you enhance your image, stay connected and manage your business with far greater flexibility and efficiency.

CONTACT:

Mike Robertson
GlobalView International
Marketing division
Robertson@ globalviewnowip.com

Another important standardized rule is the title of the e-mail. Every time you send a press release, you must repeat the header of the release adding "Press Release:" or "Press Announcement:" before the title.

For a header like:

GlobalView expands Skyper services across Europe

The e-mail's title will be:

Press Release: GlobalView expands Skyper services across Europe

This is the traditional format that indicates the nature of the e-mail as a press release. Forgetting this may jeopardize all the hard work in the press release content.

Step 5: Content Management

It is important to consider some parameters to create an effective press release content. Once you have defined the title that represents the news or event you need to announce, it is time to work on the body text of the release, and give it some logic for the editor. Remember that the structure is very standard, and you cannot modify this too much if you want the release to be published.

Check for missing data by answering the questions "who," "what," "when," "where," "why," and "how." Your text should include relevant information regarding your product, service, or event. If writing about a product, make sure to include details (not excessive) on when the product is available, where it can be purchased, and the cost.

If you are writing about an event, include the date, location of the event, and any other pertinent data.

Qualification: You can include a quote from someone who is a credible source of information; include their title or position with the company and why they are considered a credible source. Always include information on any awards they have won, articles they have published, or interviews they have given. If you do not have this type of validation, try to find some public information that relates somehow with the information of the release, in order to provide that relevancy level.

Structure: An ideal press release has a three-paragraph minimum and is 400 to 600 words. Keep your sentences and paragraphs short; a paragraph should be no more than four to six sentences.

Proofing: Use a word processing program, and spell check for errors. Do not forget to proofread for grammatical errors. The mood of the release should be factual, not hyped; do not use sales language or the press release will go in the trash.

Bottom: You might add to the last paragraph (before the "About…" text) "For additional information on (probably the subject of this release), visit **www.yoururl.com**." If you offer a sample, copy, or demo, put the information in here. You can also include details such as product availability or trademark acknowledgment in this area of the release.

Double check the message. Depending on the media's style, some editors or journalists rewrite the release. In that case, they may have a clear identification of the message; otherwise, the release is not effective. Sometimes, a journalist considers the topic really interesting and the release becomes an article. They contact the person at the bottom of the e-mail to let them know or get additional information.

Step 6: Outsourcing to Newswire Companies

Do not underestimate the value of the newswire services. Although the creation of your own media contact list is an important action, the value of hiring an external (and specialized) service is very high. Commercial newswire companies charge businesses for delivering their news and provide press consulting support. These types of companies may have agreements with a large number of media corporations and publications in order to secure the publication of the release.

This service is very helpful for distribution of press releases, mainly if your product or service is oriented to a very niche audience. I found this a very important complementary action for press campaigns, usually very affordable, and with high ROI. I obtained better results by investing in these services than in Web banner ads.

The following list represents only a few of the URL address for your reference. Type newswire services in any browser and you will see the result.

- **http://www.newswire.ca/en/content/basic/134.cgi**

- **http://www.massmediadistribution.com**

- **http://www.sbwire.com**

- **http://www.lebanon.com/news/newswire/**

- http://www.ipdgroup.com/

- http://www.majon.com/v2/advanced-pr.html

The newswire companies also provide some support services for press campaigns and all related press and media activities. It might be an interesting alternative if you need assistance with the creation of the releases or some orientation with the topic generation step.

Some newswire companies offer articles publishing services; I found this particular option a very useful action for branding propagation. If you have relevant knowledge able to be shared, consider that many publishers offer blank spaces to particular news agencies and newswire services, in order to fill the gaps with potential good material.

This is a free (or cheap) advertisement option that you may capitalize on to expose the product in a secondary way. For two of the companies I advise, I built a plan for developing, two months in advance, a series of articles of specific popular topics somehow related to the services provided or product offered. It is difficult to get commitment from high executives to write down an article; for that reason, many times I create a template that helps me interrogate them and extract the core information. An editor manages the style later on. Once the articles are finished, I distribute them to different newswire companies, waiting for the first bidder.

The key component of a promotional article is showing the topic right away. Nobody is receptive to promotional languages or topics; the article needs to identify the added value in the title and first paragraph or the reader will be gone.

Let us see, for instance, the following example from a colleague of mine:

Sample Promotional Article

Motivate Employees With Superior Work Environment

David Blissett, Vice President Dale Carnegie Institute, UK

"If you create an environment that motivates employees to turn the valve on full throttle, you can outperform any competitor any day of the week. Because when you boil it down, it's the creativity, the longevity, the loyalty of the employee base that makes it all happen." – Action-Coach Consulting.

Now that is a valuable piece of advice and it comes from one of the world's top human capital and management consulting firms. I'm sure most utilities want to motivate their employees to do their best and that some of them actually take steps to do so. But as they put fancy motivational programs together, how many of them stop to think about the impact the work environment has on motivation? Action-Coach Consulting is right – the environment in which employees must work day in and day out is extremely important.

If trying to motivate your employees individually without ever changing the environment they work in, you're probably fighting an uphill battle. Results can certainly be achieved when working one-on-one with employees to get them to perform at their best. But much can be gained by focusing on factors that influence your employees' daily routines.

There are a variety of factors to consider: your management team's skills, your employee recognition program, the utility's physical layout, your program for developing the desired skills of your staff. These factors and others shape your utility's work environment, and the conditions under which employees work have a huge influence in their motivation to perform.

Consider the following as you strive to encourage employees to do their best on the job.

Display a clear vision of your company objectives. What are your company's values? What is your utility's common purpose? Make sure everyone understands what your vision is, as sharing a clear and common vision brings people together. One simple way to do that is to have your utility's mission statement posted in every department. Better yet, give each employee their own copy of the mission statement that they can put on their desk or display on their office wall.

Continually review goals and objectives. Seeing the utility's mission statement every day is helpful, but employees also need to understand what they should be doing Monday through Friday to support the company vision. Be as specific as possible about each department's goals but also be flexible. Goals should be both short term and long term and should be reviewed at least once a month. Employees will function better when they are clear on what is expected of them. They will perform at an even higher level when they understand how their work contributes to the big picture.

Emphasize continuous training. Training is not a one-time event. Training needs to happen on a continual basis. The business world constantly changes and that has an impact on how people do their jobs. No one can possibly keep up on their own and that's where training comes into play. Please keep in mind that, during training, people are often asked to change their professional behavior. But, as humans, most of us like to stay in our comfort zone. What are you doing to support behavioral change for your staff as they go through training?

Share information. If you want to enlist your staff members as partners in your utility's success, then you should treat them like they are owners. More information is always better than less. Educate your staff on budgets, projects, challenges, trends, etc. Keep them in the know. They will appreciate it.

Make yourself available. Management should take a personal interest in their employees. Listen to their concerns and problems and support their efforts to find solutions. Listen to their ideas. The people who labor at your utility are not just simply workers. They are human beings and should be treated as such.

Provide continual feedback. Employees assume they are doing a good job if they don't hear otherwise from managers and that can lead to unexpected problems. No one likes to feel ignored or unappreciated. Employees want to know how they're doing. By offering constant feedback – both positive and negative – your employees will know how they are doing and there will be no surprises.

Ask employees for their feedback. As they go about their jobs, your employees see things that could be improved or changed. They often come up with money-saving ideas. But in most cases, employees don't offer suggestions because they don't think anyone cares. They doubt that management will do anything. Hire an outside firm to survey your employees anonymously. This will give them the opportunity to provide candid feedback on a number of issues without fear of reprisal. Use the feedback to identify the top issues that require company action. Taking action on these problems tells employees that management is listening and willing to do what needs to be done.

Reward achievements. Many managers dismiss rewards because they feel there isn't enough money to incorporate employee recognition into their budgets. Big mistake! Rewards do not need to be monetary. The single most important reward is praise and acknowledgement. Sometimes a simple "nice job" can do wonders for

---

Sample Promotional Article

morale. Still, tangible rewards are nice and have more meaning if managers identify what motivates each employee and tailor these rewards around individuals.

Empower employees to initiate projects. If you truly want employees who demonstrate an ownership attitude in their work, give them the opportunity to initiate and carry out projects. Let them give it their best shot. Above all, understand that mistakes may happen but that mistakes are part of the learning process. Employees will learn when they stumble and emerge from the experience more knowledgeable. That will make them more valuable to your utility. Allowing your staff to think and act like an owner will create self-motivated employees."

About the author: David Blissett has more than 10 years of business experience as VP of Dale Carnegie Institute, UK. He was vice president of marketing and training for Abobe Inc. and he also has experience in the insurance, real estate and banking industries. Blissett can be reached at ...

This is an interesting article for analysis. The whole objective is obviously to promote David, his knowledge and to mention the company of course, but the tactic is to allocate less than 3 percent of the text to talk about that. The majority of the content goes directly to the point that (not coincidentally) may result extremely interesting to the targeted audience.

The following set of questions are relevant for article creation, you may try to answer them with the viewed example. I know several marketers who underestimate the article strategy, considering that is not valuable enough, and as a result lost important product exposure. This action is totally worthy. Mandatory questions for testing the article are:

a.   Is it audience defined and targeted?

b.   Is the title catchy and intriguing?

c.   Does the author appear below the title, with the position and company name?

d.   Is the first paragraph solid enough to grab audience attention?

e.   Does the article mention data or quotes form relevant sources?

f.   Is the "About the author" section at the end?

g.   Does it have the contact information at the bottom?

h.   Does it have the right length? (Depending on publisher preferences, usually between 1,300 and 2,000 words)

i.   Are there plenty of links?

Step 7: Delivering Plan

The distribution of the newsletters became a significant point of the plan. We have learned the importance of newswire services as a complementary activity, and the distribution of the releases to our own media contact list, explained in step 2. There is also a third option for promotion — delivering the release directly to our CRM database. This is called "Promotional Press Release."

I have obtained extraordinary results with this technique. The audience welcomes news. For that reason, I usually modify the format of the release to make it more friendly, but without removing the sense of a press announcement.

Let us take the last press release example and convert it to a promotional press release.

Sample Promotional Press Release
"Press announcement: GlobalView expands Skyper services across Europe"
GlobalView expands Skyper services across Europe
Houston, TX, June 2007 — European conference call provider GlobalView, is extending its partnership with Skyper to provide the first ever link up of its kind across Europe. This week Skyper services will become available across Holland, Germany and France for the first time, with even more coverage to follow over the coming months.

Sample Promotional Press Release

Skyper is a free VoIP (voice over Internet protocol) solution which facilitates free telephone calls across the Internet. GlobalView is the only conference call provider to offer Skyper Y3 dial in into its conference calls, thus opening up worldwide access to conference calls for hugely reduced costs.

Robert Dimitri, director of GlobalView comments: "This is a great opportunity for all European GlobalView users. They are able to benefit from our lower dial-in rate and are now able to access this service from wherever they are in the world. We are excited to be the first European voice conferencing company to offer this unique service to our customers, achieving our goals to provide the lowest rate possible to users, in the simplest, most effective way possible."

The service is now available for Open Access, Enhanced Access, and Gold Access customers. GlobalView's innovative service centers around a simple dial-up where each invited participant calls a number and, using a PIN, joins the private voice conference. There are no bills for organizers, no contracts and each participant simply pays for their own call. The conference service is immediate, with no need to book, no registration and no conference service charge.

Learn more about GlobalView at **www.globalviewnowip.com**.

Did you notice the difference? I have modified some of the standard components that do not make sense or are irrelevant for the general audience. "For immediate release" text and the contact information have been removed; also, the "About us" section is replaced with a simple line more proactive and direct. You may observe, anyway, that the feeling of press announcement is intact. That is the important consideration.

Topic Hunting

I usually engage the topic fishing technique. Once I have defined the potential titles of the release, I look for complementary information on the net — relevant public data that helps to validate and create the release.

A good press release campaign is an organized action that alternates hidden promotional messages with relevant news in which the product or company is almost secondary. Do not be afraid of being nonspecific from the promotional perspective, a good campaign will provide long term benefits regardless.

Let us imagine, for example, we need to promote a new antivirus application. We may have already a list of all the benefits, new features and value added of the product. At this point, all of that is secondary for press release creation; first, we need to look for validation (fishing) in order to get a potent argument for engaging the releases. I usually use three different sources of information for validation:

- **Googlenews.com**

- **Wikipedia.org**

- **CNN.com**

These sources will provide enough relevant information regarding the keywords entered. At that point, we will be able to visualize past news and associate it with our product. I normally use **Google.com** and **CNN.com** to find related news and **Wikipedia.org** for relevant links.

Let us see one of the results obtained in **Computerworld.com** with some supporting potential for this topic:

Protect Yourself With Antivirus Software Before You Surf the InterWeb

Surfing the Internet can be a frightening experience for computer-using novices, especially when there are almost as many computer programs online designed to hurt, rather than to help. Viruses, worms, trojans, and other nasty pieces of code are lurking where you least expect them to be, waiting for some unsuspecting Web browserer (you) to be infected (...)

The press release has now a core argument with enough validation; this allows hooking a hidden promotion and expands the content. Let us take a look at the first cut of the release:

For Immediate Release:

The 2008 big news: Internet under attack

Palo Alto, CA, July 2007 - We all know what a computer virus is. We all know that every 3 seconds a computer virus strikes in somebody's computer in the world. Do we? Maybe this assumption is not totally correct; maybe we do not know the reality (and future) of computer viruses in detail.

According to Computerworld's report, "Surfing the Internet can be a frightening experience for computer-using novices, especially when there are almost as many computer programs online designed to hurt, rather than to help. Viruses, worms, trojans, and other nasty pieces of code are lurking where you least expect them to be, waiting for some unsuspecting Web browserer." The new features introduced by ProductN combine software development experience and advanced anti-hacking techniques to assist low lever users" (...)

Let us analyze the example. The title is more alarmist and dramatic, intensifying the effect of the information. The collected news was slightly modified in order to melt it with the release content and make it appear more natural. The added value of the product is mentioned right after the validation statement, to show the clear contrast between problem-solution formula.

Secondary Audience Plan

Many times, the marketer needs to expand his perception of "the audience" for press campaigns; meaning think in a different way about the audience. You might generate some news related to your product applicable to media channels that do not necessarily target your audience.

For instance, Peter F. Campton designed an interesting online press campaign for a large scale shoe factory in Europe. His campaign was divided by categories, and identified different audiences and media channels:

• General audience (12 percent potential customers)

• Direct audience (77 percent potential customers)

- Female general audience (253 percent influential public)

He acknowledged general audiences that did not necessarily represent the targeted audience of the product, usually named indirect buyers or indirect audience.

For those people, he created an interesting set of releases about general aspects of the products sponsored by the company brand, for instance:

- History of the shoe

- Shoes in the Roman Empire

- Evolution of the Italian shoe

- Secrets of comfortable men's shoes

- The mystery of Napoleon's favorites shoes

- Engineering laws in shoes

- Story of Winston Churchill's shoes

- Do the astronauts wear shoes?

- Physics of the shoe

- The secret Walt Disney's shoe factory

- Shoes: Fashion, style, and need

Following this concept, you may create topics of interest for online magazines such as *Popular Mechanic* or *National Geographic*, even if you are not directly promoting your product or service through the release, or not visibly to the "direct audience." The objective is providing relevancy, propagation, and eventually, customers.

Designing the Campaign

The first step is to establish the difference between hot (immediate) and cold (slow) press releases. This will allow the marketer to create a balanced campaign with recurrent presence. Hot releases are the ones that cover immediate topics, sometimes difficult to anticipate, such as product or service launching, awards, new hiring, or celebration.

Cold releases usually cover topics that might be announced any time of the year, such as product advantages, market general news regarding the product or services, or messages from some stakeholders.

An effective press campaign sends between 20 and 25 releases per year. Any number less than 20 pieces will not impact notably in the market. It is mandatory to plan ahead and define a realistic schedule.

The marketer usually starts the year with a basic list of general topics and designs the plan according to the hot and cold releases he has in his hands at the moment. I participated in monthly meetings with executives for several companies in the past, and I used to bring potential topics to discuss for one month ahead. The group voted their favorite topics, and the marketing department started to work on the content for approval.

The plan was similar to the following example:

January

5 — "Business Plan presentation" NW/CRM

12 — "Metrox introduce a new set of solutions" NW

22 — "New Director of sales of Metrox" NW/CRM

February

10 — "Metrox: A new business philosophy" NW/CRM

17 — "President of Metrox speaker at GasMart 2007" NW/CRM

March

2 — "Alliance for a new landscape" NW

12 — "Metrox participates in NY awards ceremony" NW

26 — "Metrox is silver sponsor of Platts Awards" NW/CRM

(...)

The titles on the plan are not definitive yet; at the moment of designing the schedule, the titles are referential. The NW stands for Newswire and CRM stands for the promotional database and clients. As you can see, some releases are delivered only to the newswire companies, in order to avoid stressing the audience with excessive press releases.

The plan should indicate, at least, planning date to go out, referential title or topic, and delivery method.

15

Internet Marketing Integration

What You Will Learn About in the Following Chapter

- All the options in Internet marketing

- Blog marketing and SMO

- Advertising options

- Affiliate, viral, and interactive marketing

- Internet marketing analytics

Internet Marketing Supporting Actions

As outlined in Chapter 1, Internet marketing is formed by a group of different sub-activities. Eventually, the synchronization of those activities in a solid game plan will build the Internet marketing strategy.

Internet characteristics and technological advantages have brought many unique benefits to marketing, including low costs in distributing information and media to a global audience. The interactive nature of Internet marketing, both in terms of instant response and in eliciting response, are unique qualities of the medium. A successful online marketing campaign is usually displayed in the following list of online products:

- Blog marketing

- Pop-ups ads

- Banner ads

- Affiliate marketing

- Viral marketing

Blog Marketing

In 2005, blogs become very popular. Blogs or Weblogs are Web sites written in chronological order. Promotional Weblogs are intended to provide company news and services or products characteristics with some level of periodical updating. The flexibility of the format allows developers to publish instantaneously promotional information regarding their products, in order to make it available to the public.

Search engines' spiders do not crawl blogs. There are several blog search engines, such as **blogsearchengine.com** or **IceRocket.com**, dedicated specifically to crawling the information and content in blogs.

Also, the "news" sections of Google and Yahoo! index the content of blogs, since they read Really Simple Syndication (RSS). RSS is a family of Web feed formats used to publish frequently updated content, such as blog entries, news headlines, or podcasts. RSS documents are usually called "feeds" or "Web feeds," containing either a summary of content from an associated Web site or the full text. RSS makes it possible for people to keep up with their favorite Web sites in an automated manner that is easier than checking them manually.

RSS content can be read using software called an "RSS reader," "feed reader," or an "aggregator." The user subscribes to a feed by entering the feed's link into the reader or by clicking an RSS icon in a browser that initiates the subscription process. The reader checks the user's subscribed feeds regularly for new content, downloading any updates that it finds. Links from blogs count for links relevancy, which is sometimes a useful and legal resource for providing link relevancy to sites.

SMO and Its Derivatives

The Social Media Optimization (SMO) is a set of methods for generating publicity through online communities and community Web sites. SMO's methods include adding RSS feeds, blogging, and incorporating third party community functionalities, like Facebook or YouTube. Social media optimization is a form of search engine marketing, and is in many ways connected as a technique to viral marketing where word of mouth is created not through friends or family, but through the use of networking in social bookmaking, video, and photo sharing Web sites. In a similar way, the engagement with blogs achieves the same by sharing content through the use of RSS in the blog atmosphere and special blog search engines.

The Web community or virtual community concept is very popular at present; they have emerged from the Web 2.0 and social networking experiences (such as MySpace, LinkedIn, and Friendster) and combined with advanced technology that allow users to access a new concept in virtual networking. Many Internet marketers are using these networks to promote services and products in a different level with good results. Web communities have a captive market that is extremely focused and proactive.

Pop-up Advertisement

This is a questionable form of online advertising. It works when certain Web sites open a new Web browser window to display advertisements. The pop-up window containing an advertisement is usually generated by JavaScript, but can be generated by other means as well.

This type of advertisement option, popular from 2001 to 2003, was highly criticized by many marketers for its invasive characteristics. By the end of 2003, the anti pop-up technology had designed many pop-up blocking systems, in order to protect users from this unwanted type of ad.

Pop-under ads are a variation of pop-up ads, but the ad window appears hidden behind the main browser window rather than superimposed in front of it. As pop-up ads became widespread, many users learned to immediately close the pop-up ads that appeared over a site without looking at them. Pop-under ads do not immediately impede a user's ability to view the site content, and thus usually remain unnoticed until the main browser window is closed, leaving the user's attention free for the advertisement.

I usually do not recommend the implementation of pop-up advertisement, since the effectiveness of those ads is almost non-existent.

Banner Ads

A Web banner or banner ad is a very popular form of Web advertising, embedding an ad into Web pages with the objective of attracting traffic by linking them to the sponsored site.

The advertisement is built from an image (e.g., gif, jpg, or bmp) and sometimes developed in JavaScript or multimedia languages like Shockwave or Flash, often employing animation or sound to maximize presence. Images are usually in a high-aspect ratio shape (i.e., either wide and short, or tall and narrow) hence the reference to banners. These images are usually placed on Web pages that have interesting content, such as a newspaper article or an opinion piece.

The Web banner is displayed when a Web page that references the banner is loaded into a Web browser. This event is known as an "impression." When the viewer clicks on the banner, the viewer is directed to the Web site advertised in the banner. This event is known as a "click through." In many cases, banners are delivered by a central ad server.

When the advertiser scans their logfiles and detects that a Web user has visited the advertiser's site from the content site by clicking on the banner ad, the advertiser sends the content provider a small amount of money (usually around five to 10 cents).

Web banners function the same way as traditional advertisements are intended to function — by notifying consumers of the product or service and presenting reasons why the consumer should choose the product in question, although Web banners differ in that the results for advertisement campaigns may be monitored real-time and may be targeted to the viewer's interests.

Many Web surfers dismiss these advertisements as highly annoying because they distract from a Web page's actual content or waste bandwidth. I believe that these types of ads are very effective, if your product matches the market targeted by the site. Companies like MSN and Yahoo!, for instance, offer different sections and internal categories in order to increase the benefits to advertisers looking for a particular market.

The tracking capabilities of the banner ads system are very convenient to evaluate campaign results and public response.

Figure 42.0

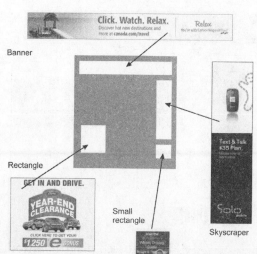

There are different types of banner ads, according to sizes, aspect ratio, and positioning on the layout. Figure 42.0 represents some of the more popular banner ads. The following list shows the conventional names and standard characteristics of those type of advertisements:

- Banner — Horizontal ad (approximately 730 x 90 pixels)

- Rectangle — Vertical ad (approximately 180 x 150 pixels)

- Skyscraper — Vertical ad (approximately 730 x 90 pixels)

- Floating rectangle — Vertical ad (approximately 180 x 150 pixels)

Some floating rectangles might vary sizes and shapes, as shown in Figure 42.5.

Figure 42.5

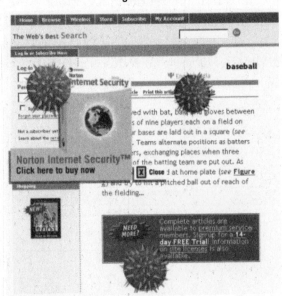

Affiliate Marketing

Affiliate marketing started as a Web-based practice introduced by CDNow in early 1994. The concept is revenue sharing as a commission payment for referrals. **CDNow.com** had the idea that music-oriented Web sites could review or list albums on their pages that their visitors might be interested in purchasing and offer a link that would take the visitor directly to CDNow to purchase them.

The idea for this remote purchasing originally arose because of conversations with a music publisher called Geffen Records in the fall of 1994. The management at Geffen Records wanted to sell its artists' CDs directly from its site, but did not want to do it itself. Geffen Records asked CDNow if it could design a program where CDNow would do the fulfillment.

Geffen Records realized that CDNow could link directly from the artist on its Web site to Geffen's Web site, bypassing the CDNow home page and going directly to an artist's music page. Affiliate marketing was used on the Internet by the adult industry before CDNow with an extraordinary marketing result. Figure 42.7 represents the affiliate marketing process.

Figure 42.7

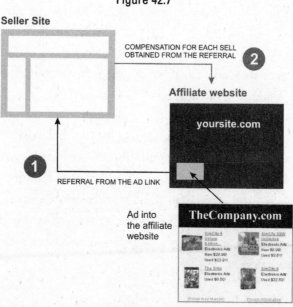

Amazon.com launched its associate program in July 1996. Amazon associates would place banner or text links on their site for individual books or link directly to Amazon's home page. If visitors clicked from the associate's site through to **Amazon.com** and purchased a book, the associate received a sell commission.

In February of 2000, **Amazon.com** announced that it had been granted a patent (6,029,141) on all the essential components of an affiliate program. The patent application was submitted in June of 1997, which was before most affiliate programs but not before PC **Flowers&Gifts.com** (October 1994), **AutoWeb.com** (October 1995), **Kbkids.com/BrainPlay.com** (January 1996), EPage (April 1996), and others.

Viral Marketing

Viral marketing and viral advertising refer to marketing techniques that use social networks to produce increases in brand awareness, through self-replicating viral processes. Internet viral marketing is a phenomenon that facilitates people to promote involuntarily by passing along a marketing message.

Viral promotions may take the form of video clips, interactive Flash games, images, digital goodies, or more.

Viral marketing is based on the natural human behavior of propagating messages by referrals, recommendations, or simply propagation by attachment (see the following Hotmail example). The goal of marketers interested in creating successful viral marketing programs is to identify individuals with high social networking potential and create "viral messages" that appeal to this segment of the population and have a high probability of being passed along.

For instance, Hotmail offers "free" Webmail service with the final objective of captivating an audience that turns into a market for different products or advertisement; the Webmail is not the service that will produce the profit, it is the media to capture the market.

YouTube, Google, Flickr, Yahoo!, Facebook, Disney, CNN, Second Life, MySpace, and InnoCentive, among many others, engage the concept of viral marketing all the time, providing value to the users for nothing in return, but that "nothing" doesn't mean necessary "free." A gigantic captivating market makes these corporations qualified enough to receive the attention (and investment) of millions of dollars (sometimes billions) from the rest of the corporations in the world, seeking market penetration and exposure.

David Rusell designed for Ford Motors Canada, a distinctive newsletter for Halloween day. The layout showed a group of windows in order to let the user watching videos with real-time broadcasting of the Halloween celebrations of the company's employees around the country. It was a very entertaining initiative that showed hundreds of people from the company, celebrating their original customs in their work location. The result — two billion people watched the videos around the globe in a one-week period. Imagine the market exposure and the secondary selling points as a result of that massive exposure.

Another interesting example of viral Internet marketing is the different experiments conducted by the people of **Eye4u.com**. I strongly recommend visiting their site and spending some time going through their portfolio of projects.

Contextual Advertisement and Google Ads

The term contextual advertising appeared in 2002, and is applied to Web ads, such as content displayed in mobile phones, where the advertisements are selected and served by automated systems based on the content displayed by the user. The system directly scans the text of the Web site looking for keywords and returns ads to that page based on what the user is viewing.

Then, an automatic request to the publisher server filters the keywords in order to pull the ads that match in content.

Google AdSense was the first major contextual advertising program. It provided Webmasters with a special JavaScript code that, when inserted into Web pages, called up relevant advertisements directly from Google's ads repository servers.

Since the beginning of AdSense, the Yahoo! Publisher Network, Microsoft AdCenter, and others have been gearing up to make similar offerings.

Contextual advertising has made an important impact on earnings of many Web sites, since is more effective than the traditional banner ad promotion. The contextual ad system offers ads placed on the page or pop-up ads. For example, if the user is viewing a site about skiing, and the site uses contextual advertising, the user might see ads for sky-related companies, such as products, promotions, or services. Contextual advertising is also used by search engines to display ads on their own search results pages based on what word(s) the user has searched for.

Paid Inclusion

During 2003, several companies became popular by offering paid inclusion services — an online marketing product where the search engine company charges fees related to inclusion of the business or company into the relevancy list. Paid inclusion products are provided by most search engine companies, except for Google.

The fee structure is both a filter against superfluous submissions and a revenue generator. Typically, the fee covers an annual subscription for one Web page, which will automatically be catalogued on a regular basis. A per-click fee may also apply. Each search engine is different. Some sites allow only paid inclusion, although these have had little success. More frequently, many search engines, like Yahoo!, mix paid inclusion (per-page and per-click) with results from Web crawling. Others, like Google and **Ask.com**, do not let Webmasters pay to be in their search engine relevancy listing.

Some detractors of paid inclusion allege that it causes searches to return results based more on the economic standing of the interests of a Web site, and less on the relevancy of that site to end-users. The line between PPC advertising and paid inclusion is debatable. Some have lobbied for any paid listings to be labeled as an advertisement, while defenders insist they are not actually ads since the Webmasters do not control the content of the listing, its ranking, or even whether it is shown to any users.

Another advantage of paid inclusion is that it allows site owners to specify particular schedules for crawling pages. In the general case, one has no control as to when their page will be crawled or added to a search engine index. Paid inclusion proves to be particularly useful for cases where pages are dynamically generated and frequently modified.

Some supporters of paid inclusion allege that the system allows them to be listed immediately, instead of redefining the site's content, making it SEO friendly, and waiting months to be included in the relevancy list.

Web Analysis – Making Sense Out of the Statistics

The most important complementary information, regarding Web site traffic, is provided for the statistical data of the site. The usage of this kind of information (and its analysis) is part of the every day activity of Internet marketers.

Every operating system of Web servers provides stats and tracking applications that allow the administrator to get some approximation of traffic (and related information). Usually, those tools read the visitor log files, stored in the server, and perform a mathematical calculation that provides the following data:

- Daily traffic, per hour

- Approximate geographical data of visitors' servers

- Referral linking (from where the visitor arrived to our site)

- Durability of visits

- Web pages loaded

- Files downloaded

The quality of the data extracted for these applications is not good enough to design any market intelligence strategy. The objective of the statistical data collection, from the marketing standpoint, is to recognize trends, navigational problems, user location, and behavior. A detailed set of information is able to provide the mentioned set of data and qualify visitors as potential Internet prospects or Web leads.

Web leads

This is a new term created as a derivation of the term "phone-leads" or "sales leads," typically linked to phone cold-calling in sales. A Web lead is a Web visitor who qualifies as a potential customer. The Internet marketer, in the role of analyst, must investigate in detail the information of the visitors, with the intention of recognizing how close those visitors are to becoming customers.

Web leads analysis is an important activity, but cannot be performed with the statistical information provided from the common tracking applications mentioned before. I will show you the options for professional Internet marketers. There are many services that provide access for getting Web leads information; those services request you to become a member of the service, and then they do the following:

- Allocate a space in their servers in order to gather information from your site

- Ask you to add a piece of code (Java) in the page or pages you want to track

- Give you secure access to a friendly interface with the statistical information and calculations about your site

The code captures detailed information of the user's visit and sends it directly to their server (where is stored). You have personal access to your own account in order to monitor that data. There is a free service that offers Web leads data and other types of relevant info, called **Statcounter. com**; I strongly recommend subscribing to their service. **Statcounter.com** is part of an interesting experimental project conducted by Aodhan Cullen, initiated in 2000.

There are also paid services that offer the same help as **Statcounter.com**. Some of them are precise and have much added value to their interface, in order to facilitate the analysis and comprehension of the data. Some of the companies specializing in providing this type of service are: E-analyst (**http://www.evisitanalyst.co.uk**), Net-results (**http://www.net-results. com**), Google Analytics (**http://www.google.com/analytics/**), Sitemeter (**http://www.sitemeter.com**), and XITI (**http://www.xiti.com/**).

Figure 42.9

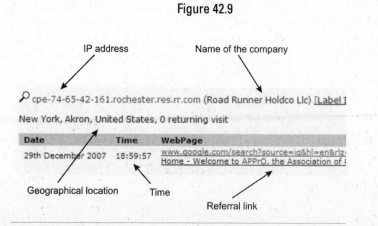

The most important information collected for these services is a detailed explanation of the visitor location, in a more broad way than the typical data extracted from the server visitor logs. Figure 42.9 shows a typical result of the Web lead services result page.

The Internet marketer is usually looking for these important elements:

- **Lead name** — Name of the company that visited the site (very important for business to business products or services)

- **Location** — City and state of the company

- **SE data** — Search engine and keywords used

- **Path** — Pages viewed in order

- **Time details** — Time spent on each page

The access to this particular set of information allows the marketer to design a strategy of post-actions or correct the Web site as a result of the definition of visit trends and visitor general behavior.

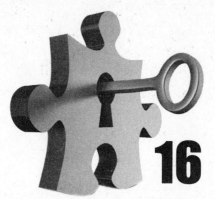

E-commerce Strategy & Development

16

E-commerce Considerations

I would like to outline what I call the five e-commerce considerations for successful developments. Any Internet marketer must consider these points before engaging in any project of electronic commerce over the Internet.

1. People look for specifics.

2. One product per site increases the chances to sell.

3. Think of the site as nothing but a storefront.

4. Use every single element of the layout to motivate the user to "buy."

5. Be specific and show credentials that demonstrate a high level of reliability.

History

Simplistically, we may say that the beginning of e-commerce was **Amazon.com**, since it set the example that motivated thousands of organizations and companies to initiate the first steps in online e-commerce. Figure 43.0 provides solid evidence of the magnitude of this increasing industry with an extraordinary future.

Amazon was founded in 1994, spurred by what Jeff Bezos referred to as his "regret minimization framework." Bezos wrote its business plan while he and his wife drove a 1988 Chevrolet Blazer from Fort Worth, Texas to Bellevue, Washington. The company began as an online bookstore called **Cadabra.com**, a name that Bezos quickly abandoned due to its sounding like "cadaver." While the largest brick-and-mortar bookstores and mail-order catalogs for books might offer 200,000 titles, an online bookstore could offer many times more. Bezos renamed his company "Amazon" after the world's most voluminous river.

The company was incorporated in 1994, in the state of Washington, began service in July of 1995, and was reincorporated in 1996 in Delaware. The first book ever sold by **Amazon.com** was Douglas Hofstadter's "Fluid Concepts and Creative Analogies: Computer Models of the Fundamental Mechanisms of Thought." **Amazon.com** had its initial public offering on May 15, 1997, trading on the NASDAQ stock exchange under the symbol AMZN at an IPO price of US $18 per share.

Figure 43.0

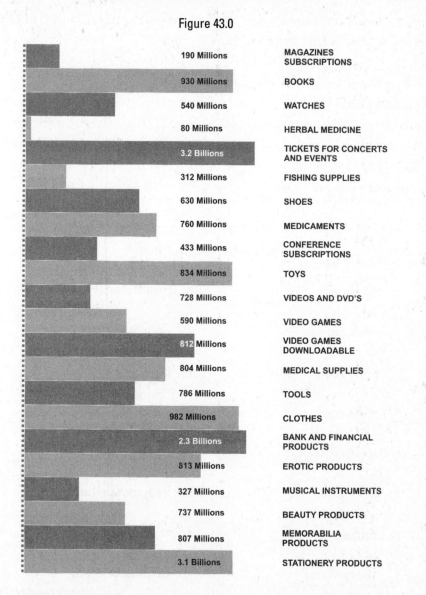

190 Millions	MAGAZINES SUBSCRIPTIONS
930 Millions	BOOKS
540 Millions	WATCHES
80 Millions	HERBAL MEDICINE
3.2 Billions	TICKETS FOR CONCERTS AND EVENTS
312 Millions	FISHING SUPPLIES
630 Millions	SHOES
760 Millions	MEDICAMENTS
433 Millions	CONFERENCE SUBSCRIPTIONS
834 Millions	TOYS
728 Millions	VIDEOS AND DVD'S
590 Millions	VIDEO GAMES
812 Millions	VIDEO GAMES DOWNLOADABLE
804 Millions	MEDICAL SUPPLIES
786 Millions	TOOLS
982 Millions	CLOTHES
2.3 Billions	BANK AND FINANCIAL PRODUCTS
813 Millions	EROTIC PRODUCTS
327 Millions	MUSICAL INSTRUMENTS
737 Millions	BEAUTY PRODUCTS
807 Millions	MEMORABILIA PRODUCTS
3.1 Billions	STATIONERY PRODUCTS

VOLUMES OBTAINED FROM ONLINE TRANSACTIONS WORLDWIDE, BETWEEN DECEMBER 2004 AND JANUARY 2006.
VALUES IN AMERICAN DOLLARS

DATA FROM SMITH AND SMITH BUSINESS RESEARCH

Amazon's initial business plan was unusual; the company did not expect to turn a profit for four to five years. In retrospect, the strategy was effective. Amazon grew at a steady pace in the late 1990s, while many other Internet companies grew at a blindingly fast pace. Amazon's slow growth caused a number of its stockholders to complain, saying that the company was not reaching profitability fast enough.

When the dot-com bubble burst and many e-companies went out of business, Amazon persevered and finally turned its first profit in the fourth quarter of 2002: a meager $5 million, just $.01 per share, on revenues of over $1 billion, but it was important symbolically. *Time Magazine* named Bezos its 1999 Person of the Year in recognition of the company's success in popularizing online shopping.

Along with **Amazon.com**, many other e-commerce companies began to experiment in the new terrain of online business:

- **eBay.com**
- **dash.com**
- **productopia.com**
- **wine.com**
- **theknot.com**
- **disney.com**
- **djin.s**
- **shoeguru.ca**
- **uo.com.au**

- **onsale.com**
- **mysimon.com**
- **petopia.com**
- **carsdirect.com**
- **rocketcash.com**
- **drugstore.com**
- **teetonic.com**
- **furioustees.com**
- **sintaxclothes.com**

Promo Portals

About 97 percent of Internet marketing strategies are to promote an e-commerce development and finally produce sales.

The promo portal is a very important concept that the user needs to incorporate in order to achieve two major objectives:

1. A successful marketing campaign

2. Sale of the product or service promoted

Promo sites are single-product oriented Web sites, created with the objective of promoting and selling exclusively that product. If you have three products to sell, you need to create three vertical sites, and treat the three products separately from each other. This is the basic concept of niche marketing; oriented to engaged a more focused promotional activity in order stimulate the customer buying desire by communicating a direct message and avoiding any additional distraction.

Figure 43.5

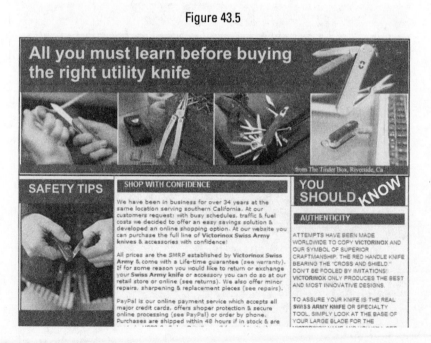

Figure 43.5 shows a good example of a promo portal. The only objective of the site is to promote and sell the popular Victorinox utility knife. Although the company manufactures several other products (e.g., watches, accessories, and sport-tools), the site is oriented to send a focused message

directly to potential buyers of the utility knife, without confusing their attention with other offerings. Promo portals are extremely effective in terms of selling, with a very high ROI value.

Vertical Portals

Also called vortals, these Web sites provide a gateway to information related to a particular industry, such as health care, insurance, automobiles, or food manufacturing. A vertical industry is one that is focused on a relatively narrow range of goods and services, whereas a horizontal industry is one that aims to produce a wide range of goods and services. Because most industry tends to specialize, most industry tends to be vertical.

Figure 43.7

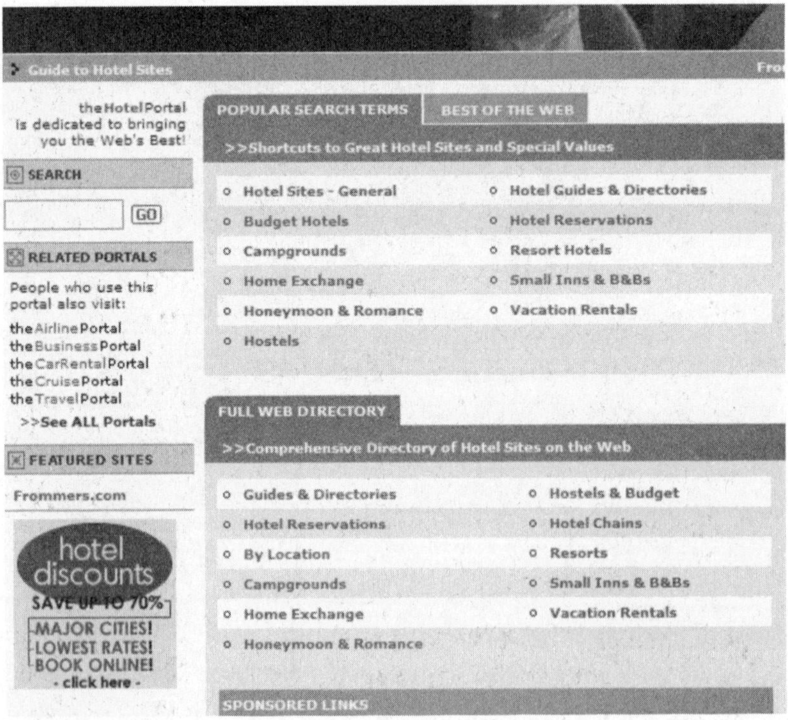

A term that might also be used is interest community Web site, since any vertical industry brings together people sharing an interest in buying, selling, or exchanging information about that particular industry. Vertical portals are also seen as likely business to business communities. For example, small business people with home offices might be attracted to a comprehensive vertical portal that provided ideas and product information related to setting up and maintaining the home office. Figure 43.7 shows a vertical portal of the hotel industry, with a very specific set of information and data regarding that industry.

Integration of Internet Marketing and E-commerce

Being specific is the most important element in the development of any e-commerce site. Many people arriving to the site are coming from an online directory, vertical site, or a search engine results page; think about that and try to see the most beneficial approach for convincing an interested user. As I outlined at the beginning of the book, the user coming from search engine results pages is "looking for something" — an answer to their need.

A successful e-commerce site is the one that creatively integrates the following components in its structural concept:

- **Web site brand** — Header with Web site name and logo. Recommended high of between 35 and 90 pixels.

- **Menu** — Horizontal and vertical menus facilitate enormously the navigation on the site; menus must be present all the time in the Web site.

- **Up-front benefit** — It is important to outline the benefit. Why the customer will have an advantage buying this product, what the advantage is, and what problems it can resolve. Do not outline the questions; just provide the answers in the simplest language.

- **Search feature** — High-quality e-commerce Web sites offer a search box feature in some corner of the layout. The internal search engine allows the user to look for any data within the entire site, facilitating access to all the products and associated information.

- **Additional information** — All the offerings in the site must be structured in a consistent and detailed way to help the user evaluate better the characteristics of the product or service. Figure 43.9 shows a good example of complementary information usually displayed in e-commerce layouts, in order to stimulate the buyer's desires.

Figure 43.9

Additional information such as products details, characteristics and price

- **Pricing** — The price is a key factor of any sell. For some particular consulting services or professional services (like Web sites), it is not recommended to expose the price upfront; this is always a consideration that the marketer faces. But the pricing needs to be exposed sooner or later, in order to engage a positive sales process. At that point, make sure the price is clear, and detailed enough.

- **Payment** — The payment system must be transparent and disclosed upfront, if you really want to make any sell online. Any good e-commerce site is proactive and tries to generate an immediate reaction on the potential buyer. Figure 44.0 represents a fair example.

Figure 44.0

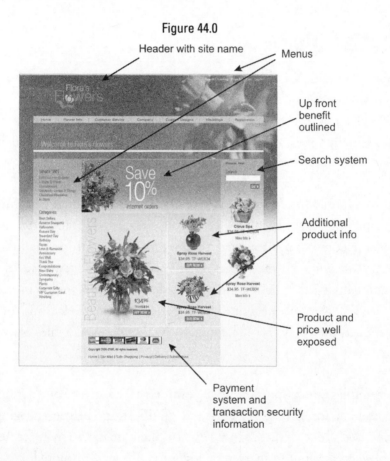

Header with site name

Menus

Up front benefit outlined

Search system

Additional product info

Product and price well exposed

Payment system and transaction security information

Click Level

A general rule among e-commerce developers is the click level or click-profundity; an evaluation performed on the navigational structure of the Web site, with the intention of estimating how many clicks the user needs to execute to reach the information requested. The 1-click deepness is the standard best limit. Many clicks disappoint and fatigue users looking for price, product details, or shipping information.

If the site offers many products or variations of the products, the developer needs to seriously evaluate the best design in order to show all the information (without overwhelming) and let the user click as little as possible to facilitate the access to the right information, such as buying options, product detail, and shipping information.

Free Sample

Jason Craver said, "My wife and I go to Costco every Saturday for shopping. When we are out of the store we do not even think about dinner; these people give more food samples than anyone could imagine. My wife, not coincidentally, buys almost 20 percent of the products sampled in the store."

The free sample concept is a derivative of permission marketing techniques. Its adaptation to the e-commerce universe occurred around 1999, when popular e-commerce sites tried to dominate competitive markets with products of similar characteristics. **Disney.com** is a good example. In 2000, the company tried to gain a big market share of games online by offering full free access to all the games for a period of two weeks; this model is still applied these days for the company, with an amazing sales conversion rate.

Free samples are important in e-commerce ventures, considering that visitors look forward to benefits and gratifications before engaging any buying decision. Marketers need to use their imagination to create free samples, no matter the characteristics of the product promoted.

Another good example is the approach of **gotomypc.com**, created by Citrix Systems, which offers a remote control software service that enables the user to operate a computer from another computer via the Internet. Their 100 percent online trial version is the key component of the entire sales model of the product, with impressive results.

The most popular online market of free samples is the software industry, since the delivery might be totally online and very easy. Adobe Corporation, for instance, offers all its software packages online in downloadable trial versions with expiration day restrictions, in order to let the user play with the tools. After the trial time is finished, the user is able to purchase the license and unlock the software for good. This frequently implemented system has facilitated enormously the selling process of software companies around the world in the last couple of years; even complex software installations for business (i.e., business objects products) have implemented this model for years with important results.

Trials and Tours

The trial concept was initiated for the software industry around 1998, capitalizing the online business for delivering an evaluation version of the promoted application. The freeware, shareware, evaluation copy, and others were deviations of the trial concept, which is the clean adaptation of the free sample technique to the online business.

Marcus Robertson was one of the first developers in trying to design a business model based on trial applications. In late 1998, he planned a neat strategy for Ambrosia Software, a pioneer company of video games delivering a CD-ROM with the game valid for 15 days (at that time, the download was not a valid delivery option yet). After the trial period expired, the user was able to buy the unlocked key online, which was a unique alphanumerical code delivered by e-mail.

Trial versions are also applicable to other type of products, not necessarily related to the software development industry. Look at the following list of examples:

Amazon.com— They introduced the "Look Inside" initiative, as a valid tactic to stimulate sales by giving to the potential buyer the possibility of viewing some relevant parts of the book. The online device provided extraordinary results to the company; more than 40 percent of the buyers use this option before buying the product.

Ford Motors — The automotive corporation (and many others) started, in 2000, to promote online intensive test drives by geographic dealer location, with additional prizes and gifts for all the interested public. This type of promotion has become very popular for this industry in the last seven years.

Herbalife — The company directly offered free products online, by capturing the IP address of the visitor, and giving them a unique code along with the contact information of the representative. The promotion increased 6 percent of the sales in 2003.

iTunes — The revolutionary mp3 (and now also movies) selling concept introduced in 2001 for Apple. The iTunes application, totally free, allows users to organize and play mp3s and other audio formats under Mac and Windows operating systems. The company launched iTunes to promote a solid business of selling mp3 downloadable files for a convenient price.

MOMA — The Museum of Metropolitan Art of New York implemented in 1999 the first virtual tour to some of the rooms in a 360 degree online console. In this way, the visitors were able to navigate some particular exhibits. Also, Royal Caribbean International started developing the same concept in order to share the feeling of their cruise areas onboard.

Kellogg's Rice Krispies — The popular cereal product initiated an original campaign created by the advertiser Tim Demanstri to promote the interaction of the young audience and the company Web site. The promotion started with a puzzle in the TV commercials, and then the kids were asked to look for a specific code inside the cereal box, which resolves the puzzle once the Web site is visited and the user is asked for the code. Along with the puzzle, the site offered prizes and fantastic gifts.

Although the promotion was not exactly a free sample concept, it is an interesting deviation of that idea that has been copied by many competitors, and interpolated to other types of products.

Hoover's Inc. — The business research company, owned by D&B, has provided information on North American and European companies and industries since 1990. Their phenomenal online model provides a tailored free information system to the general audience, but with restrictions strategically designed to encourage visitors to become members, for full access.

Hoovers also provides additional online products, such as Hoovers Index, which looks like a very efficient free online market watch portal in real time; but it is really a facade of a paid product.

Deviations of "Free Sample"

For some particular products that are difficult to adapt to the trial or free sample concept, marketers have created good initiatives, such as 100 percent money-back guarantee or buy it now pay 30 days later. Typical concepts created originally for non-online businesses now have been incorporated to the online model.

When the Free Sample Become a New Business

Universities online are excellent examples of shy initiatives that suddenly become a new offering. Today, 23 percent of the academic services in North America are online; thousands of students choose online courses as a convenient option. This started originally as a free sample product in order to give a taste of the potentiality of some academic institutions looking to promote their services. Radio stations began in 2001 to broadcast their shows online as a kind of free sample technique, until all of a sudden the market adopted the modality of broadcasting 24/7, as a new propagation channel.

Payment: The Definitive Funnel

This is a topic that must have your attention. Charles Cornwell from Midphase demonstrated, in 2006, that 67 percent of the e-commerce users abandon a buying process in the payment stage. The reason is a lack of trust. The payment area of the site needs to qualify, in order to convince the user to finalize the process initiated. Now that we know how to make the people get interest in our site and drive them to it, it is time to end the process and turn users into customers.

The following rules are "must" components of any successful e-commerce site:

- **Rule 1:** Open a Paypal account and incorporate it to your site, but never use it as the only payment method. The idea e-commerce site offers both systems: Paypal (for members of the service) and direct credit card payment.

- **Rule 2:** Use reliable and proven shopping cart and payment system services (i.e., LML Payment Systems Corp, BeanStream — **http://www.beanstream.com**).

- **Rule 3:** Offer credentials for payment guarantees (i.e., Verisign).

- **Rule 4:** Allow excessive access to the shopping cart, from every page of the site.

- **Rule 5:** Remember that the shipping system and costs (in case your Web site requires this option) are sometimes as relevant as the payment credentials for engaging the potential customer. The next chapter provides detailed coverage about shopping carts and online payment modules for Web sites.

Figure 44.7

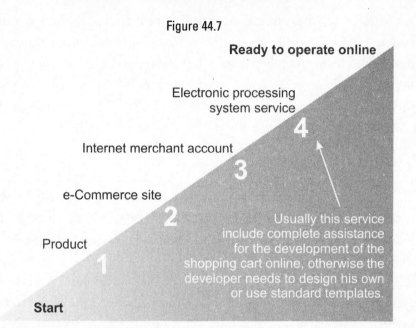

Figure 44.7 represents a diagram with the necessary steps to be able to engage online transactions for any product. After the product and Web site has been defined, the next step is to acquire an Internet merchant account; almost any bank in North America provides this service.

Bill-Me-Later.com

If your site concentrates an important number of visitors, you may also consider the implementation of a bill-me-later system, a distinctive payment method created by Gary Marino, an innovative entrepreneur, around 2004. More than 1000 e-business companies (such as Wal-Mart, Lenovo, Toy-R-Us, CD Universe, and **Onlineshoes.com**) use this method.

The system considerably reduces internal cost of e-commerce companies, generated by the fees of the credit card monopoly, also known as "plastic planet." The user does not need to use a credit card or e-check to pay through bill-me-later; the system is the Internet-age equivalent of asking the neighborhood warehouse store to put the light bulbs on your tab. Users are required to enter their last four digits of their Social Security number and date of birth. If the credit information is good, the system validates the transaction in advance. The user is billed two weeks later, with the option of paying by mail, at the bank, or even online. Bill-me-later is expecting to process $1 billion in online purchases for 2008.

The eBay Storefront

eBay offers a very attractive option recommended by e-commerce experts in the last year: The eBay Stores. Before explaining the details of this interesting offering, let us learn more about eBay positioning and history.

This online auction Web site was founded in San Jose, California on September 3, 1995 by computer programmer Pierre Omidyar. The original objective was to launch an auction Web online service, as part of a larger personal site project. The first item sold on eBay was a broken laser pointer for $14.83. Astonished, Omidyar contacted the winning bidder and asked if he understood that the laser pointer was broken. In his responding e-mail, the buyer explained: "I am a collector of broken laser pointers."

Chris Agarpao was hired as eBay's first employee and Jeffrey Skoll was hired as the first president of the company in 1996. In November 1996, eBay entered its first third-party licensing deal, with a company called Electronic Travel Auction to use SmartMarket Technology to sell plane tickets and other travel products. The company officially changed the name of its service from AuctionWeb to eBay in September of 1997.

Originally, the site belonged to Echo Bay Technology Group, Omidyar's consulting firm. Omidyar had tried to register the domain name **echobay. com** but found it already taken by the Echo Bay Mines, a gold mining company, so he shortened it to his second choice, **eBay.com**. eBay went public in 1998, and both Omidyar and Skoll became instant billionaires. In an extraordinary strategic move, the company purchased PayPal on October 14, 2002.

The launching of the eBay stores was a big initiative to allow people to create their own storefront supported by eBay infrastructure, technology, and merchant/marketing advantages. I would not recommend building an e-commerce strategy exclusively using the eBay Stores, but I believe this is an extraordinary complementary action that helps generating a second gateway to the original Web site.

When the Product Is a Service

Capitol Research, a reliable Houston based consulting firm that provided important stats of Internet and users' behavior, shows that 29 percent of the Web sites worldwide sell services; this is a significant amount of sites. The same firm stated that services' Web sites sold almost $17 billion in 2006 only in North America; another significant number.

Many times, I have been asked about the applicability of traditional online storefront concept to companies that only sell services. You need to make the service a product as much as you can. This is the key. The user needs to identify the service as a product in order to engage an online buying process. Even if the objective is just promotional, the best chances of coming across with the message are to make the service a product, and conceive it as a tangible product.

Breaking the abstract concept of a service is one of the most difficult strategies to engage, considering that some services are customized, and the effort to make them a product may modify the spirit of the service. Look for your competitor and collect information. Deloitte & Touche (**http://www.deloitte.com**) is a great example. The company has approximately 150,000 professionals at work in over 148 countries, delivering audit, tax, consulting, and financial advisory services for the most important companies in the world. Their Web site approach is a clear example of the service understood as a product and explained consistently in that way.

.biz and the New Standard

The extension .biz is a generic, top-level domain intended for domains of business. In 2001, the Internet Corporation for Assigned Names and Numbers (ICANN) designated this option as a result of a market need for alternative URL names. Although the .com extension is still the most popular and representative of all the options, it is expected that .biz will clearly represent the business domains by 2015.

Considering the propagation of preventative domain name registration (people who register hundreds of names with the objective of re-selling them to the highest bidder later on), the .biz option is a good mitigation route.

17

The Shopping Cart

What You Will Learn About in the Following Chapter

- Importance of the shopping cart in e-commerce
- Characteristics of the shopping cart
- Implementation of the online shopping cart

The electronic shopping cart is a valuable instrument of the e-commerce process, sometimes the most relevant. As I mentioned before, the chances of the customer leaving at this point are high and the results catastrophic. This is a critical component that must not fail under any circumstances. Technically, the online shopping cart is software used in e-commerce to assist people making purchases online, analogous to the American English term "shopping cart."

This software allows online shopping customers to place items in the cart. Upon checkout, the software typically calculates a total for the order, including shipping and handling (i.e., postage and packing) charges and the associated taxes, if applicable.

Shopping cart applications typically provide a function of capturing a client's payment information, but in the case of a credit card, they rely on the software module of the secure gateway provider, in conjunction with the secure payment gateway, in order to conduct secure credit card transactions online. The gateway provider may have its own shopping cart provider, but we are not forced to use it.

Some setup must be done in the HTML code of the Web site, and the shopping cart software must be installed on the hosting Web server, or on the secure server, which accepts ordering information. Online shopping carts are usually implemented using HTTP cookies or query strings. In most Web server based implementations, however, data related to the shopping cart is kept in the "session object" and is accessed and manipulated on the fly, as the user selects different items from the cart. Later, at the process of commitment, the information is accessed and an order is generated against the selected item, thus clearing the shopping cart.

Although the simplest shopping carts strictly allow for an item to be added to a basket to start a checkout process (e.g., the free PayPal shopping cart), most online shopping cart software actually provides additional features that an Internet merchant uses to fully manage an online store. Data (e.g., products, categories, discounts, orders, and customers) is normally stored in a database and accessed in real time by the software.

Shopping Cart Basic Structure

Online shopping cart software is typically formed by two components:

Storefront — The area of the Web store that is accessed by visitors to the online shop. Category, product, and other pages (e.g., search or best sellers) are dynamically generated by the software based on the information saved in the store database.

Administration — The area of the site store that is accessed by the merchant to manage the online shop. The amount of store management features changes depending on the sophistication of the shopping cart software. In general, a store manager is able to add and edit products, categories, discounts, and shipping and payment settings. Order management features are also included in many shopping cart programs.

The developer usually may choose between two options of shopping cart software offering:

1. Licensed software

2. Hosted service

Licensed software — The software is downloaded and installed on a Web server. This is most often associated with a one-time or initial fee, although there are many free products available as well. The main advantages of this option are that the merchant owns a license and therefore can host it on any server that meets the server requirements, and that the source code can often be accessed and edited to customize the application.

Hosted service — The software is directly provided by a hosted service provider and is generally paid for on a monthly or annual basis; also known as the application service provider (ASP) software model.

Some of these services also charge a percentage of sales in addition to the monthly fee. This model often has predefined templates that a user can choose from to customize their look and feel. In this model, users typically trade less ability to modify or customize the software with the advantage of having the vendor continuously keep the software up-to-date for security patches, as well as having new features added.

The following links are for some referential vendors in the current market:

*   **http://www.fortune3.com/**

*   **http://www.volusion.ca/**

- http://www.clicshop.com

- http://www.x-cart.com/

- https://www.ecartsoft.com

- http://www.netsuite.com

- http://www.techwave.com/

- http://www.uburst.com/uStorekeeper/

- http://www.hwg.org/services/classes/phpclass3.html

- http://www.cartscience.com/

18
CMS Under the Magnifying Glass

What You Will Learn About in the Following Chapter

- Characteristics of CMS

- Different types of CMS

- Detailed overview about CMS and SEO

If you are not familiar with content management systems (CMS), I strongly recommend you read Appendix C, at the end of the book, for a detailed explanation and overview of this topic.

Why CMS?

A Web CMS covers the complete lifecycle of the pages on your site, from providing simple tools to creating the content, through to publishing, and finally, archiving.

It also provides (and enhances) the ability to manage the structure of the site, the appearance of the published pages, and the navigation provided to the users. Please note that in some circles, these systems are also called Web Management Systems (WMS), which is more correct than CMS.

Considering the current dynamic of Web development, and the requirements of the modern internal business processes, CMS is a solid solution for content administration and displaying. I generated savings (thousands of hours of development per year) for several companies by implementing this type of solution.

Business Benefits

There are a broad range of business benefits that can be obtained by implementing a CMS, including:

- Improved site navigation

- Reduced duplication of information

- Faster turnaround time for new pages and changes

- Greater consistency

- Streamlined authoring process

- Reduced site maintenance costs

- Increased site flexibility

- Support for decentralized authoring

- Increased security

- Greater capacity for growth

As additional value, CMS also can help to improve sales, increase user satisfaction, or assist in communicating with the public. Once a page has been created, it is saved into a central repository in the CMS. This stores all the content of the site, along with the other supporting details.

This central repository allows a range of useful features to be provided by the CMS, for instance:

- Keeping track of all the versions of a page, and who changed what when

- Ensuring that each user can only change the section of the site they are responsible for

- Integrating existing information sources and IT systems

- Most importantly, the CMS provides a range of workflow capabilities

When the page is created by an author, it is automatically sent to their manager for approval, and then to the central Web team for their editorial review. It is finally sent to the legal team for their sign-off, before being automatically published to the site.

Publishing

Content management systems have powerful publishing engines which allow the appearance and page layout of the site to be applied automatically during publishing. It may also allow the same content to be published to multiple sites; this is an interesting alternative considering that the different CSS could manage different appearance for each site.

These publishing capabilities ensure that the pages are consistent across the entire site, and enable a high standard of appearance. CMS can also provide a number of features to enhance the quality and effectiveness of the site itself and also makes it easy to support multiple browsers, or users with accessibility issues. The CMS can be used to make your site dynamic and interactive, thereby enhancing the site's impact.

CMS Objectives to Consider

Site flexibility — Corporate Web sites must quickly adapt to match new products, services, or corporate strategies. The CMS supports easy and trouble-free restructures and interface redesigns. This includes updating all pages to reflect a new corporate brand or image.

Information accuracy — The overall quality of the information is to be improved by these types of systems, gaining added value in accuracy, up-to-date information, and comprehension.

Usability — CMS organizes the people involved in the content generation and Web design, since the editor may manage the content through the administrative interface, without touching (or knowing) HTML code or Web development components.

Marketing support — Facilitates the delivery of marketing material and supports current brands and corporate identity.

Reduced duplication of information — The conventional HTML structures have an outstanding weakness for content duplication, mainly for big sites. Duplication of information across the company notably increases maintenance costs and error rates.

Improved customer experience — CMS enhances the ability to provide a rich environment for Web site visitors from the navigation and friendliness stand point.

Sales support — E-commerce sites are one of the most important beneficiaries of CMS, since they allow a solid method for instant content updating (e.g., prices and product details), most of the CMS' applications offer strong e-commerce support and features, providing further sales features (and infrastructure) to enhance the sales impact of the Web site.

Streamlined information updates — Replacing the current manual (slow and inefficient) process for updating Web site information with an automated, dynamic, and fast system.

Web site growth support — There is a strategic need to substantially increase the amount of information published on corporate Web sites. The CMS delivers efficiency and management benefits to support the goal of Web site growth.

Increased flexibility to change — Due to the dynamic nature of the applications.

Improved business responsiveness — Support the development of new products and services, as well as other changes in corporate direction. This is achieved by providing fast and efficient mechanisms to update internal corporate information and resources.

Improved publishing process — Ad-hoc publishing processes prevent effective management and tracking. CMS improves on this and provides greater transparency and accountability.

Reduced legal exposure — All information presented on the corporate Web site exposes the business to legal liability. This should be reduced by establishing greater control and accountability over the review and publishing processes.

Captured business knowledge — It is recognized that the loss of key staff reduces the knowledge available within an organization. The CMS supports the capture of this information in a documented form.

Improved knowledge sharing — Staff "peer-to-peer" sharing of information is one of the most effective ways of spreading knowledge.

Knowledge discovery support — Many staff members are now confronted with "information overload." By providing powerful searching, browsing, and filtering, the CMS allows staff to find and track key information.

Improved staff efficiency — Staff efficiency can be improved by supporting key business processes with sufficient information. The CMS aims to provide staff with the information they need, when they need it. This will translate into direct time savings by avoiding fruitless searches for required information.

Reduced customer support costs — Customer support requirements are reduced, by providing more accurate and comprehensive information to customers.

Reduced publishing costs — Many business manuals are still produced in paper form. Direct cost savings would be realized by replacing these with online resources.

Reduced Web site maintenance costs — By replacing the current labor-intensive maintenance activities, the CMS reduces the need for Web site administration staff, and other associated costs.

Increased Web site audience — The CMS allows a wide audience to access the corporate Web site. All customers of the business will then benefit from the site. (This includes non-English speakers.)

CMS and SEO

This is a critical topic in any CMS application, regardless of the technology or features. SEO, as we learned before, is based on the recurrent activity of the SE spiders and their functionality. The spiders crawl the information stored in the server with some particular characteristics (e.g., file formats or location).

All CMS work with dynamic connection to a database that stores all the content of the Web site. Spiders are unable to access the databases and index that information. For that reason, the majority of the Web site content is hidden from the spiders, making all the SEO efforts almost useless.

Not even typical SEO Web site components like page titles or image ALT attributes are accessible to the spiders, since even those are stored in the CRM's database. In order to compensate this downside, the developer needs to implement a strategy I will explain in detail.

Optimization of the main file — Although the CMS site is dynamic (e.g., PHP or ASP) there are some formatting structures where the dynamic components will work together to display the information. Those structures are readable for the spiders. For instance, the formatting structure in Mambo is an index.php file. That file might be optimized in order to meet the standards of SEO (Appendix C shows the optimization code for that particular file). Title and meta-tags are able to be optimized in that file, as well as the title, additional text, and other embedded objects.

Supporting Gateways

The most effective mitigation technique is the supporting gateway. This compensates well for the lack of SEO in CMS applications. The idea is to develop identical HTML pages to some of the critical pages of the site and post them directly on the root of the server.

White Papers

Publishing of SEO documents (e.g., DOCs or PDFs) is another common technique for increasing the chances of being detected by the spiders. If the Web site is built with CMS, I usually publish a significant number of additional white papers.

Mini-Web Site Technique

This is a strategy very useful for CMS sites. I frequently select some critical content (not displayed on the home page) and develop an entire mini-Web site in order to expand that content, formed by three or four pages with a pure HTML structure and super optimized for SE.

Note It is very important to publish these supporting mini-Web sites from different servers or Virtual Personal Servers (VPS) in order to generate a different IP address for the spiders.

Traffic Markers

The Numbers of the Results

Anne Lhyn from PeopleSoft said, "It is not about traffic, it is not about numbers, it is about customers, it is about sales." Some marketers seem to forget this important fact that makes all the difference in terms of getting the right results.

In 1995, I had an interesting meeting with a publishing company from Mexico; they managed an impressive set of print-catalog products for the pharmaceutical industry. My objective was to induce them to move 70 percent of their operation to online products in a two-year project.

They laugh about it. Their polite negative response was something like this: "Mr. Todaro, we have deep respect of your knowledge and trajectory, but this business has been growing steadily for the last 17 years, making us one of the most important and recognized publishing companies in this field. We do not believe that there is a need to move our products to an Internet version."

Twenty months later, they were forced to move to an online format in order to face the aggressive online competition from smaller companies with more innovative vision. They contacted me and their concern at that time was traffic — making the right people come to their site.

Internet marketing war is all about traffic or audience. The distress about people coming to the site was removed after the year 2000. Today's worry is the quality of the audience and the chance to make them convert from potentials to clients. This is an important distinction. We need to recognize the high value of "good traffic," not simply "traffic."

As Mark Stevens suggests, "Today there is no effective promotional campaign if the marketer is unable to identify the return of every single penny invested." In the '80s and early '90s, marketers designed over-invested marketing strategies, aiming for a big audience in hope of getting some sales as a residual effect of their promotion. This is no longer an option. The increasing number of competition and multi-channels of promotion around the world created new rules that force marketers to approach a conscious strategy, defining metrics to get data about results and market reaction. The accuracy of the information collected by marketers represents, these days, an important evidence of success that helps to define (and adjust) the marketing strategy in any company.

Small companies invest their marketing budget in a smarter way than big companies. I analyzed Google's promotional actions since the beginning of the company through the present, and I am certain that Google wastes 30 percent of their marketing investment in activities with no return and no image propagation.

Oracle is a perfect example of this. In early 1981, Oracle was a midsize corporation with big aspirations, but a conservative budget for promotion and sales engagements. Almost every strategic move in that area required explanation to the investor's board in order to allocate funding. The investment regarding promotional activities was extremely tight, and the marketing actions used to be very ingenious.

As the company started to grow significantly, the marketing budget lost the original criteria of the old times. I collaborated with Oracle Latin-American division in late 1993, and the company invested more than 80 percent of its marketing money in actions with no ROI at all, aiming at wrong markets and non-profiled customers. In 2000, after the Oracle9i Application Server was released, the corporation re-aligned the strategy for marketing investment, increasing their online presence (more than 45 percent) in response to good competitive moves from their competitors and reduced their marketing budget by almost 50 percent, gaining market share for about 12 percent.

Qualification

Traffic qualification is an important part of Internet marketing strategy. Traffic is not an abstract concept, applicable to the marketer's analysis as a piece of a metric formula. The traffic is thousands people, each with different expectations, desires, and reactions. Traffic changes all the time. Some marketers seem to forget that a market is not easy to quantify under any measures.

The question is how to filter and find customers. All the SEO and additional online actions will conduct people to the site, but let me give you some advice about professional techniques oriented to filter and qualify visitors. Audience is formed by groups of people, classified by similar behavior and expectations, usually represented by degree or interest levels, as described in the following list:

- **Degree one** — The customers: People who are ready to buy, proactive, and interested in the product offered. They have a 90 percent chance of buying.

- **Degree two** — Potential customers with a high level of interest in the offering. They have a 70 to 80 percent chance of buying.

- **Degree three** — Intrigued audience: Potentials with less than a 30 percent chance of buying. They may become degree two in a reasonable period of time, or they may dismiss you.

- **Degree four** — People looking for similar products or a deviation of yours. They have less than a 10 percent chance of becoming buyers.

- **Degree five** — Accidental visitors: They are looking for something different, and they arrive to the site misled or by mistake. No chance of buying.

By engaging a classification of the audience, the marketer is able to identify the common characteristics and group behavior of the potential customers; this information is relevant for designing the traffic strategy of the site. A good example is the exercise conducted by the online advertiser Thomas Smith-Ellison for several of his clients that profiled high executives as audience. Smith-Ellison discovered that a high percentage of that particular market visited frequently specialized cruises and tourism sites. He built an advertising strategy based on banner ads for those sites, driving an immense traffic (mainly degree one and two) to his clients' Web sites.

The first elements that marketers consider in order to engage a fair audience classification are their common factors, common stimulations, desires, and expectations. You must avoid thinking about the market in terms of personal analysis. If I tell you that there is a huge online market for thermometers, you may think I am crazy, just because you cannot believe there is a big market for such a product. People commonly qualify based on personal perceptions. In marketing, this leads to hundreds of mistakes.

Traffic Services

This is a sensitive topic. I have never gotten a satisfactory result from these types of services. Some of them are just a scam; some of them provide an interesting model, but not customers.

Originally, these services were offered by companies called "surfers buyers;" they offered money to people for navigating on particular sites. These companies had a very good administrative formula in order to split the fee charged to their clients among their market (people willing to surf and get money for that). The service works, since the people actually go to the sites, but there is no segmentation and real stimulation in that visit. As a result, the traffic does not provide any real value.

20
Last Notion Before Goodbye

The following are points I would like you to bear in mind, and constantly review in your personal adventure with Internet marketing.

Remember:

- Proactively market the site

- The value of a visitor to your site

- The conversion rate is the key

- Do not try to control all the eyeballs, just your customers'

- Identify your market

- One product per Web site is the key

- Customers buy on impulse

- Success follows when customers come first

- Be where your buyers are and your competitors are not

The most important thing I want you to consider is that online shopping is only 3.8 percent of all retail sales worldwide, but in the next 15 years, this number is going to increase significantly, defining a new scenario that will impose new rules in the economy and thousands of professional activities, such as marketing, programming, and Web design. Be ready.

Appendix A:
Flash & SEO

I always use Flash in my Web site projects. I am also an advanced ActionScript developer, fascinated with all the extraordinary power of the interactive optionally of that application. Flash must be applied in a smart mode, considering its disadvantages for SEO optimization.

Flash files are coded in their own programming language, the browser requires a special plug-in in order to understand their content (unrelated to HTML code). Search engines' spiders are unable to penetrate flash movies. My advice is simple:

- Never overuse Flash

- Try to break the HTML page into small Flash files

- Alternate Flash with HTML all the time (i.e., use Flash for multimedia effects and use hypertext for all the text)

- Never engage an entire Flash site if you want to successfully market the site

- Use interactive effects in JavaScript instead of Flash, for small effects (**http://www.w3schools.com/**)

- Use XML and text sourcing as external variables for loading content into Flash

In the following article, Jonathan Hochman (**www.jehochman.com**), a very knowledgeable Internet marketer, provides important advising for make Flash projects more SEO friendly:

Flash gets a bad rap, undeserved in my opinion, for harming search engine visibility. Why are search engine optimization (SEO) practitioners concerned about Flash, and how can we SEO Flash content? The main problem with Flash is that search engines do not yet understand it, and probably will not in the near future. Flash includes logic and can take input from the visitor, but search engines are designed to handle static content. Flash is actually a running program, so it is much harder to analyze than plain HTML code.

The leading Web development tool, Adobe Dreamweaver, embeds Flash in Web pages with code that fails to provide accessibility for visitors or search spiders who cannot handle Flash. Instead of using the default code, my recommendation is to hand code Flash pages with primary HTML content, and a method of automatically testing for Flash support before attempting to insert the movie. The primary HTML content can be search optimized as if the Flash was not there, while the Flash provides an enhanced user experience for those visitors who have the necessary Flash player.

The April 11, 2006 release of Microsoft's popular Internet Explorer (IE) browser includes an update ("Eolas") that prevents ActiveX-based Flash controls from working properly. When the user attempts to interact with the Flash, a tool tip appears, stating, "Click to activate and use this control." That extra click is an annoyance. Fortunately, the programming technique described in this article solves the Flash Eolas problem.

Requirements for Successful Use of Flash

Flash animation is a great way to present complex content because it allows the designer to put more content in a finite space, without wrecking page design. For technology sites, Flash is an ideal way to present a slide show or movie explaining a complex product. At the other end of the spectrum, art and entertainment sites have a real need for multimedia, and Flash is the perfect solution.

When using Flash, satisfy each of these objectives:

- Clean design

- Search Engine Optimization

- Accessibility for a wide variety of browsers, including screen readers and mobile phones

- Code validation and standards compliance

- Correct functionality with IE

SEO Flash Programming

My recommended Flash SEO method uses a DIV with search-engine-accessible, primary content, and a Javascript function called SWFObject() to detect when browsers are capable of viewing Flash. When an appropriate version of Flash player is present, the Javascript manipulates the page's document object model (DOM) to replace the primary content with the Flash movie. Most search engine spiders cannot handle Flash, so they will elect to view the primary content. The primary content may contain links, headings, styled text, images — anything we can add to an ordinary HTML page. With SEO copyediting and coding skills applied to the primary content, Flash becomes a non-issue.

Flash accessibility programming is not spamming, as long as the primary content and the visible movie are essentially the same. The World Wide Web Consortium (W3C) Web Accessibility Initiative (WAI) specifically states that multimedia content should have an alternative representation available. Accessibility programming creates the benefit of presenting visual information without losing the visitors and search engines who depend upon textual content.

In July of 2007, I discussed this method with Dan Crow of Google. He warned this programming method could draw attention because of the possibility for abuse. If you use this method, make sure the alternative content is a faithful representation of the Flash content, and avoid combining this with other coding methods that could be abused. While this SEO method is not abusive, it is aggressive because there is a small risk the search engines could mistakenly decide the primary content is a form of cloaking.

SWFObject and UFO

Please visit Geoff Sterns' blog at **http://blog.deconcept.com/swfobject/** for a full explanation of SWFObject() and to download the SWFObject.js file required for this solution. Another open source solution, UFO (Unobtrusive Flash Objects), is available from Bobby van der Sluis. Both are conceptually similar.

Example: Making Flash Home Page and Flash Menus Spiderable

The sample code below shows part of the Flash heading and menu code of Marc Abrahms Photography. The interior pages of this site are now indexed because search engines can find the links in the primary content.

```
<head><!--snip-->
<script type="text/javascript" src="/jscript/SWFObject.js"></script>
</head>
```

```
<body>
<!--snip-->
<!--primary content, for non-Flash visitors-->
<div id="flash" align="center">
  <p><a href="/gallery/index.php?category=gallery/1_Prints">prints</a> |
    <a href="/gallery/index.php?category=gallery/2_Posters">posters</a> |
    <a href="/gallery/index.php?category=gallery/3_Books">books</a> |
    <a href="/gallery/index.php?pageId=115&amp;start=0">my account</
a>
    <!--snip, for brevity-->
  </p></div><!-- Flash player detection and Flash insertion -->
<script type="text/javascript">
    var fo = new SWFObject("homepage_v1.swf",        "flash", "680",
"390", "5", "#3a403c");
  fo.write("flash");
</script>
```

Flash accessibility programming will not magically cause a site to rise to the top of the rankings, but this Flash SEO method will eliminate any ranking disadvantages associated with Flash.

Example: Making Flash Slide Show Content Visible to Search Engines

A second example, from the Virtutech Web site, shows how to insert rather long content into a fixed space. We use a DIV, and set its CSS property "overflow:auto" to create a scrolling text area. This prevents the page layout from breaking when the alternative content is displayed.

```
<div id="movieAlt"><div id="movieAltInner">
    <h2><a href="/products/index.html">Simics</a> is
    used to develop the embedded
    software that runs electronic devices such as:</h2>
    <li>Aerospace hardware</li>
    <li>Automobile control systems</li>
```

```
<li>Telecommunications infrastructure</li>
<li> High-end servers</li>
</ul>
<p><em>Hardware:</em> <strong>Satellite Control
System</strong></p>
<p><em>Challenge:</em> Unable to test software with satellites
on orbit.  How
to verify new software?</p>
<p><em>Resolution:</em> Using Simics, the developers
can run software
quality tests on the ground, to ensure that the software works correctly
before it's installed.</p>
<h2>Industry: Automotive</h2>
<p><em>Hardware:</em> <strong>Electronic Control
Unit</strong></p>
<p><em>Challenge:</em> Need to develop software now, but the ECU
won't be available for months</p>
<p><em>Resolution:</em> Simics enables programmers to
develop and test
the software before the hardware is available, reducing time to market.</
p>
<h2><em>Industry:</em> Telecommunications</h2>
<p><em>Hardware:</em><strong> Wireless Network Equipment</
strong></p>
<p><em>Challenge: </em> You have twenty programmers. Each
needs a complete
system for testing. They cost MILLIONS.</p>
<p><em>Resolution:</em> Using Simics to create a model of the target
hardware, each programmer can have his or her own virtual device for
software testing and debugging, without breaking your budget.</p>
<h2>Industry: Internet</h2>
<p><em>Hardware:</em> <strong>Network servers</strong></p>
<p><em>Challenge:</em> Software bugs keep popping up.
Some take weeks to
```

reproduce and fix. You are running out of time.</p>
<p><em>Resolution:</em> With Simics, programmers can run the program forward and backward to quickly identify, recreate and repair bugs.</p></div></div><script type="text/javascript">   var fo = new SWFObject("flash/virtutech_intro.swf", "mymovie", "497", "287", "7", "#ffffff");   fo.write("movieAlt"); </script>

The CSS code:

```
#movieAlt {
     height: 287px;
     width: 497px;
     overflow: auto; /*Scroll bar on HTML content div*/
#movieAltInner {    /*For IE's faulty box model*/
     padding: 10px 20px;
```

In addition to these sites, we have used this Flash SEO method on many other high traffic sites. The code has been served hundreds of thousands of times with virtually no complaints. Sites using this Flash SEO method have achieved top rankings for keywords found only in the Flash content.

All Flash Sites

A site built entirely with Flash suffers a great disadvantage because it lacks page structure to organize the content, internal linking, and unique page titles. One remedy is to create distinct HTML pages to represent each Flash "page," and install the Flash movie on each and every HTML page. When a visitor requests the page, they will see Flash if they can handle it. Otherwise, a non-Flash visitor, such as a search engine, will be able to spider the site. If a user follows a search result onto one of the inner pages, they will get the same Flash experience because the movie is available on every page. Another approach is to divide the Flash into pieces and put the relevant piece on each page.

Slicing up the Flash can result in page transitions that do not provide the seamless effect that you want to create. To get the best of both worlds, pass a parameter into the Flash movie using FlashVars. The same movie can appear on each HTML page, but depending on the parameter value, the movie can start at an appropriate point to show the Flash content that corresponds to that page. To get rid of all the extra pages, but still be able to reference different parts of the Flash piece, add a "#" and a tag to the end of each URL, and pass that tag into the Flash. This approach can make the back and forward buttons work properly, and allow people to bookmark specific parts of the Flash site.

It is also possible to use PHP scripts to pull both the primary HTML content and the Flash content from a MySQL database. This approach would greatly simplify the maintenance of an accessible Flash site by storing only one representation of the content.

Appendix B: Drop Shipping Technique

Drop shipping is a typical supply chain management method in which the retailer does not keep goods in stock, but instead transfers customer orders and shipment details to manufacturers or wholesalers, who then ship the goods directly to the customer. The retailers make their profit on the difference between the wholesale and retail price.

Some drop shipping retailers may keep "show" items on display in stores, so that customers can inspect an item similar to those that they can purchase. Other retailers may provide only a catalogue or Web site.

Retailers that drop ship merchandise from wholesalers may take measures to hide this fact to avoid any bad consequence or to keep the wholesale source from becoming known. This can be affected by "blind shipping" (shipping merchandise without a return address), or "private label shipping" (having merchandise shipped from the wholesaler with a return address customized to the retailer). A customized packing slip may also be included by the wholesaler, indicating the retailer's company name, logo, and/or contact information.

Many sellers on online auction sites, such as eBay, also drop ship. Often, a seller will list an item as new and ship the item directly from the wholesaler to the highest bidder. The seller profits from the difference between the winning bid and the wholesale price, minus any selling and merchant fees from the auction site. A seller is permitted to list items that are currently not in his/her own possession, provided that he/she follows eBay's policy on pre-sale items.

A new emerging trend in the drop ship business is private label drop shipping, in which a manufacturer produces a custom item for a retailer and drop ships it. The range of private label drop shipped items varies from simple key-chains and T-shirts with custom logos or pictures to customized formulations for vitamins and nutritional supplements.

The two main benefits of drop shipping are:

- No upfront inventory to purchase.

- Positive cash flow cycle, because the seller is paid when the purchase is made.

The seller usually pays the wholesaler using a credit card or credit terms. Therefore, there is a period of time in which the seller has the customer's money, but has not yet paid the wholesaler.

Visible Risk

As in any business, some risks are involved in drop shipping. For example, back ordering may occur when a seller places a shipment request with a wholesaler, but the product is sold out. Back ordering may be accompanied by a long wait for a shipment while the wholesaler waits for new products, which may reflect badly on the retailer. A good wholesaler will keep retailers updated, but it is the business owner's job to be aware of the quantities that the wholesaler has available.

Advantages of Online Drop Shipping

Drop shipping can be a very simple and effective way to get started in e-commerce. Many online merchants find drop shipping strategies are good way of minimizing stock holding, decreasing overall shipping costs, and cutting down on delivery times to customers. As I mentioned before, drop shipping allows Web site owners to send single or low-quantity unit orders gathered on their Web sites to manufacturers, or wholesale warehouses, who in turn ship the items directly to the customers of the Web site owner. Typically, you take care of the promotion and collect the payment, and the drop shipper looks after order fulfillment.

Drop shippers can buy in huge volumes, which means they will be able to offer you the best prices on products and shipping, usually wholesale. There is no capital investment, no need to invest in stock, and no danger of you suddenly having large stocks you are unable to sell. You can sell a wider product range without buying stock. Using drop shipping allows you great flexibility in terms of product range. Promote as much or as little as you wish.

Disadvantages of Drop Shipping

If you are interested in proceeding with a drop shipping strategy, shop around. It is important to know all the costs involved so you can calculate your profit margins accurately. Any wholesale company that wants to charge you a regular "participation" fee should be avoided; the only time you should have to pay a drop-ship company anything is in connection with a specific order. Ask whether the drop shipper is using a reputable shipping company to deliver the goods, and where will they ship to.

Important Considerations

- Return policy of the drop-shipper

- Written guarantees associated with the products

- Directories of wholesale suppliers or manufacturers of products: **www.thomasnet.com**

Appendix C: Content Management System (CMS)

A content management system (CMS) is an application used to manage the content of a Web site. Content management systems are deployed primarily for interactive use by a potentially large number of contributors. For example, the software for **Wikipedia.org** is based on a Wiki system, which is a particular type of content management system designed specially for the development of that site and offered to the public as an open source format named Tikiwiki.

The content managed includes computer files, image media, audio files, electronic documents, and Web content. A CMS makes all the files available through an interface over the Web. Many companies use a CMS to store files in a non-proprietary form. Companies use a CMS to share files with ease, as most systems use server-based software, even further broadening file availability. As shown below, many CMSs include a feature for Web Content, and some have a feature for a "workflow process," which refers to moving an electronic document along for approval, or for adding content.

Some CMSs will easily facilitate this process with e-mail notification and automated routing. This is ideally a collaborative creation of documents. A CMS facilitates the organization, control, and publication of a large body of documents and other content, such as images and multimedia resources.

The Web content management system was designed originally by newspaper companies, looking for a friendly system to publish the content online and reduce the internal production cost with digital technologies.

Conceptually, the CMS works with a standard database as a repository format of all the content displayed in the site. Dynamic HTML (DHTML) languages are used to display the content on the browser.

The following list is a fair report of the most popular CMSs in the current market:

- Typo3 — Open source content management system

- Xaraya — Open source content management system

- Plone — Open source content management system based on Zope and Python

- PostNuke — Open source content management system

- Vignette — Enterprise content management system

- Zope — Open source application server for building content management systems

- Textpattern — Open source content management system by Dean Allen

- PHPwcms — Open source content management system based on PHP and MySQL

- PHP-Nuke — Popular open source content management system based on PHP

- Xoops — Open source content management system based on PHP and MySQL

- Bricolage — Open source content management system

- CMSimple — Open source content management system

- DotNetNuke — Open source content management system based on ASP.NET

- WordPress — Open source content management system based on PHP and MySQL

- Drupal — Open source content management system

- eZ Publish — Open source content management system by eZ Systems

- Mambo — Open source content management system by Miro International

- Metadot — Open source portal server

- phpWebSite — Open source content management system based on PHP by the Web Technology Group at Appalachian State University

- RedDot — Enterprise content management system

- SPIP — Open source content management system based on PHP and MySQL by the minirezo

- Alfresco — Open source, J2EE-based content management system

- Site Executive — Content management system by Systems Alliance

- Vertical Site — Content management system based on J2EE by Enonic

- Back-End — Open source content management system for small/ medium s based on PHP and MySQL

- CMS400.NET — Content management system based on .NET by Ektron

- e107 — Open source content management system based on PHP and MySQL

- Freestyler — Content management system by Datalink

- NQContent — Content management system based on Coldfusion by NetQuest

- Kwiki — Open source wiki-type content management system based on Perl

- CityDesk — Content management tool by Fog Creek

- Caravel — Open source content management system based on PHP

- QP7 — Content Management System by Quantum Art

- Tikiwiki — Open source content management system

- WebGUI — Open source content management system by Plain Black

- Website Baker — Open source content management system based on PHP

- SMBCMS — Small business content management system

- Miraserver — Content Management System based on PHP and MySQL by PC Media

- Artiphp Velocity — Open source content management system also known as Artiloo

- AssetNow — Content management system by Orbital

- Clever Copy — Free content management system based on PHP and MySQL.

- Colony — Content management system to create accessible Web sites by Red Ant Development.

Mambo

I am very familiar with Mambo (**http://www.mamboserver.com/**). I have engaged quite a few projects using Mambo CMS and I truly recognize its reliability. I consider Mambo a fantastic open source application for Web content management. As I outlined before, there are many CMS applications on the market; some are open source, some are freeware, and some are paid applications. I recommend spending some time playing with several of them, until you get comfortable with one.

Mambo was originally released by The Mambo Foundation, a non-profit entity established under the laws of Australia. The Foundation is based on Eclipse and GNOME and is controlled by the members of the Foundation via an elected board of directors. The Mambo Foundation's brief is to foster the development of the Mambo system and to shelter the project from threats and misuse. The Foundation was formed in August of 2005. The Mambo Foundation also has forums addressing the latest issues within Mambo, including the deployment of the coming next version, Mambo 5.

Mambo is released under the terms of the GNU General Public License (GPL) and is written with the PHP programming language. The database support of Mambo is a MySQL database. Mambo can be installed and run in servers based on Apache or Windows IIS systems, but only the Apache version has been fully tested. People often refer to Mambo as Joomla!, a project initiated for a group of experimental programmers in order to create a divergence of Mambo. Joomla! offers almost the same functionality and consistency as Mambo.

Mambo and SEO

Mambo has an SEO friendly component (only for Apache version); this is a very basic Linux functionality that makes Mambo language optimize the .htaccess file in the site's root for SE spiders. This feature is not enough to achieve SEO relevancy; usually the developer and the marketer must define a supplementary strategy, as outlined in Chapter 18. OpenSEF is an open source solution oriented to provide SEO support for Joomla! by enabling automatic and manual text-based search engine friendly URL core components and third party developer components.

If you are familiar with Mambo, I would like to give you a tip. Instead of adding the meta-tag keywords from Mambo's control panel (Global Configuration), do it directly in the index.php code, as follows:

Mambo Example

```
<?xml version="1.0" encoding="iso-8859-1"?><!DOCTYPE html PUBLIC "-//W3C//
DTD XHTML 1.0 Transitional//EN" "http://www.w3.org/TR/xhtml1/DTD/xhtml1-
transitional.dtd">

<html xmlns="http://www.w3.org/1999/xhtml">

<head>

<title>Meridian Travel Company - Home</title>

<meta name="description" content=""Australia, New Zealand, low Airfares, Cruises,
Cheap, Discount, Downunder, travel agents, caribbean cruises, tours, vacation
packages, european vacation, Business Class, Fiji, Tahiti">

<meta name="description" content="Looking for flights, travel packages, tours,
cruises, or hotels to Australia, New Zealand, Europe, Fiji, Tahiti, or Hawaii? Plan
Your Dream Vacation with Experienced Agents. Over 28 Years."><meta http-
equiv="pragma" content="no-cache"/>

<meta name="Generator" content="Mambo - Copyright 2000 - 2006 Mambo
Foundation. All rights reserved." />

<meta name="robots" content="index, follow" />

<link rel="shortcut icon" href="http://www.Taorr.com/images/favicon.ico" />

<meta http-equiv="Content-Type" content="text/html; charset=iso-8859-1" />

<link href="http://www.meridian.com/templates/ _model/css/template_css.css"
rel="stylesheet" type="text/css"/>

<link href="http://www.meridian.com/templates/ _model/css/tabs.css"
rel="stylesheet" type="text/css"/>

<link href="http://www.meridian.com/templates/ _model/css/meridian_tabs.css"
rel="stylesheet" type="text/css"/>

<script type="text/javascript" src="http://www. group.com/meridian_3_test/flash/
tabber.js"></script>

<script type="text/javascript" src="http://www. group.com/meridian_3_test/flash/
meridian_tabs.js"></script>

<script type="text/javascript" src="http://www. group.com/meridian_3_test/flash/
img_viewer.js"></script>
```

Mambo Example

```css
<style type="text/css">

<!--

body {

        background-image: url();

        margin: 5px 0px 0px 5px;
```

Bibliography

"Confessions of an Advertising Man" by David Ogilvy and Sir Alan Parker

"Wikinomics: How Mass Collaboration Changes Everything" by Don Tapscott and Anthony D. Williams

"Your Marketing Sucks" by Mark Stevens

"Effective SEO" by Steve Barry

"The Digital Economy: Promise and Peril In The Age of Networked Intelligence" by Don Tapscott

"C++ Primer Plus" by Stephen Prata

"Search Engine Optimization" by Richard John Jenkins

About the Author

Miguel Angel Todaro is originally from Buenos Aires, Argentina. He has been an advisor to important corporations in marketing, multimedia, and e-commerce projects.

He is an expert in software development, with a strong background in graphic design, multimedia programming, and marketing.

In 1997, he developed one of the first automotive e-commerce projects on the net for the Italian company, Fiat Auto International Corporation. As a consultant he helped major organizations, such as UNICEF, AIGA,

Oracle, and IBM. He also developed experimental multimedia e-learning ventures for different companies in North America, including BP and Methanex Corp.

Glossary

ADN (Advanced Digital Network): Usually refers to a 56Kbps leased-line.

ADSL (Asymmetric Digital Subscriber Line): A DSL line where the upload speed is different from the download speed. Usually, the download speed is much greater.

Ajax (Asynchronous JavaScript and XML): A way of including content in a Web page in which javascript code in the Web page fetches some data from a server and displays it without re-fetching the entire surrounding page at the same time (hence the 'Asynchronous'). It is common for Ajax applications to update the Ajax content multiple times without the surrounding page needing to be updated even once.

Apache: The most common Web server (or HTTP server) software on the Internet. Apache is an open-source application originally created from a series of changes ("patches") made to a Web server written at the National Center for Supercoputing Applications, the same place the Mosaic Web browser was created.

Apache is designed as a set of modules, enabling administrators to choose which features they wish to use and making it easy to add features to meet specific needs, including handling protocols other than the Web-standard HTTP.

ARPANet (Advanced Research Projects Agency Network): The precursor to the Internet, developed in the late '60s and early '70s by the US Department of Defense as an experiment in wide-area-networking to connect together computers that were each running different system so that people at one location could use computing resources from another location.

ASCII (American Standard Code for Information Interchange): This is the default world-wide standard for the code numbers used by computers to represent all the upper and lower-case Latin letters, numbers, and punctuation. There are 128 standard ASCII codes, each of which can be represented by a 7 digit binary number: 0000000 through 1111111.

ASP (Application Service Provider): An organization (usually a business) that runs one or more applications on its own servers and provides (usually for a fee) access to others. Common examples of services provided this way include Web-based software, such as calendar systems, human resources tools (e.g., timesheets and benefits), and various applications to help groups collaborate on projects.

Bandwidth: How much stuff you can send through a connection, usually measured in bits-per-second (bps). A full page of English text is about 16,000 bits. A fast modem can move about 57,000 bps. Full-motion, full-screen video would require roughly 10,000,000 bps, depending on compression.

BITNET (Because It's Time NETwork or Because It's There NETwork): A network of educational sites separate from the Internet, although e-mail is freely exchanged between BITNET and the Internet. Listservs®, a popular form of e-mail discussion groups, originated on BITNET. At its peak (in the late 1980s and early 1990s), BITNET machines were usually mainframes, often running IBM's MVS operating system. BITNET is probably the only international network that is shrinking.

Blog (Web LOG): A blog is basically a journal that is available on the Web. The activity of updating a blog is "blogging" and someone who keeps a blog is a "blogger." Blogs are typically updated daily using software that allows people with little or no technical background to update and maintain the blog.

Broadband: Generally refers to connections to the Internet with much greater bandwidth than you can get with a modem. There is no specific definition of the speed of a "broadband" connection, but in general, any Internet connection using DSL or via Cable-TV may be considered a broadband connection.

Browser: A Client program (software) that is used to look at various kinds of Internet resources.

CGI (Common Gateway Interface): A set of rules that describe how a Web server communicates with another piece of software on the same machine, and how the other piece of software (the CGI program) talks to the Web server. Any piece of software can be a CGI program if it handles input and output according to the CGI standard.

Cgi-bin: The most common name of a directory on a Web server in which CGI programs are stored.

Cookie: The most common meaning of "cookie" on the Internet refers to a piece of information sent by a Web server to a Web browser that the browser software is expected to save and to send back to the server whenever the browser makes additional requests from the server.

Depending on the type of cookie used, and the browser's settings, the browser may accept or not accept the cookie, and may save the cookie for either a short time or a long time. Cookies might contain information such as login or registration information, online "shopping cart" information, or user preferences.

When a server receives a request from a browser that includes a cookie, the server is able to use the information stored in the cookie. For example, the server might customize what is sent back to the user, or keep a log of particular user requests.

Cookies are usually set to expire after a predetermined amount of time and are usually saved in memory until the browser software is closed down, at which time they may be saved to disk if their "expire time" has not been reached.

Cookies do not read your hard drive and send your life story to the CIA, but they can be used to gather more information about a user than would be possible without them.

CSS (Cascading Style Sheet): A standard for specifying the appearance of text and other elements. CSS was developed for use with HTML in Web pages but is also used in other situations, notably, in applications built using XPFE. CSS is typically used to provide a single "library" of styles that are used repeatedly throughout a large number of related documents, as in a Web site. A CSS file might specify that all numbered lists are to appear in italics. By changing that single specification, the look of a large number of documents can be easily changed.

Cyberspace: The term was originated by author William Gibson in his novel Neuromancer. The word "cyberspace" is currently used to describe the whole range of information resources available through computer networks.

DHCP (Dynamic Host Configuration Protocol): DHCP is a protocol by which a machine can obtain an IP number (and other network configuration information) from a server on the local network.

DHTML (Dynamic HyperText Markup Language): DHTML refers to Web pages that use a combination of HTML, JavaScript, and CSS to create features such as letting the user drag items around on the Web page, some simple kinds of animation, and many more.

DNS (Domain Name System): The domain name system is the system that translates Internet domain names into IP numbers. A "DNS Server" is a server that performs this kind of translation.

Domain Name: The unique name that identifies an Internet site. Domain Names always have two or more parts, separated by dots. The part on the left is the most specific, and the part on the right is the most general. A given machine may have more than one domain name, but a given domain name points to only one machine.

Firewall: A combination of hardware and software that separates a network into two or more parts for security purposes.

Gateway: The technical meaning is a hardware or software set-up that translates between two dissimilar protocols. For example, America Online has a gateway that translates between its internal, proprietary e-mail format and Internet e-mail format. Another, sloppier meaning of gateway is to describe any mechanism for providing access to another system,. For example, AOL might be called a gateway to the Internet.

GIF (Graphic Interchange Format): A common format for image files, especially suitable for images containing large areas of the same color. GIF format files of simple images are often smaller than the same file would be if stored in JPEG format, but GIF format does not store photographic images as well as JPEG.

Host: Any computer on a network that is a repository for services available to other computers on the network. It is quite common to have one host machine provide several services, such as SMTP (e-mail) and HTTP (Web).

HTML (HyperText Markup Language): The coding language used to create Hypertext documents for use on the World Wide Web. HTML looks like old-fashioned typesetting code, where you surround a block of text with codes that indicate how it should appear.

The "hyper" in Hypertext comes from the fact that in HTML, you can specify that a block of text, or an image, is linked to another file on the Internet. HTML files are meant to be viewed using a "Web browser." HTML is loosely based on a more comprehensive system for markup called SGML, and is expected to eventually be replaced by XML-based XHTML standards.

HTTP (HyperText Transfer Protocol): The protocol for moving hypertextfiles across the Internet. It requires an HTTP client program on one end, and an HTTP server program (such as Apache) on the other. HTTP is the most important protocol used in the World Wide Web (WWW).

Hypertext: Generally, any text that contains links to other documents – words or phrases in the document that can be chosen by a reader and which cause another document to be retrieved and displayed.

IP Number (Internet Protocol Number): Sometimes called a dotted quad. A unique number consisting of four parts separated by dots, for instance, 165.113.245.2. Every machine that is on the Internet has a unique IP number – if a machine does not have an IP number, it is not really on the Internet. Many machines (especially servers) also have one or more domain names that are easier for people to remember.

ISDN (Integrated Services Digital Network): A way to move more data over existing regular phone lines. ISDN is available to much of the USA and in most markets it is priced very comparably to standard analog phone circuits. It can provide speeds of roughly 128,000 bps over regular phone lines. In practice, most people will be limited to 56,000or 64,000 bps. Unlike DSL, ISDN can be used to connect to many different locations, one at a time, just like a regular telephone call, as long as the other location also has ISDN.

ISP (Internet Service Provider): An institution that provides access to the Internet in some form, usually for money.

Java: Java is a network-friendly programming language invented by Sun Microsystems. Java is often used to build large, complex systems that involve several different computers interacting across networks, for example, transaction processing systems.

Using small Java programs (called "Applets"), Web pages can include functions such as animations, calculators, and other fancy tricks.

JavaScript: JavaScript is a programming language that is mostly used in Web pages, usually to add features that make the Web page more interactive. When JavaScript is included in an HTML file, it relies on the browser to interpret the JavaScript. When JavaScript is combined with CSS, and later versions of HTML (4.0 and later), the result is often called DHTML.

JDK (Java Development Kit): A software development package from Sun Microsystems that implements the basic set of tools needed to write, test, and debugJava applications and applets

JPEG (Joint Photographic Experts Group): JPEG is most commonly mentioned as a format for image files. JPEG format is preferred to the GIF format for photographic images, as opposed to line art or simple logo art.

LAN (Local Area Network): A computer network limited to the immediate area, usually the same building or floor of a building.

Linux: A widely used, open source, Unix-like operating system. Linux was first released by its inventor, Linus Torvalds, in 1991. There are versions of Linux for almost every available type of computer hardware from desktop machines to IBM mainframes. The inner workings of Linux are open and available for anyone to examine and change, as long as they make their changes available to the public. This has resulted in thousands of people working on various aspects of Linux and adaptation of Linux for a huge variety of purposes, from servers to TV-recording boxes.

Login: Noun: The account name used to gain access to a computer system. Not a secret (contrast with Password).

Log in: Verb: The act of connecting to a computer system by giving your credentials (usually your "username" and "password").

Mail-list or Mailing List: A (usually automated) system that allows people to send e-mail to one address, whereupon their message is copied and sent to all of the other subscribers to the mail list. In this way, people who have many different kinds of e-mail access can participate in discussions together.

Mashup: A Web page or site made by automatically combining content from other sources, usually by using material available via RSS feeds and/or REST interfaces.

Meta Tag: A specific kind of HTML tag that contains information not normally displayed to the user. Meta tags contain information about the page itself, hence the name ("meta" means "about this subject"). Typical uses of meta tags are to include information for search engines to help them better categorize a page. You can see the meta tags in a page if you view the page's source code.

MIME (Multipurpose Internet Mail Extensions): Originally a standard for defining the types of files attached to standard Internet mail messages. The MIME standard has come to be used in many situations where one computer programs needs to communicate with another program about what kind of file is being sent. For example, HTML files have a MIME-type of text/html and JPEG files are image/jpeg.

Modem (MOdulator, DEModulator): A device that connects a computer to a phone line. A modem allows a computer to talk to other computers through the phone system. Modems do for computers what a telephone does for humans. The maximum practical bandwidth using a modem over regular telephone lines is currently around 57,000 bps.

NIC (Network Information Center): Any office that handles information for a network. The most famous of these on the Internet was the InterNIC, which was where most new domain names were registered until that process was decentralized to a number of private companies. Also means "network interface card," which is the card in a computer that you plug a network cable into.

NNTP (Network News Transport Protocol): The protocol used by client and server software to carry USENET postings back and forth over a TCP/IP network. If you are using any of the more common software, such as Netscape, Nuntius, or Internet Explorer to participate in newsgroups, then you are benefiting from an NNTP connection.

Node: Any single computer connected to a network.

Open Source Software: Open source software is software for which the underlying programming code is available to the users so that they may read it, make changes to it, and build new versions of the software incorporating their changes. There are many types of open source software, mainly differing in the licensing term under which (altered) copies of the source code may (or must) be redistributed.

PHP (PHP: Hypertext Preprocessor): PHP is a programming language used almost exclusively for creating software that is part of a Web site. The PHP language is designed to be intermingled with the HTML that is used to create Web pages. Unlike HTML, the PHP code is read and processed by the Web server software (HTML is read and processed by the Web browser software.)

Ping: To check if a server is running. From the sound that a sonar system makes in movies when they are searching for a submarine.

Plug-in: A (usually small) piece of software that adds features to a larger piece of software. Common examples are plug-ins for the Netscape® browser and Web server. Adobe Photoshop® also uses plug-ins.

Podcasting or pod-casting: A form of audio broadcasting using the Internet, podcasting takes its name from a combination of "iPod" and "broadcasting." iPod is the immensely popular digital audio player made by Apple computer, but podcasting does not actually require the use of an iPod.

Podcasting involves making one or more audio files available as "enclosures" in an RSS feed. A pod-caster creates a list of music, and/or other sound files (such as recorded poetry or "talk radio" material) and makes that list available in the RSS 2.0 format. The list can then be obtained by other people using various podcast "retriever" software, which reads the feed and makes the audio files available to digital audio devices (including, but not limited to iPods) where users may then listen to them at their convenience.

Portal: Usually used as a marketing term to describe a Web site that is or is intended to be the first place people see when using the Web. Typically a "portal site" has a catalog of Web sites, a search engine, or both. A Portal site may also offer e-mail and other service to entice people to use that site as their main "point of entry" (hence "portal") to the Web.

Proxy Server: A proxy server sits in between a client and the "real" server that a client is trying to use. Clients are sometimes configured to use a proxy server, usually an HTTP server. The client makes all of its requests from the proxy server, which then makes requests from the "real" server and passes the result back to the client. Sometimes the proxy server will store the results and give a stored result instead of making a new one (to reduce use of a network). Proxy servers are commonly established on LANs.

RSS (Rich Site Summary or RDF Site Summary or Real Simple

Syndication): A commonly used protocol for syndication and sharing of content, originally developed to facilitate the syndication of news articles and now widely used to share the contents of blogs. Mashups are often made using RSS feeds. RSS is an XML-based summary of a Web site, usually used for syndication and other kinds of content-sharing. There are RSS "feeds," which are sources of RSS information about Web sites, and RSS "readers," which read RSS feeds and display their content to users.

Security Certificate: A chunk of information (often stored as a text file) that is used by the SSL protocol to establish a secure connection.

SEO (Search Engine Optimization): The practice of designing Web pages so that they rank as high as possible in search results from search engines.

Server: A computer or software package that provides a specific kind of service to client software running on other computers. The term can refer to a particular piece of software, such as a WWW server, or to the machine on which the software is running; for example,

"Our mail server is down today, that's why e-mail is not getting out." A single server machine can (and often does) have several different server software packages running on it, thus providing many different servers to clients on the network.

Sometimes server software is designed so that additional capabilities can be added to the main program by adding small programs known as "servlets."

Servlet: A small computer program designed to add capabilities to a larger piece of server software. Common examples are "Java servlets," which are small programs written in the Java language and added to a Web server. Typically, a Web server that uses Java servlets will have many of them, each one designed to handle a very specific situation; for example, one servlet will handle adding items to a "shopping cart," while a different servlet will handle deleting items from the "shopping cart."

SMTP (Simple Mail Transfer Protocol): Main protocol used to send e-mail from server to server on the Internet.

SMTP is defined in RFC 821 and

modified by many later RFCs.

Spyware: A somewhat vague term generally referring to software that is secretly installed on a user's computer and that monitors use of the computer in some way without the user's knowledge or consent. Most spyware tries to get the user to view advertising and/ or particular Web pages. Some spyware also sends information about the user to another machine over the Internet. Spyware is usually installed without a user's knowledge as part of the installation of other software, especially software such as music sharing software obtained via download.

SQL (Structured Query Language): A specialized language for sending queries to databases. Most industrial-strength and many smaller database applications can be addressed using SQL. Each specific application will have its own slightly different version of SQL implementing features unique to that application, but all SQL-capable databases support a common subset of SQL.

SSL (Secure Socket Layer): A protocol designed by Netscape

Communications to enable encrypted, authenticated communications across the Internet.

Unix: A computer operating system (the basic software running on a computer, underneath things like word processors and spreadsheets). Unix is designed to be used by many people at the same time (it is multi-user) and has TCP/IP built-in. It is the most common operating system for servers on the Internet. Apple computers' Macintosh operating system, as of version 10 ("Mac OS X"), is based on Unix.

URL (Uniform Resource Locator): The term URL is basically synonymous with URI (Uniform Resource Identifier). URI has replaced URL in technical specifications.

XHTML (eXtensible HyperText Markup Language): HTML expressed as valid XML. XHTML is intended to be used in the same places you would use HTML (creating Web pages), but is much more strictly defined, which makes it much easier to create software that can read it, edit it, and check it for errors. XHTML is expected to eventually replace HTML.

XML (eXtensible Markup Language): A widely used system for defining data formats. XML provides a very rich system for defining complex documents and data structures, such as invoices, molecular data, news feeds, glossaries, inventory descriptions, and real estate properties. As long as a programmer has the XML definition for a collection of data (often called a "schema"), they can create a program to reliably process any data formatted according to those rules. XML is a subset of the older SGML specification — the definition of XML is SGML minus a couple of dozen items.

Index